HEALING STRESS IN MILITARY FAMILIES

HEALING STRESS IN MILITARY FAMILIES

EIGHT STEPS TO WELLNESS

Lorie T. DeCarvalho
and Julia M. Whealin

WILEY

John Wiley & Sons, Inc.

Published by John Wiley & Sons, Inc., Hoboken, New Jersey.
Published simultaneously in Canada.

Library of Congress Cataloging-in-Publication Data:

DeCarvalho, Lorie T.
    Healing stress in military families : eight steps to wellness / Lorie T. DeCarvalho and Julia M. Whealin.
        p. cm.
    Includes bibliographical references and index.
    ISBN 978-1-118-03821-5 (pbk. : alk. paper)
    ISBN 978-1-118-21862-4 (ebk)
    ISBN 978-1-118-21863-1 (ebk)
    ISBN 978-1-118-21864-8 (ebk)
    ISBN 978-1-118-23209-5 (obk)
        I. Whealin, Julia M.   II. Title.
        [DNLM: 1. Family Therapy—methods—United States.   2. Military Psychiatry—methods—United States.   3. Family Relations—United States.   4. Military Personnel—psychology—United States.   5. Stress, Psychological—United States.   6. Veterans—psychology—United States. WM 110]
    616.89156—dc23
                                                                                                2011039270

Printed in the United States of America

10 9 8 7 6 5 4 3 2 1

We dedicate this book to our military families. We acknowledge and honor all of the sacrifices you make every day, which often go unrecognized or unnoticed. We thank our service members, National Guard Members, reservists, and veterans for their service to our country. And we thank the loved and loving family members who stand beside them along the way. We pay tribute to your patience, steadfastness, loyalty, and courage. And we appreciate and respect those who are serving our country's military families.

Table of Contents

The 8 Steps to Healing and Wellness

Appendices: Handouts for Families and Clinicians

Preface

There are more than 3.1 million individuals who are part of a military family, including 2 million children. About 900,000 children have one or both parents who have been deployed multiple times (DoD, April 2010). Active-duty service members, National Guard members, and Reservists bear a heavy weight as they serve our country. But sometimes, as civilians, we may forget that for every service member and veteran affected by active duty, a family is also impacted.

Military family members are the silent witnesses to their loved ones' sacrifices and pain. The family members sit in front of the television, praying that their loved one will not become a statistic covered up by the camouflage of a body bag. The family deals with separation from their loved ones for months to years at a time. They manage the family affairs and household needs. They open their arms when their loved ones return. Military children go to school every day, not knowing when mom or dad will be back to play ball or hear about how their day at school went. The family stands by as the returnee readjusts to seemingly mundane daily life outside of a combat zone. The family sacrifices in ways that often go unnoticed by the rest of the world. Their pain tends to lie hidden, though it is very real.

Being a military family comes with the cost of learning to adjust to change. Many families move through their transitions with relative ease, but many others struggle with trying to negotiate the challenges at different phases, with each relocation, deployment, redeployment, and reunion. The struggles associated with deployment are taking a toll on military families. As with any difficulties in life, those experiences can either strengthen or weaken an individual. In a relationship, those challenges can bond the individuals together and solidify that connection, or they can separate them so that they become more disconnected from one another.

In our previous books, the *Clinician's Guide to Treating Stress After War: Education and Coping Interventions for Veterans* and *Strategies for Managing Stress After War: Veteran's*

Workbook and Guide to Wellness (John Wiley & Sons, 2008), we provided step-by-step guidelines to promoting wellness in returnees and veterans. But we felt that more needed to be done to help our nation's military families, so in this book, *Healing Stress in Military Families: Eight Steps to Wellness,* we offer answers to the family's pain that comes not only from war but also from other related issues facing today's military families. We wrote this book as a guide for clinicians, chaplains, academicians, as well as for active-duty service members, veterans, spouses, family members, friends, and loved ones.

You may be a clinician who is trying to understand how best to serve those who serve our country. Or, maybe you are a loved one who is looking for answers as you struggle in your family relationships. Whatever your situation, we are honored that you chose this book to be part of your life's process. We wrote this book with the military family at heart, and we hope that you will find the information, tools, and skills will empower you to move ahead.

It is our ultimate goal that with this book, military families can more easily reconnect, heal, and become stronger and more resilient as they go through life. We wish all of the healing and wellness to our courageous military families.

And now onto wellness . . .

Acknowledgments

As is true of any major process in life, there will be certain people who play an important part along the way. We would like to say thank you to individuals who assisted in the formation of this book.

We both thank the amazing team at John Wiley & Sons, Inc., for their passion for wanting to help our military service members and families. We give special thanks to our team: Patricia Rossi, our Executive Editor, for your consistent support, invaluable feedback, and for going the extra mile in this and our past two books. We are very grateful and honored for the opportunity to work with you. Thank you to Kara Borbely, our Editorial Program Coordinator, for joining together the many facets of book making, including manuscript editing, production, design, marketing, and many more. You made the process a smooth one! Thank you Leigh Camp, our Production Editor, for all of your expert assistance in copyediting, page proofing, and production. Thank you Ginjer Clarke for your attention to detail in the review of our manuscript, and for your expert feedback.

A special thank you to Lynda Shanahan-Trent, for generously giving your time to review the book and meticulously tuning into the big and small details in the editing of hundreds of pages of manuscript more than once.

A thank you from Dr. Whealin: Thank you to my friends, family, and wonderful husband Kevin for their support and understanding during my weekends and late nights of work. Thank you especially to our courageous service members and their families for their everyday sacrifices, large and small.

A thank you from Dr. DeCarvalho: Thank you to my family and friends, for your unending, unconditional support and understanding, when I had no time or life to share with you because I was consumed in creating and writing this book. Thank you to my staff for graciously rearranging my schedule on more than one occasion so I could have time. To all of the service members and veterans who I have worked with over the years, saying thank you does not seem adequate for all of the sacrifices you make and the pain you endure to serve our country. It has been a supreme privilege and honor to work with you and share in your lives.

And a joint thank you: Thank you to the many military families who shared their experiences with us. It has been an honor to witness your fortitude in the face of stress, worry, loneliness, and pain. Your experiences served as the catalyst in the creation of this book. Know that your pain and courage has not gone unnoticed, and it is now being paid forward to heal the many thousands of other military families who face similar hurts. We are more than touched and honored to know you and serve you in your journey.

How to Use this Book

The fact that you have picked up this book says a lot. It means that you would like to be equipped with the tools, knowledge, and skills to help today's military families. Military families go through frequent readjustment phases with each deployment, redeployment, and relocation. In addition, military spouses and children experience fear and worry for their loved one who is deployed to a war zone or traveling overseas on missions. The military family is expected to rapidly and easily adjust to all of the changes they are required to make in order to be a healthy family. However, the adjustments are not so easy, and many military families struggle through this process.

Our purpose for writing this book is twofold. First, we want to provide a very informative, practical tool that clinicians can use to understand the unique issues faced by today's military families, and we will provide very specific ways that clinicians can help the family. Second, we write this book with the hope that family members (spouses/partners, children) will work through the steps provided here to find healing and grow as a family. We also hope that significant others in the family's life (parents, extended family, friends, and other loved ones) will use this book as a resource to learn more about what their loved ones are experiencing, in order to be better sources of support for them.

Focus of the Book

The entire focus of this book is to work with the inherent strengths of individuals in military families. We do not believe it is useful to emphasize illness or dysfunction. Our focus is on empowering people to wellness. As clinical psychologists, we have worked with individuals, couples, and families for more than 30 years. This book is in alignment with the way we practice as clinicians. We will focus on the strengths that are already there, we will help build upon them and, as a result, make the family unit stronger.

Who Can Benefit From Using This Book?

We wrote this book for clinicians—those working with military service members and their families. We have written the book in a non-jargon format for ease of use by a variety of providers and academicians in military, VA-based, and civilian settings. We believe the book should be incorporated into professional clinical training programs for internship and postdoctoral programs in psychology, counseling, social work, and marriage and family therapy to prepare clinicians to help returnees and their families. Chaplains (both civilian and military) can benefit from this book. Likewise, physicians and specialists (e.g., physical and occupational therapists, speech therapists, pain specialists) in a variety of practice settings, such as hospitals, clinics, or private practice, and medical trainees (e.g., predoctoral interns, residents, and postdoctoral fellows) would provide improved care if they incorporated this knowledge into serving military families.

In addition, we believe that family members and friends can greatly benefit from reading the book on their own. Having said that, we would also like to make it clear that any therapeutic interventions should be used by trained mental health professionals. We do advise military families to work with a counselor or therapist as they go through the steps and exercises in the book.

What You Will Get From Using This Book

In working through this book, you will learn very practical steps toward rebuilding the family. Families can work and rework through the eight steps, and by doing so, they will achieve many positive results. Some of those results are that they will rebuild a stronger connection among members, improve communication, and cope with stress in healthy ways. Ultimately, they will become a resilient family, with healthier and emotionally stronger individuals within their family.

How to Use the Book

We recommend going through the book from front to back, working through the steps one by one. The steps are designed to build on one another. It will be important to master each step before moving onto the next one. By doing it this way, family members will get the most benefit from using the book, and they will heal more. Skipping steps will not help. It is possible to work through the steps once, then to reread the book and go back and work through any of the steps that family members feel they need to address further.

Clinicians can strongly benefit from taking the information in the book to another level by employing the Making It Real sections as exercises in family sessions with their clients. In addition, we have included all of the exercises in handout form, as well as access to the exercises online at www.wiley.com/go/decarvalho. Please use these hand-outs and exercises with family members.

The best way to use this book is to take your time to work through it with the family, working the steps for as long as you need to. There is no race to the finish line. Healing can take time, and rushing through the steps would make it more likely that issues will be left unresolved. We recommend using the book as though you are going through a journey or process. It may take a little longer to get through the book, but it will be worth the extra time and effort.

Format of the Book

The following are the different sections you will find throughout this book. Please do not skip around in the book. You will gain the greatest benefit by going through the exercises and steps in the order they are written.

Quote of the Chapter

Each chapter begins with a quotation. Every quote relates to and encompasses the gist of that particular chapter.

Family Scenario

Each chapter begins with a scenario of a military family. In the scenario, we provide some details about issues that the military family is facing. We include dialogues from therapy sessions with the families, which will provide common situations you may face with the military families with whom you work.

Setting the Stage

In this section, we provide an overview of what we will cover in the chapter.

For Your Information

Each chapter will include at least two of these sections. In this section, we provide relevant research and recent clinical findings that relate to the key issues faced by today's military families.

Making It Real Exercises

In every chapter, we include Making It Real exercises. Each chapter will have a few exercises that you can do with your military family. As we mentioned earlier, these exercises should be done in sequence, because they build on each other. Please do not pick and choose which exercises to do. Please go through and complete all of the exercises with the family. They will gain the most benefit from using all of the exercises. In this section, we provide reasons why the exercise helps, any materials needed, detailed instructions, and scripts.

Talking Points

You will notice that Talking Points will follow the Making It Real exercises. In Talking Points, we illustrate how the exercises worked for the family. You will get to experience real dialogues from therapy sessions. This section will demonstrate how you can therapeutically guide the family in their healing process. You will also be able to see the transformation of the family as you go through the successive steps of the book.

Final Thoughts

In this brief section, we give our final thoughts by summarizing and highlighting the most significant changes that have occurred for the military family. We will reinforce the progress they have made by working through the step, as they head into the next one.

Keys to Family Wellness

Keeping with our focus on wellness and resilience, we provide keys to the reader about how to maximize wellness and healing in military families. These keys will also provide practical, how-to-live summaries of significant points covered in-depth within the chapter.

Taking Action

At the end of every chapter, you will find Taking Action steps. We believe that healing continues after the sessions. It is crucial that the family practices what they have learned and take it a step further on their own. To help the family do this, we have included three steps that they can do in the week that follows. They should do each of the steps to hone their knowledge, but especially to further bond as a family. These action steps, combined with their sessions with you, will help the family to reconnect, heal, and grow.

Handouts and Resources

In Part Three, you will find three appendices. The first appendix includes all of the handouts and exercises, which we have written in worksheet form so that family members can fill them out as they work through the steps in the book. In Appendix B, we have provided you, the clinician, with a host of resources that you can utilize as you work with military families. Finally, in Appendix C, we provide you with a lot of important and helpful resources for military families, based on their specific needs.

Special Online Access to Book Materials

With the purchase of this book, you are also entitled to special access to all of the materials contained in the book in online form. This way you can print out the worksheets, exercises, or resources to facilitate your work with military families. You can find these resources at www.wiley.com/go/decarvalho. You simply enter the username HealingStress and password EightSteps and will be directed to a web page where you can download the materials.

Cautions

Military families may use this guide on their own; however, we advise the family to consider going through this book with a trained mental health professional. It is not possible to predict how someone in the family may react while participating in some of the exercises in the book. Returnees may be experiencing mental and emotional aftereffects of war, including PTSD, traumatic brain injury, depression, anxiety, or other problems. In the book, we have advised when additional help should be sought out. However, we would like to caution you, as a provider or family member, to please be aware that it is possible that individuals may experience emotional discomfort as they share their thoughts and feelings. At any point, if family members become emotionally distraught or decompensate, or if any family members express any thoughts of hurting themselves or someone else, please **seek help immediately** from a trained mental health professional!

All in the Family: Sources of Stress

The Stress of Military Life

Courage is the price life exacts for granting peace.

—Amelia Earhart

Imagine yourself sitting in front of the television watching the 6:00 news. You see a news clip come on where the anchor says, "Another roadside bombing occurred today in Kabul. It is confirmed that 25 more U.S. soldiers were killed." The anchor changes the topic and talks about something else. But what is it like for the wife who just got married to her military husband, expecting to have their first child? Could this be the end of their relationship? Is he safe? Did he make it out alive?

What about to a 6-year-old girl? Her heart races and drops in her chest, as she cries to her mom, "Mommy, is Daddy dead?" This happens every time they hear bad news. She is young, but she knows that her dad is fighting in a war. She feels the stress every day. When she sits at her desk in school, trying to focus on her homework, her mind wanders to the days when her dad was at home and safe. Now, it seems like all she worries about is whether or not he is alive. Will her daddy come home for her next birthday, or for Christmas?

They just got new orders from their command. She is getting deployed overseas, while her husband and 3-year-old daughter stay behind for a year. This is her third move in five years. Her daughter will learn to read without her. Will her daughter remember who she is when she gets back? What will her little girl think of her? Will she think that her own mother doesn't love her, or that she abandoned her for a year of her life?

Their 19-year-old son just got deployed to Afghanistan for the first time. He just joined this past year and finished boot camp. His mother, father, and sisters get the word that he has been injured in the line of duty, but no one will tell them how badly he has been hurt. Where is he? How is he? What happened? Can he come home? So many questions are left unanswered. So much silence in the room. What is there to say at a time like this?

They are sitting at the dinner table having a family dinner, but no one feels like eating. It is the dinner hour they will never forget as long as they live. They had a knock at the door with a message from a military officer that their 22-year-old son was killed by a roadside bomb in Afghanistan. The military will be making arrangements for the body to be flown over for a military memorial service. The body? His parents, who are in their 50s, sit dumbfounded. Sure, everyone knows it could happen—but not to their son. They were supposed to go first—not the other way around. It wasn't supposed to be that way.

The Reality for Military Families

These are all experiences that a typical civilian family can't dream of going through. Yet, to a military family, it is everyday life. It is typical. It is frequently hard, with lots of uncertainties, lots of change, and a lot of adjustments to be made. This is what it is like for more than 3.1 million individuals who are part of a military family. This is the experience of more than 2 million children. How do they do it? Being a military family comes with the cost of learning to adjust to change.

Many families move through the transitions with relative ease, but many others struggle with trying to negotiate the challenges at different phases, with each relocation, deployment, redeployment, and reunion. Because of repeated deployments, the current veterans of Operation Enduring Freedom and Operation Iraqi Freedom (OEF/ OIF) are at a high risk for mental health problems (e.g., Hoge et al., 2004), including high rates of posttraumatic stress disorder (PTSD), depression, drug and alcohol abuse, and traumatic brain injury (TBI). Recent research shows that spouses of active-duty soldiers deployed to war also are at a high risk for mental health problems compared to spouses whose husbands did not deploy (Mansfield et al., 2010). Specifically, wives of soldiers who deployed for less than 11 months had an 18% higher rate of suffering from depression compared to wives whose husbands did not deploy. The rate was 24% higher when soldiers were deployed 11 months or longer. Therefore, it is apparent that the struggles associated with deployment are taking a toll on families.

As with any difficulties in life, those experiences can either strengthen or weaken an individual. In a relationship, the challenges can bond the individuals together and solidify that connection, or they can make family members become more separate and disconnected from one another.

Military Culture and Therapy

A common criticism that service members have about mental health clinicians is that civilian clinicians have little knowledge about the military or about the wars in which the returnees may have participated. Service members sometimes resent having to explain military acronyms, command structure, the differences between services, and facts about the OEF/OIF wars to their therapists. Therefore, civilian clinicians who work with military families should make themselves familiar with military life, activities, and culture.

Military Branches and Values

Whereas all U.S. military services follow the same general structure of ranks and responsibilities for enlisted personnel, noncommissioned and commissioned officers, each service and branch of the military has its own culture and language. In order to understand what's going on with a career Marine, for example, it is important to understand Marine culture, history, and language. This may include having an understanding of Marine ranking labels, use of acronyms, and stated values. Taking the time to learn about military culture and the experiences that clients may have had serving our country will facilitate rapport and validate the returnee's internal frame of reference.

Military Beliefs and Help-Seeking

A crucial point to understand is that the beliefs held by service members can directly impact their family members and hinder them from seeking mental health care. Some strong belief systems include gender role identity and those related to mental health stigma. These beliefs can also greatly affect the relationships among military family members.

Gender Role Identity

Not surprisingly, many personal beliefs held by service members are consistent with ideologies underlying masculine gender role identity. Individuals who hold masculine gender role ideals tend to value attributes such as independence, self-reliance, competition, power, strength, and emotional control. These values can impact the therapeutic relationship as well.

On the one hand, such values can positively impact the therapy environment by helping service members be proactive in participating in their therapy process. On the other hand, it is important to be aware that those individuals who hold traditionally masculine ideals often run a greater risk of developing health problems and tend to utilize health care services less often than those without these ideals (Bowman & Walker, 2010). This is particularly true for mental health problems. The belief that one ought to be able to handle mental health problems on one's own is much higher in men who have traditional masculine values (e.g., Sayer et al., 2009; Stecker, Fortney, Hamilton, & Ajzen, 2007). These masculine military values often trickle down to the family members. Knowing about and appreciating the values that military families can bring to the therapeutic environment will help build rapport.

It is important to note that individuals who endorse traditional male role values, including service members, often view suppression of emotions as an appropriate means for dealing with stress (Lorber & Garcia, 2010). In an "open letter" to "military wives everywhere," one service member discusses military culture and how the repression of emotions is "deeply learned through repetitious training and experience." He writes:

> Another change *(that differentiates civilian culture from the military culture)* is that emotions are distrusted and shunned. The mission comes first, orders are given

and are expected to be carried out, and there is no place where emotional concerns come to bear. Therefore the soldier seeks to repress emotions in order to get the job done. (*Military Culture: A Primer*, 2011)

Individuals who hold traditionally male values often view coping tactics that help them suppress their emotions (such as heavy drinking or other addictive behaviors) as a suitable means for coping with problems (Lorber & Garcia, 2010). However, coping strategies focused on suppressing emotions are counterproductive once service members return from war, and doing so tends to exacerbate mental health problems. For example, research shows that, compared to former service members who share their emotions, those who willfully suppress their emotions have higher levels of disturbing thoughts and emotions like those associated with PTSD (Shipard & Beck, 2005).

Mental Health Stigma

Service members may hold stigma-related beliefs about mental illness, such as the belief that having mental health problems is a sign of weakness (e.g., Hoge et al., 2004; Pietrzak et al., 2009). Unfortunately, stigma-related beliefs about mental illness are highest among service members who screen positive for mental health issues (e.g., Hoge et al., 2004; Whealin et al., 2011).

In one large study, less than one-third of service members, including Marines who acknowledged a need for mental health care, actually accessed available services. When asked about the barriers to obtaining treatment, the service members who said they needed mental health care endorsed stigma-related beliefs about treatment as the greatest barrier to seeking services (Hoge et al., 2004). In therapy, clients who hold traditional male gender role values and stigma-related beliefs may be more likely to conceal or underreport mental health problems. We will discuss these types of beliefs in more detail in Step 4.

Mental Problems as a Sign of Weakness

Research also suggests that OEF/OIF returnees who screen positive for mental health problems (compared to those without symptoms) are more likely to believe that their family members would have less confidence in them if they knew they had mental health problems, and would see them as weak (Whealin et al., 2011). In some cases, family members actually do have these attitudes. When this is the case, family members may discourage each other from openly talking about their problems (Lorber & Garcia, 2010). However, at other times, family members do not hold such beliefs, even if their service member believes they do. These families simply may be stuck in patterns that keep them from openly discussing mental health issues. Such families will need encouragement and modeling from the therapist to begin to share candidly with each other.

Unfortunately, service and family members who feel they must conceal mental health problems often experience guilt and shame about having such problems. These negative emotions often compound the problem, in that the individual suffers from the original symptoms as well as from additional emotional distress caused by shame and guilt. When others in their social environment keep symptoms to themselves as well, a family member may feel that she or he is the only one with a problem. Although such attitudes among military families are changing with time and educational outreach by the U.S. Departments of Defense and Veterans Affairs, guilt and shame about having a mental health problem are still common.

Military Culture and Treatment

The military culture vastly differs from that of civilian culture. Sometimes those common beliefs held by military service members not only prevent the military family from seeking help but can also create difficulties during treatment. It is important to recognize this issue and adapt treatments as you work with military families.

Views About Sharing Emotions

In treatment, it will be important to assess for mental health symptoms among service and family members. At the same time, we suggest exploring clients' attitudes about mental problems and about sharing emotions. If someone does endorse stigma-related beliefs, it is helpful to openly discuss their values with them. To illustrate, if a service member reports that self-reliance and emotional control are important to him or her, talk about both the pros and cons of such ideals in the context of what it means to be a Marine, Soldier, Airman, or Coast Guardsmen. We recommend validating the fact that such values have benefits for those who possess them, including success, discipline, and in some circles, respect. Then discuss how these values can also have a downside. When applied too rigidly, such values can be maladaptive.

If relevant, talk more specifically about how military training and culture may be at odds with discussing emotions. However, emphasize that emotions have very important functions and are necessary to solve problems. Additionally, let clients know that sharing emotions is appropriate within the context of therapy. The act of suppressing emotions in the military environment may be appropriate and necessary; however, doing so in the therapeutic context prevents military returnees from overcoming difficulties and hinders their ability to connect with family members. Similarly, if a returnee or family member suffering from mental health problems endorses mental health stigma, it will be helpful to normalize how common mental health symptoms actually are. In such cases, openly discuss how it is typical to feel discomfort talking about mental health problems at first. Explore any other fears that clients may have that prevent them from talking about their feelings. Once individuals feel that they have permission for sharing emotions and discussing symptoms, they will be better able to thrive individually and as a family member.

Resources for Civilians

A variety of resources are available to help civilian therapists better understand and effectively communicate with service members and their families. The U.S. Department of Defense, for example, offers an interactive online course in military culture addressing organizational structure, rank, branches of service, core values, and demographics, as well as the similarities and differences between the active and reserve components. This course is located at: http://deploymentpsych.org/training/training-catalog/military-cultural-competence.

Additionally, the U.S. Department of Veterans Affairs National Center for PTSD has an online course on military culture that includes military demographics, branches, rank, status, treatment, and stressors. It also addresses assessment and treatment hints for therapists. That course is located at: http://www.ptsd.va.gov/professional/ptsd101/course-modules/military_culture.asp.

Traumatic Brain Injury and Polytrauma Syndrome

In this section, we provide an overview of traumatic brain injury (TBI), mild traumatic brain injury (mTBI), and polytrauma syndrome. This section is only an overview, but we hope it will give you further insight into how prevalent traumatic brain injuries are and how they relate with chronic pain and PTSD. Thousands of military families have been and are affected by their loved ones sustaining injuries and requiring short-term, intermediate, and sometimes long-term care. So you will encounter military families who are experiencing the ramifications of these injuries. This chapter will give you a cheat sheet for identifying the conditions, symptoms, and treatments to help service members and returnees.

Unique Injuries in OIF/OEF

As society has advanced, protective military equipment such as Kevlar helmets, flack jackets, and advanced front-line battlefield medical care have been developed. With these advances, soldiers have been able to survive wounds that may have killed them in other wars (Gawande, 2004). On the other hand, technological advances have also included upgrades in military equipment. Subsequently, the development of devices with blast mechanisms, such as improvised explosive devices (IEDs), have resulted in an increase in the occurrence of traumatic brain injuries (TBI), mild traumatic brain injuries (mTBI), and polytrauma syndrome (Wade, Dye, Mohrle, & Galarneau, 2007). In fact, researchers have determined that there is a greater proportion of head and neck injuries in OIF and OEF veterans when compared to past wars, including World War II, the Korean War, and the Vietnam War (Zouris, Walker, Dye, & Galarneau, 2006).

Traumatic Brain Injuries

Traumatic brain injuries are being called the "signature wound" of OIF/OEF (Hayward, 2008). Mild TBIs affect approximately 300,000 returning service members (Benge, Pastorek, & Thornton, 2009). However, other researchers have found that more than 50% of soldiers injured in combat sustain head, neck, and facial injuries (Wade, Dye, Mohrle, & Galarneau, 2007). The study supported earlier findings that 59% of the service members who were injured and hospitalized at Walter Reed Medical Center had sustained TBIs (Okie, 2005).

Prevalence of TBI

Traumatic brain injuries appear to be far more common in returnees from OIF/OEF than any other wars (Zouris, Walker, Dye, & Galarneau, 2006). In a very recent study, researchers compared the rates of TBI among active-duty personnel between the U.S. military branches. They found that Marines ran a greater risk of sustaining TBIs than those in the Army, Air Force, or Navy (Heltemes, Dougherty, MacGregor, & Galarneau, 2011). Heltemes et al. (2011) inferred that this may be so because the Marines "are an expeditionary force primarily deployed during periods of high combat intensity, and as such, it may be expected that their rates of injury due to combat are higher than the rates of injury of other services" (p. 134).

Definitions of the Conditions

As you treat service members and their families, it will be helpful to have a better understanding of the presentation for TBI or mTBI and polytrauma syndrome. We will also talk about postdeployment multisymptom disorder (PMD), a newly proposed classification for service members. In this section, we provide descriptions and definitions of these conditions.

Mild Traumatic Brain Injury

Service members who have sustained a *mild traumatic brain injury (mTBI)* experience loss of consciousness for 30 minutes or less, loss of memory for less than 24 hours (termed *posttraumatic amnesia*), or feeling dazed or confused for less than 24 hours after being injured (Defense Veterans Brain Injury Coalition, 2006). Service members' recovery time from a typical mTBI can range from a few days to a few months after being injured.

Most service members return to normal functioning within one to three months (Alexander, 1995). However, nearly 39% of service members with a mTBI still have symptoms and problems associated with their injury up to a year later (Terrio et al., 2009). Other service members experienced significant neuropsychological problems for years after they were injured. This is called *post-concussion syndrome* or *post-conconcussive symptoms (PCSx)*, which is defined as "a persistent constellation of symptoms marked by cognitive, emotional, and physical complaints for many months to years after injury" (Benge, Pastorek, & Thornton, 2009).

Polytrauma Syndrome

Because OIF/OEF veterans may incur so many injuries that require care, the Department of Veterans Affairs and the Veterans Health Administration (VHA) now classify more complex cases as *polytrauma syndrome* (Department of Veterans Affairs, 2009). Service members who present with polytrauma syndrome have sustained injuries to multiple body systems, which may or may not include TBI. When service members present with symptoms that cannot be clearly categorized, this is referred to as *medically unexplained symptoms (MUS)*, which can include physical, psychological, or cognitive problems (Uomoto & Williams, 2009).

Postdeployment Multisymptom Disorder

Researchers have suggested that it is typical for returning service members to have the combination of postconcussive syndrome, chronic pain, *and* PTSD (Clark et al., 2007; Clark et al., 2009; Lew et al., 2009). Furthermore, researchers have concluded that this combination is unique to OIF/OEF returnees (Walker, Clark, & Sanders, 2010). Lew et al. (2009) found that 42% of returning service members had chronic pain. There appears to be an overlap of these symptoms in OIF/OEF returnees (Clark et al., 2009). As such, Walker, Clark, and Sanders (2010) proposed that this multisymptom presentation should be called *postdeployment multisymptom disorder (PMD)*, which may include problems such as sleep disturbance, irritability, concentration and attention difficulties, fatigue, headaches, musculoskeletal problems, affective disturbance, apathy, personality changes, substance abuse, avoiding activities, problems in work or school, problems in relationships, and hypervigilance.

Blast Injuries

Improvised explosive devices (IEDs) cause what are called "blast injuries," which appear to be more unique to the OIF/OEF wars (Moore & Jaffee, 2010). There are four levels of blast injuries: primary, secondary, tertiary, and quaternary. We briefly describe them here.

Primary Blast Injuries

Primary blast injuries are typically caused by what is referred to as "barotrauma." That is, when an IED explodes, the pressure of the blast causes trauma to the tissues. Service members who sustain primary blast injuries can have any of the following (or combination of injuries): ruptured ear drums, pulmonary embolism, ruptured colon, ruptured small or large intestine, damage to the kidneys, spleen, or liver, facial fractures, or serious eye damage or blindness (DePalma, Burris, Champion, & Hodgson, 2005).

Secondary Blast Injuries

When the explosion has settled to some degree, fragments and chunks of metal can cause serious shrapnel wounds and penetrating injuries. These are considered to be secondary blast injuries and have been found to be the leading cause of death and injury in service members and civilians (DePalma, Burris, Champion, & Hodgson, 2005).

Tertiary Blast Injuries

Tertiary blast injuries are caused by structures collapsing, such as vehicles and buildings, and "they result from people being thrown into fixed objects by the wind of explosions. Any body part may be affected, and fractures, amputations, and open and closed brain injuries occur" (DePalma, Burris, Champion, & Hodgson, 2005, p. 1338).

Quaternary Blast Injuries

Quaternary blast injuries are essentially any injuries that were caused by the force of the blast, which did not fall into one of the other three classifications. Quaternary injuries may include burns, poisoning from chemicals and gases emitted from the explosion, asphyxiation, or exposure to radiation or asbestos.

Treating Wounded Service Members and Their Family Members

The point to understand is that service members can sustain one or more than one level of blast injury. They may sustain serious second- or third-degree burns requiring skin graft surgeries. They may be deaf or blind as a result of the blast. They may have mild or serious TBI. It is likely they will have chronic pain and PTSD. As such, returning service members will have a lot of physical as well as mental healing to do after these events. Once they have been medically discharged and sent home, their rehabilitation will continue. It is imperative that the family be educated and supported as well, so they can support their loved one. However, that process begins with you having information about how to help the service member and family, from the clinical presentation to assessment and treatment.

Clinical Presentation

Once service members have gone home, their treatment will continue. Assuming it is a few months after they were injured, they will present with some ongoing problems related to TBI, pain, or PTSD. As stated earlier, it is very common for service members to have mTBI, PTSD, *and* chronic pain (Clark, Scholten, Walker, & Gironda, 2009). And you will find that there is some symptom overlap when returnees have polytrauma syndrome. Here are symptoms and problems that seem to occur in both mTBI and PTSD:

- Distractibility
- Attention deficits
- Poor working memory
- Slower processing speed
- Problems with executive functioning

➤ Impulse control problems

➤ Irritability

➤ Reduced verbal processing

(Adapted from Campbell et al., 2009; Cooper et al., 2010; and Morrow, Bryan, & Isler, 2011.)

Confounds With Diagnosing TBI Versus PTSD

Sometimes it can be difficult months after service members have been wounded to differentiate whether they have residual symptoms of TBI, or if it is PTSD. That is because there is an overlap between symptoms. For example, Kennedy, Leal, Lewis, Cullen, and Amador (2010) found that, "There is something about mTBI itself that conveys risk for subsequent PTSD" (p. 228). The authors suggest that clinicians address the reexperiencing symptoms from PTSD in order to ameliorate the TBI. Because of the overlap of symptoms, clinicians who assess returning service members after the traumatic events may have difficulties teasing apart and differentiating which condition is which.

Other researchers have pointed out the problems with confounding variables when assessing and diagnosing returning service members. For example, Summerall and McAllister (2010) stated: "Many service members today are exposed to multiple psychological and biochemical traumas, occasionally during the same combat episode. Clinicians evaluating these conditions should bear in mind these limitations to the current diagnostic schema" (p. 564).

Assessment Guidelines

It can be helpful to administer screening instruments to assess for specific symptoms and presentation. In addition, it is important to obtain a very detailed history. A detailed clinical assessment may include the following components:

➤ PTSD symptom checklist (Military), PCL-M

➤ Trail-making test, Part B

➤ Structured diagnostic interview

    ➤ Military history (where they served, how long, how many deployments)

    ➤ Psychosocial functioning before injury

    ➤ Specifics about events causing injuries (what happened before, during, and afterward)

    ➤ Medical history

    ➤ Developmental history (past school performance, history of head injuries, learning disabilities or difficulties)

    ➤ Substance abuse history

➤ Trauma history
➤ Current psychosocial functioning (relationships, current stressors, living situation, etc.)
➤ Current functioning (symptoms, disabilities, conditions)

Treatment Considerations

Some researchers suggest that rehabilitation and treatment efforts should focus on reducing reexperiencing symptoms with prolonged exposure therapy (e.g., Kennedy et al., 2010). However, other researchers suggest that when service members have reduced verbal processing speed, therapies such as prolonged exposure and cognitive processing therapy may not be as effective (Campbell et al., 2009). Campbell et al. (2009) suggest that "treatment for those with comorbid TBI/PTSD may require adapting these evidence-based therapies to include slower verbal processing" (p. 802). Other researchers suggest that "a recovery-oriented approach emphasizing that improvement in one functional domain can lead to improvement in another should inform treatment planning" (Summerall & McAllister, 2010, p. 568).

An extremely important consideration is that the returning service members will not go through treatment in isolation. They will reintegrate into society and into their family. This can pose several challenges (Whealin, DeCarvalho, & Vega, 2008a; Whealin, DeCarvalho, & Vega, 2008b). The added stress of injury, mTBI or TBI, chronic pain, and/or PTSD further complicates the treatment picture. The service member will face a lot of challenges in his or her rehabilitation process.

Supporting the Military Family

It is imperative that the family members, from spouse or partner to parent(s), to siblings, to extended family and friends, provide support. Having said that, it is equally important to ensure that the family is supported as well, because it can be incredibly stressful, frustrating, and emotionally painful for family members to watch their loved one suffer. At times, military family members may feel frustrated and helpless because they can't fix the situation, and they sometimes can't do much to help their loved one. Military families can go through huge adjustments when their loved one is injured, medically discharged, and then having long-term physical and/or psychiatric difficulties because of war experiences.

Effects on the Military Family

Because the returnee may not be fit to work any longer, a spouse may need to be retrained for a job or shoulder some or most of the financial burden. Financial strain can sometimes lead to foreclosure and further relocation. Family members may feel isolated from other loved ones because of the time, energy, and focus that goes into rehabilitation. Some spouses may not know how to handle it if their loved one loses his or her temper or says inappropriate things because of a brain injury. Some spouses may provide secondary gain when their loved one bows out of doing household chores or having responsibilities because of their chronic pain condition(s). These are just a few of many potential difficulties the military family may face, and they are all very important scenarios to consider as you turn your attention toward helping military families to heal.

Vicarious Trauma in the Military Family

Vicarious traumatic stress is a term that refers to someone developing traumatic stress symptoms by *hearing about* someone else's trauma secondhand and being impacted over time by someone who is suffering from PTSD. Vicarious traumatic stress can come about gradually from listening to stories or news reports about traumatic events. It can also come about by living with someone who is suffering from PTSD.

Vicarious Trauma in Family Members

Family members who develop vicarious traumatic stress can develop the same types of symptoms their service member is experiencing.

Symptoms Family Members May Experience

Some family members may find themselves thinking about upsetting stories or images even when they are not trying to think about them. Others may have dreams or nightmares about the events their service member has experienced. Like the service member, family members may feel like they have to be on guard all the time. They may become startled following sudden noises, feel very anxious, or have trouble falling or staying asleep. Family members of service members may also experience avoidance and go out of their way *not* to think or talk about deployment or other war-related topics. Family members can experience emotional numbing and begin to feel detached from other people, or they may feel fewer positive feelings, such as happiness.

Transfer of Beliefs to the Family

In addition to vicarious trauma, family members may experience direct stress that results from a service member's PTSD symptoms. For example, trauma survivors who have developed hypervigilance may attempt to teach their families to be afraid of crowded or unknown environments. During deployment, service members adapted to living in a dangerous and/or foreign environment. As a result, they may have developed new beliefs and behaviors, which they can transfer to their families without even knowing it. For example, a service member who does not go to shopping malls because he has learned that crowded places can be very dangerous may pass on his fear of crowded malls to his daughter. He may be very overprotective and forbid his daughter to go to shopping malls. Over time, his daughter may adopt hypervigilant behavior and begin to avoid crowded places as well.

Other Effects on Family Members

A service member's combat stress symptoms can also directly harm, and even traumatize, family members, especially when combined with other problems. For example, research has shown that families experience the most distress when their service member with PTSD has difficulty regulating anger and other emotions (Galovski & Lyons, 2004). When a service member is highly irritable and/or cannot control his or her anger, family members often become targets of that anger, leading to conflict and sometimes abuse. It is not surprising that postdeployment families experience more problems and divorce than other families. This is why it is extremely important for everyone in the family to understand how and why a service member's PTSD is affecting them, and they need to take action to not harm one another.

Other Forms of Vicarious Traumatization

There are other ways that military family members can be affected by the service member's stress. These are referred to as secondary traumatic stress and compassion fatigue.

Secondary Traumatic Stress

A term related to *vicarious* traumatic stress is *secondary* traumatic stress. Although the terms are often confused, secondary traumatic stress refers to stress reactions that are caused by *directly witnessing* another person's exposure to trauma (Ruzek, 1993). The viewer's life is not threatened, but he or she experiences fear, helplessness, or horror as a result of looking at pictures, a video, or being a bystander during a traumatic event.

Compassion Fatigue

One other related term, usually applied to those in professional caregiving positions, such as nurses, is *compassion fatigue.* Compassion fatigue refers to the negative changes that can occur over time when a person cares for someone who is suffering from psychological or physical ailments. Symptoms of compassion fatigue include hopelessness, a decrease in experiences of pleasure, anxiety, and a negative attitude.

The 8 Steps Visited

> *As long as you live,*
> *Keep learning how to live*

> —Seneca, 4 B.C.–65 A.D.

In our lives, we can keep going along as we always have, expecting that things will change or improve. In the addictions or chemical dependency field, there is an adage. It states that the definition of insanity "is to keep doing the same thing over and over, but to expect different results." As you are aware, expecting different results from doing the same thing is rather ridiculous and pretty contradictory. The reality is that if we want to grow in life, we need to be willing to change at various points in our lives. Usually, painful or joyful life experiences serve as catalysts that help us make life changes. Other times, boredom or dissatisfaction with how things are causes us to question why we are doing what we are, and to explore other options. This book is about exploring options. It is about offering solutions and different, healthier ways of doing things.

The 8-Step Approach to Healing the Military Family

The 8 Steps are essentially the roadmap to better relationships for the military family. As is part of life, there will always be normal setbacks and milestones, but within the unique culture of the military, the family experiences numerous added stressors that create significant challenges. We will help the family solve these problems, meet their challenges head on, and successfully master them.

In the diagram that follows, you can see that we have defined the steps in the context of a pyramid. Within the pyramid, you will find the *processes* that military families will go through as they conquer each of the steps. In using this top-down approach, families

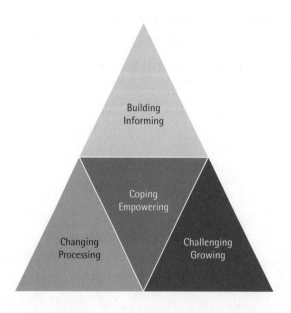

will begin with building and informing, moving down to coping and empowering, then changing and processing, and finally challenging and growing. Throughout this book you will see this pyramid highlighted for the specific process through which you will lead your family.

At the core of this healing and strengthening process is positive coping and empowering. Dealing with stress in a healthy manner, and being empowered to move ahead and conquer higher challenges, are central facets in the 8 Steps. When families know how to handle stress as it impacts them, and know they have what it takes to deal with it, they will more confidently move ahead in life. They will also be stronger and more resilient in meeting life's challenges.

Here is a sneak peak at the 8 Steps. Within each of the steps, there are very specific *key issues and challenges* that commonly occur within military families, so the goal is for family members to work through those issues together.

Building/Informing

At the beginning of this process, the family will start with reconnecting. The family will learn to build the connection and inform/explain their perspective. In **STEP 1**, family members will **CONNECT** with one another again. You will guide them through the process of building the connection and improving communication.

Once they have reestablished a positive connection with one another, the family will arrive at **STEP 2**, wherein they **EXPLAIN** their perspective to each other. In Step 2, you will guide the family through the process of learning how to effectively and sensitively communicate and become more informed about each other's experiences.

Coping/Empowering

In **STEP 3**, you will help military family members to **DISCOVER** what helps in their relationship, and what coping skills will help them to more effectively deal with life's stress. Their process will involve discovery and practice of powerful coping skills. By taking good care of themselves, the family can move to the next level.

In **STEP 4**, you will help **EMPOWER** family members. In this step, the family learns to focus on one another's strengths. They learn to use those strengths to deal with the key issues they will face.

Changing/Processing

At this point, the family faces challenges with trust and intimacy. Family members may have inaccurate perceptions or thoughts about others in the family, which may be leading to anger and resentment. In **STEP 5**, you will help the family **IMPROVE** their thoughts, beliefs, feelings, and behaviors. You will guide them through the process of becoming more aware of their negative thoughts and beliefs, which are particularly relevant to sexual intimacy. The family will learn to break the habits of negative thoughts and beliefs and change the course of their relationship at a deeper, more intimate level.

In **STEP 6**, we provide healthy ways that the family can share their intimate fears, thoughts, and feelings. You will learn how to **PROCESS** painful experiences that military family members may have had, which to this point have prevented the family from moving ahead in their lives. The family will work together to understand and unconditionally accept one another.

Challenging/Growing

The family is now equipped to set powerful, higher-level goals for themselves because they have conquered all of the core issues that were previously holding them back. With newfound energy and trust, family members learn in **STEP 7** to set positive, powerful, short- and long-term goals as individuals and as a family. You will learn how to help the family **CHALLENGE** themselves and work together as a family toward achieving their most important goals in life. Meeting new challenges will help the family to reach the final step—growth.

In **STEP 8**, the family is ready to **GROW** together and become resilient. They learn how to further reinforce their individual and collective strengths as a family. They learn to become resilient, able to face new challenges in their lives in ways that are now positive, healthy, and empowering for everyone.

The Road to Healing in the Military Family

Our intent is not to point out faults, focus on problems, or to judge. Our intent is to highlight areas that can be improved upon. No one is perfect. Everyone has problems. That is not the issue. The key to healing and becoming stronger as individuals and as families is to acknowledge those areas of difficulty, then to adapt and adjust accordingly. In the words of Thomas Edison, "There is a better way to do it. Find it."

We would like to offer better ways of doing things for the family. By taking these steps and practicing these new, improved methods of interacting with one another, the family will quickly be on their way to healing, wellness, and success in their relationships. This is what we hope every military family will achieve as a result of working through this book. Now let's get started!

THE 8 STEPS TO HEALING AND WELLNESS

Connect

Building the Relationship

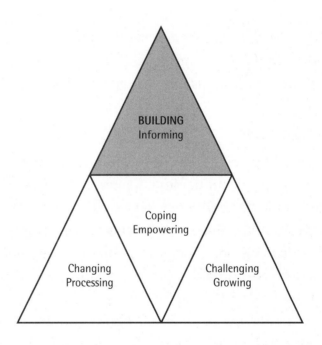

The strength of a nation is derived from the integrity of its homes.

—Confucius c. 551–478 B.C.

John and Amy got married 10 years ago and have a 9-year-old daughter. John is on active duty in the U.S. Marines. A squad leader for an infantry company, John is a well-seasoned combat Marine. Since they married, John has been deployed to Afghanistan three times and Iraq once. His wife (Amy) and daughter (Ashley) can count how many days they have spent together.

As if being apart at the beginning of their relationship is not enough, the couple has also relocated across the country in the past few months. John and Amy sit across from me in my office. There is a silence looming in the room, which Amy hesitatingly breaks.

> *"You just don't understand!" she says emphatically.*
>
> *"Understand what?" John says, looking off to the side, with a disconnected look on his face.*
>
> *"You come back, and you just think everything is the same as when you left? You think you are the* only one *who is hurting? You think* you *are the only one who has it rough?" she retorts, her voice starting to climb.*
>
> *"Don't fucking tell* me *what* hard *is! You have* no *idea* what hard *is! You have been here, at home, in the comfort of our house, with our daughter. I am the one who was off on deployment! I'm the one who has suffered! You have had it easy!" he yells back.*

The screaming match continues and plays back and forth for a few minutes before I play referee and break up the fight. Both John and Amy are fuming, and the conversation has come to a screeching halt. The silence in the room has now thickened.

The Stress on Military Families

As immature and inflamed as this interaction may sound to the outside observer, it is a true story (as we said, with names changed). We have seen it time and time again in our work with families. The difference here is the circumstances. Not to say that civilian families lack stress in their lives, but in general, active-duty military families experience a plethora of added stressors, including deployments, relocations, war, and reunions. And the stress does add up after a while, creating a host of issues and problems to be dealt with and resolved by the family.

As we stated earlier, the point of this book is not to emphasize dysfunction. It is certainly not to judge. The purpose of this book is to inform you of the most common difficulties faced by today's military families. We provide clear and practical suggestions you can use to help families reconnect, become stronger, and more cohesive. As the slogan for Lowe's says, "Let's build something together!" Let's rebuild the military family. But first, we want to provide you with important information about the specific challenges military families face.

Setting the Stage

In this chapter, we discuss the types of challenges military families face when they reunite after war or other long-term deployments. The types of problems faced by families following reunion include feelings of disconnection from each other, barriers in communication, and changed roles in the family. Step 1 sets the foundation to help rebuild the connection and improve communication among family members. In this step, we describe strategies that can help families deal with these problems to begin to reconnect, learn to rebuild the connection, and improve communication.

The Important Roles of the Family

Because of frequent relocations, the service member and spouse often rely upon each other to be the primary sources of emotional support. The family serves as an extremely important support mechanism in dealing with deployment-related stress (see Family Handout Step 1.1 located in Part Three, Appendix A). In fact, a large body of research shows that being in a relationship can help buffer many deployment-related problems, including PTSD and depression (Galovski & Lyons, 2004). This is because families and friendships provide companionship and a sense of belonging. Here are some other important roles of the family (see Family Handout Step 1.2). Families do the following:

> ➤ Provide practical support for solving problems (benefit: increased self-efficacy)
> ➤ Help service members reconnect to the community, other friends, or with extended family
> ➤ Provide emotional support and stability when coping with life stressors
> ➤ Buffer feelings of isolation
> ➤ Help family members feel like they belong
> ➤ Increase a sense of safety
> ➤ Boost self-esteem

Different Folks, Different Strokes

It may be expected that service members who return from deployment should easily and smoothly transition back into home life. Unfortunately, this is sometimes far from the case. One example of this was the very common experience of John and Amy. As you can see, family members can have lots of difficulties relating with one another. Couples frequently struggle with communication in the postdeployment phase. Service members and spouses have very unique experiences before, during, and after deployment, and they subsequently adjust in different ways. Of course, after being apart for several months, both individuals may have changed considerably, and they may each be struggling with their own difficulties. Let's go back to John and Amy's argument.

From John's Point-of-View (Service Members)

If you recall, John argued that he was the one who suffered the most. Indeed, the deployment experience is filled with chronic and, often, severe stress, especially when deployment involves direct combat, responding to attacks, and involvement with casualties or similar threats. Intense, life-threatening situations often cause service members to connect closely with their military comrades. In life-threatening situations, they learn to trust each other in ways that others cannot imagine or understand if they have not experienced this sense of chronic life-threat.

Consider a game where you are blindfolded and you have a friend who is leading you around an obstacle course. You must rely on that person to keep you safe. You would need to quickly learn to trust your friend, and, in a sense, put your life in his or her hands. Now extrapolate upon this scenario. In combat, John (and other service members like him) had to learn to put his life in his comrades' hands. He literally had their back, and they had his. His "men" shielded him from flying bullets and rocket-propelled grenades. They shot oncoming enemies so that he would live. No doubt, service members grow close. Now, when John gets back home, how does he unlearn his combat training? How can he—and other service members—put aside those life-and-death experiences? Is there a switch they can use to automatically shut off those feelings and experiences? Of course not. Yet, that is what they are expected to do.

From Amy's Point-of-View (Military Spouses)

Similarly, Amy and other spouses share the experience of adjustment. Amy has supported her husband and moved to different states in the United States for his military career. She has raised their child as a single mother would when John was deployed, playing the part of both mother and father. She has been fully responsible for taking care of all household chores. She has made sure the household bills have been paid. She has had to learn again and again to sleep in bed alone at night.

During deployments, Amy's life has essentially been her own. Yet, she has worried for her husband's safety every day. Then, redeployment brings John back to the family again after being gone for so long. Amy is expected to adjust, to be excited that he is back. And she is, because he is safe and in one piece. Yet, on a deeper level, she feels like he is a stranger who has come back to her bed. And now, *he is changed*. But then again, she has changed too. She, too, is different on many levels.

The Common Ground for the Family

Whereas military couples and families all have unique experiences, they also share some universally common experiences. Specifically, most family members have been apart from each other because of deployments. They have had to adjust in their own unique responsibilities. Most family members have changed in terms of their outlook and priorities in life. Things that used to be important to family members before deployment may change during deployment and be vastly different after reuniting.

Following deployments, family members may struggle with being able to communicate with each other. They may be challenged by renegotiating their sense of trust in other family members. Members of the family have become used to functioning independently in separate contexts; as such, they all must learn to function together as a unit again. For example, members of the family need to adjust to changes in family household chores and responsibilities. In addition, the service member and the spouse may struggle with feeling awkward with intimacy and find it difficult to reconnect sexually.

Not surprisingly, family members often deal with hurt feelings because of a disconnection between each other's needs and experiences. All family members are unique individuals, trying to rediscover their identities after their experience apart. This is the common struggle that can be overcome within a therapeutic relationship. The key is to help the family reconnect in the process, and that is where we are heading in the rest of this chapter.

Rebuilding the Foundation of Trust

It is crucial that the service member and family members cut each other some slack during the redeployment period and be patient with each other. It takes time and commitment to reconnect. What does that mean for the clinician, exactly? It means that family members may need to be guided to try to understand each other's points of view. Additionally, family members may need to be encouraged to make an effort to respect and accept each other, even when they see things differently. This is part of the process of healthy communication.

Fostering Healthy Communication

As you know, without a good, solid foundation of being able to communicate, a relationship will not survive. Even more important, without mutual respect and appreciation, a relationship is destined to fail. Back to the example of John and Amy, it is clear that some points were lacking in the arena of communication. Right?

Amy started out trying to let her husband know that she felt that he did not understand her feelings. John rebutted by asking what he should understand. However, his body language communicated that he had no interest in what Amy had to say. The argument blew up further when Amy shot back accusations, and it was all downhill from there. At that point, both of them felt misunderstood and insulted, and they were not able to listen anymore. They both focused on getting their points across, rather than on understanding where the other person was coming from.

For Your Information: Communication 101

Communication involves more than just talking. Communication requires that a person send a message and that the second person hears the message. But, when you break down the process of communication, there are six key components involved. Look at the following figure, and you can see what is conveyed during communication.

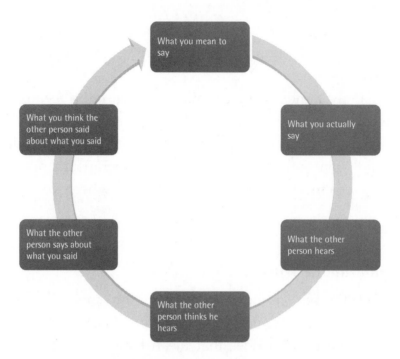

What you mean to say

What you actually say

What the other person hears

What the other person thinks he hears

What the other person says about what you said

What you think the other person said about what you said

Taking this figure a step further, there is the communication; then, there is respect and appreciation for other family members' views. Essentially, to be successful, family members need to make an effort to act in a way that makes others feel listened to, safe, and respected. They listen without interrupting or making judgments. They value others' opinions, even if they are different from their own.

It's important to know that family members may resist sharing their experiences. This usually happens if family members emotionally shut down from feeling overwhelmed, if they feel like there is no point, or if they are trying to make the other person feel bad or guilty. In working with military families, it is important to reinforce that family members each have their own unique experiences, but they also have shared experiences. In John and Amy's exchange, was there healthy communication? Was there respect? Was there appreciation for the other's experience at all? The obvious answer is "No!" on all points. Let's get back to assisting this couple.

Reframing and Redirecting Toward Positive

To reiterate, an extremely important key to rebuilding the connection between family members is not only enhancing communication, but also improving the level of respect and appreciation family members have for each other. With John and Amy, the part of the session you did not see yet will shift the content toward a more positive direction.

Finding the Common Ground

After John and Amy stopped screaming at each other and sat stewing, I allowed the silence to set in, and then said,

THERAPIST: John and Amy, it is clear you both feel very angry and misunderstood right now. Right?

Both John and Amy nod in agreement.

THERAPIST: (I continue.) You both share the experience of anger. You both feel alone in your experiences. In some ways, even though you had very different experiences, you both are feeling similar things. Can you see that?

They pause, and then nod in agreement again.

THERAPIST: Maybe we can spend some time working on understanding how each other is feeling.

Making sense of this, your goal is to take the family members' disagreement and find the common ground. The family members have similar feelings. These can be pointed out to help each member begin to understand the others' perspectives. Each have different experiences, but if family members make more effort to try to empathize with each other's points of view, they can turn a corner and respect one another in their differences.

Keys to Reconnecting and Rebuilding the Family

With support, family members can better appreciate what other family members have gone through. They can appreciate them for who they are and what they bring to the family unit. As simple as it may sound, the respect and appreciation are the keys to reconnecting and rebuilding the family.

We now introduce our first Making It Real exercise. You will find these exercises in all of the chapters. These exercises are designed to help your military families to reconnect, heal, and grow as a family. Please note that we have included copies of all Making It Real exercise worksheets in Part Three of this book. For those exercises where we ask family members to write out their answers to questions first, space is provided on the worksheet to do this.

Making It Real: Practicing Healthy Communication

The goal of this exercise is to help family members attentively listen and communicate better with each other. It requires that the therapist begin to help them refrain from making accusing remarks, degrading, or discounting what other family members have to say.

Instructions: Please use Family Handout Step 1.3.

➤ Use a stress ball (or a regular ball) for this exercise. Give a family member the ball. This means the ball is in their court. They have the floor. Have them communicate their experience. The recipients cannot respond until the person who is talking passes the ball to them. When the recipient gets the ball, they first need to summarize what they heard from the other person. Each member repeats this until all members have expressed themselves.

➤ Family members pass the ball back and forth until they have communicated and respected each other's abilities to speak.

➤ Have family members share their thoughts and feelings about the following:

> My experience with deployment has been . . .
>
> The most challenging part of deployment for me was . . .
>
> I feel concerned about . . .

Talking Points

Here is how some of this exercise went for John and Amy.

THERAPIST (handing Amy a ball):	Amy, why don't you go first? Go ahead and tell John what it's been like for you with him being gone on deployment. John, you are the listener first. You get to hear Amy out. When she's finished, she'll pass you the ball. Then you can say everything you want to say back, okay? (He nods, appearing quite disinterested.)
AMY (appearing irritated):	Okay. I don't think that was fair at all, John—saying that things were rougher for you. How can you possibly know what it has been like for me? You have been gone for months at a time. I have been here, yes! I haven't been out in a warzone, but I have been here playing mother and father to our daughter, taking care of the house, paying all of the bills, making sure things don't fall apart. Maybe that sounds easy to you. But I'd like to see you try it for a day. How do you think it is for me, not knowing if you are alive? You think it's easy to go through the day wondering if you are safe? Praying that you are okay? Being this far away from you? (Pauses). You just don't get it.
JOHN (irritated, looking away):	I guess I just don't get it then. I could handle it. (Stops and hands the ball back.)
THERAPIST:	Hold on a second, John. Would you look at Amy and tell her what you heard her say.
JOHN (starting to get angry):	What she said? She said . . . (looks at Amy). You said it's hard for you. You said I couldn't handle a day of what you put up with. I think that's complete and total fucking shit! I went to war! I can handle one day at home, Amy!
THERAPIST:	John, what else did you hear Amy say?

JOHN:	She said . . . you said you have a lot to do. So do I.
THERAPIST:	Anything else?
JOHN:	I don't know! This is stupid! What a fucking waste of time! I don't know.
THERAPIST:	Amy, help John to hear what you are saying to him. What is it that you want him to understand?
AMY:	I want him . . . (looks at John) . . . I want you to make an effort to step out of your shoes for a minute, to consider my needs and my experience, John. You being gone scares the shit out of me! And I feel like I have to hold it together all of the time because I can't fall apart. I don't get to fall apart. I can't. And keeping the house functioning, doing everything you get to leave behind for months at a time. It doesn't just get done on its own. I feel like a single mom. Now I understand . . . (starts to cry). I get it now. It's just . . . hard. It's really hard on me.
JOHN (breathing calm, face relaxing, quiet and listening intently)	
AMY (face softened, tone quieter):	I love you, John. We love you so much. We worry about you. I feel lonely. And I feel overwhelmed a lot.
JOHN (face soft, tone quiet, looks down and sighs):	I didn't think you had it bad. You didn't deploy, Amy (pauses). I didn't think you could feel this way. I mean, I feel lonely being gone (looks at his wife).
THERAPIST:	John, putting yourself in Amy's shoes, what do you think she was feeling while you were gone?
JOHN:	I think I would be feeling worried (pauses), sad (pauses). Stressed out. You've had to deal with a lot of shit while I was gone. And on top of it, you don't know if I'm okay. That would stress me out if it were me here.
AMY:	It was hard. We hate being away from you. We worry about you. I know it's hard for you, John. I can see you feel different. It must be hard for you. It's kind of confusing. You went through a lot too. We went through stress, but had to deal with it apart.
JOHN:	Yeah, it is confusing (relaxed body language, nodding, sighing). Amy, I'm sorry. Maybe we need to stop trying to go off on each other.
AMY:	I'm sorry too, John.

A First Step

Even though we only presented you with a brief session script, hopefully you got a sense of the transformation that occurred for both John and Amy. As you can see, when John and Amy were focused on topping off the other's experience, they became more and more frustrated with each other. The first step was to focus on John (who, in this situation, was more emphatic about his experience being worse). I did this by helping him to repeat the gist of what Amy was saying, narrowing down more and more on her discomfort as well.

Reframing and Building Empathy

The key was to reframe the situation for them by helping to build insight and empathy in both of them. It was crucial that both John and Amy develop an understanding for what the other was feeling—to step out of their own shoes and into the other's for awhile. As they felt empathy for the other, their body language and tone softened. They became more open-minded about what the other was saying.

When John and Amy were able to realize that they were *both* feeling alone, angry, and misunderstood, this was the catalyst that helped turn the tide. The focus then became finding common ground. And from there, they expressed appreciation for each other. The conversation improved from that point forward. So, the first step to rebuilding the family is using healthy communication, with lots of respect and appreciation for the others' experiences. With the next exercise, we help the family get more connected by realizing times when they were supported by their loved ones.

Making It Real: Providing Support

The goal of this exercise is to help family members continue practicing healthy communication, and also to practice the art of support for each other.

Instructions: Please use Family Handout Step 1.4.

➢ Use a stress ball (or a regular ball) for this exercise. Give a family member the ball. When they have the ball, it signifies the ball is in their court. They have the floor. Have them communicate their experience. The recipients cannot respond until the person who is talking passes the ball to them. When the recipient gets the ball, they first need to summarize what they heard from the other person. The family repeats this until all members have expressed themselves.

➢ Family members pass the ball back and forth until they have communicated and given each other the opportunity to speak.

➢ Have family members share their thoughts and feelings about the following:

> Describe in detail a time when you felt most supported by your family members. (What did they do or say?)

Talking Points

In this last exercise, John and Amy realized that they had received a lot of unconditional support from each other over the years. John acknowledged that he had not really paid attention to how much Amy had supported him throughout his military career. Amy recalled specific experiences when John had been back from deployment, and she was in bed sick. She recalled that John took charge of the house, cared for their daughter, and did anything that needed to be done so she could get better. She recalled that he also made her meals, brought her water and juice throughout the day, and prepared a warm bath with candles lit all around the tub. Amy realized that in these moments, she felt closer to the man she had married. We then did the final Making It Real exercise for this chapter, that of Practicing Appreciation.

Making It Real: Practicing Appreciation

The goal of this exercise is to help family members continue practicing healthy communication, and also to practice the art of appreciation.

Instructions: Please see Family Handout Step 1.5.

➤ Use a stress ball (or a regular ball) for this exercise. Give a family member the ball. This means the ball is in their court. They have the floor. Have them communicate their experience. The recipients cannot respond until the person who is talking passes the ball to them. When the recipient gets the ball, they first need to summarize what they heard from the other person. They repeat this until all members have expressed themselves.

➤ Family members pass the ball back and forth until they have communicated and respected each other's abilities to speak.

➤ Have family members share their thoughts and feelings about the following:

> I appreciate how you . . .
>
> I appreciate that you . . .
>
> I appreciate your . . .

Talking Points

By doing this exercise, John and Amy honed in on very specific traits they appreciated about one another. By the end of the session, they were both smiling more and left making eye contact with each other. Of course, this session does not cure or erase the problems in this family. They still have a lot of work to do with each other. However, by practicing some of these exercises during the week and weeks to come, they will be more apt to notice the positives in one another. And as they practice daily appreciation, they will be more likely to focus on things they like and appreciate about each other.

Practice Makes Perfect

You know the saying "Practice makes perfect"? There is some truth in the statement that can be applied to working with military families. It is imperative that families keep the momentum going from the sessions with you. Some of the work and progress occurs in the session. However, without practicing what they have learned, family members will be more likely to remain stuck, or they will have difficulties progressing in their treatment. To help the military family practice what they have learned and take it to a new level during the week, we have included two additional sections in every chapter.

You will find Keys to Wellness at the end of this and other chapters, as well as Taking Action steps. Please have the family do the steps listed in the Taking Action sections to further reinforce and practice these positive relationship-building skills.

We feel that both of these components are vital to helping the family heal. Reinforce the importance of going through these steps every week. Let them know that, while they may make gains during therapy sessions, the most important progress continues outside of session, in their own home. When the family does the homework, they take the initiative to work together and help each other, and this builds an individual and collective sense of accomplishment and self-efficacy.

Final Thoughts

We have made some progress with our military family. They have learned to communicate in a healthier manner. They have learned to reframe their situation. They are reconnecting and beginning to respect and appreciate each other. This family is on their way to healing. They are on their way to getting to know each other again.

Keys to Family Wellness

➢ It is common for service members and family members to expect an easy transition during reunion, but reunion is often a difficult process for the family. Family can be a source of support, but if members are disconnected from one another, family can be a source of stress.

➢ Communication is more than speaking. Family members need to make an effort to speak with each other in a way that makes others feel listened to and respected.

➢ Making the effort to communicate and reconnect can be learned. While reconnecting may be slow at first, it will help to resolve family problems.

—————— **Taking Action** ——————

Taking action will help rebuild the family. Please check off each step as the family accomplishes it.

❏ Family members should make time for each other this week. This could be in the form of a family date night. They should practice one of our suggestions for improving communication and respecting one another.

❏ The family should take time to talk about and find ways of supporting one another. Family members should each describe a time when they felt supported by others in the family.

❏ Family members should practice becoming more in tune with each other. They should practice providing support to each other this week.

2

Explain

Informing of Experiences

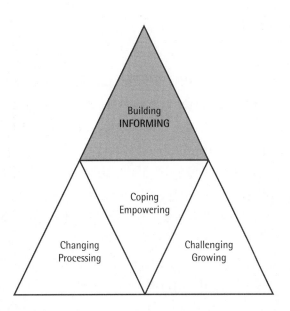

Friendship is a plant of slow growth and must undergo and withstand the shocks of adversity before it is entitled to the appellation.

—George Washington

Josh and Sarah appear confused, estranged, and almost like they are fighting to get back to the people they were before he went to war. This young couple has struggled in many ways since Josh was medically discharged from the Navy due to a mild traumatic brain injury (mTBI) and knee injury a little over two months ago. Sarah was used to Josh being gone on extended deployments, but she was relieved to have him home in one piece. However, Sarah can't help but feel that Josh is different from how he was before he deployed. She wonders what happened this time that changed him so much. When he left, Josh was nurturing, affectionate, and emotionally present in their relationship. But since he's returned, he has been emotionally distant. It's like he doesn't want to be around her. She has been making efforts to make love, but he nods and pushes her away saying he is too tired. She knows he must be tired because Josh hasn't been sleeping well at all. He tosses and turns, thrashes in his sleep, and wakes up screaming sometimes. Sarah wants to understand. Josh says he doesn't want to talk about it because "she just wouldn't understand."

Josh and Sarah's experience is shared by thousands of military couples. The postdeployment period can be a very emotionally confusing time for both the returnee and the spouse, as well as for the children. Here you have a situation where the family is feeling thankful that their loved one is home safe and sound, and the returnee feels grateful to be with the family. However, many returnees don't feel right inside, and they don't understand why. The family desperately wants to understand what is going on, but they may also feel uncomfortable crossing that bridge to broach the topic.

Setting the Stage

Homecoming can be a very difficult and challenging time for the military family. It would seem that being together after months apart should be like a bed of roses, but instead, it is often like a bed of thorns. The family may feel like they are tiptoeing around each other, not wanting to create more stress. One obvious difficulty about this period for the family is that the returnee is safe. This, in itself, should be a cause for relief and excitement. Whereas relief is a common feeling once the returnee is home, after a few weeks have passed, many families start having problems getting along or talking with one another.

Like Josh, it is common for returnees to be significantly affected by their experience in war, and they may relate differently than they previously did. Like Sarah, family members may feel like their loved one doesn't love them as much. They may feel emotionally isolated or betrayed. On the whole, the family may feel very disconnected.

The way to help the family is to bridge the gap at the level of informing and explaining. We want to help open the doors of healthy communication between family members so they can begin to form an understanding of what each other is going through.

The purpose of Step 2 is to help the family to emotionally connect on a deeper level than they did in Step 1. With Step 2, we will facilitate healthy, intimate communication among family members and help shed some light on what the returnee's experience is upon return. We will help family members mutually share their feelings in an atmosphere of trust, to ease the transition, and provide exercises the family can use to grow closer and understand one another. And we provide important and practical communication exercises to nurture the bond that will develop as family members mutually respect, understand, and appreciate each other's perspectives.

For Your Information: Marital Satisfaction

In order for you to help the military family, it is very important for you to have some more information about why the returnee is reacting and interacting differently with the family. That's why, throughout this book, you will see sections called For Your Information. In these sections, we provide you with an overview, based upon clinical research and our own clinical experiences, of what the military family members are going through. This is designed to educate and inform you, as you guide the family through this process of getting to know each other better.

A great deal of research has been done this past decade, which has clearly shown that veterans are at significant risk for depression, PTSD, anxiety, and other postwar conditions (e.g., Cozza, 2005; Hoge et al., 2004). As far as satisfaction in the marriage, returnees' trauma symptoms significantly predict their own as well as their partner's level of marital dissatisfaction (Goff, Crow, Reisbig, & Hamilton, 2007). For example, soldiers who have more dissociative, sexual, and sleep problems tend to feel most dissatisfied in their relationship (e.g., Goff et al., 2007; Simmons, Maconochie, & Doyle, 2004).

One very important point to understand is that when returnees are experiencing high levels of trauma symptoms, because they may be immersed in their own pain and discomfort, it may also be difficult for them to have the emotional ability to give their spouses and children the nurturance that they need. Beyond this, when spouses of returnees perceived greater levels of symptoms in their loved one, they consequently experienced symptoms (Renshaw, Rodrigues, & Jones, 2008), and this, in turn, reduces marital satisfaction.

The Trust Factor

It is common for returnees to feel emotionally disconnected after they return from combat and reintegrate with their family, friends, and society. Several factors can make it difficult for returnees to communicate their distress with their loved ones. Understanding returning service members' experiences puts things into perspective and clarifies some of the key issues faced by today's military families.

Isolating From the Family

Returnees who are depressed may isolate from others and may not want to talk about their problems. Other returnees with PTSD may also isolate from other people, but they can also have difficulties feeling positive emotions such as happiness, joy, or love. Conversely, returnees may have trouble feeling sadness or expressing it in the form of crying. Loved ones may perceive this inability as the returnee being unloving, emotionally detached, cold, or distant. Sometimes, because returnees don't know why they are feeling this way, they may cope by withdrawing from other people, including their family.

Difficulties With Intimacy

As a result of having trouble with loving feelings, some returnees may have a very hard time being sexually intimate or romantic with their partner or spouse. As a result, the spouse may worry that their partner doesn't love them anymore, or they may feel emotionally rejected. Similarly, when the returnee isolates or has trouble being affectionate, their children may feel rejected, as if their parent does not love them anymore.

Difficulties Sharing Their War Experiences

Another key problem that military families experience is that returnees may be having difficulty accepting things that happened while they were deployed. They may have very traumatic memories and experiences that they frequently relive. In addition, returnees commonly feel camaraderie with their military squad members because they can relate to the horrors they experienced. Returnees may believe that if they shared their feelings with military buddies, they would understand, whereas their family members would not. As a result, many returnees hesitate in sharing how they feel for fear of being judged, misunderstood, or told that they should be feeling a different way. The resulting problem is that the returnee bears a burden and feels disconnected from the family, and the family often feels like their loved one does not trust them and is emotionally detached from them.

Feeling Disconnected From the Family

The confusing dilemma here is that, though the returnee is back in the family's life and home, family members may feel like their loved one is less a part of their lives than ever before. Likewise, the returnee may feel removed from the family and unsure of how to reconnect with them. The therapeutic challenge at Step 2 is to help the family unite and learn how to trust each other again, to help them feel like an integrated system, not separate individuals in the home.

Josh and Sarah's Family Struggles

Josh and Sarah were high school sweethearts. They tied the knot and married shortly after graduation, then had their first child less than a year later. Amanda is now 8 years old, and they have a 6-year-old son, Tyler. When he was in the Navy, Josh had been deployed and the family relocated twice. Now Josh is home for the first time in a very long time. This is really the longest time Josh has spent with his family in one continuous stretch. It should be quality time, but it doesn't feel that way to anyone in the family.

Even though Josh and Sarah are only in their late 20s, this young couple has experienced their share of hurt and pain. Sarah is beginning to wonder where the love has gone. Their daughter wants to spend more and more time at her friend's house, because it has been feeling kind of awkward around the house for her. Sarah has been reading up on PTSD because she wants to understand if PTSD might have something to do with the change in Josh's behavior. Then again, the doctors at the base said he could "act different" for a few months. They said his recovery process was complicated and could take longer because Josh's lack of sleep and PTSD exacerbate the effects of his brain injury.

She has been noticing that Josh gets angry a lot, and has outbursts where he "goes off" on her for no reason. His memory is okay, but he sometimes seems to space out and disconnect from her. Sarah feels like she is at a loss and questions how their relationship is going to survive.

A Note About Children in the Sessions

Josh and Sarah bring Amanda and Tyler into this particular session. We would like to add in a quick note about whether or not to allow children into a session(s). While some of the exercises in the book can be very therapeutic for the entire family, including the children, there may also be times when the focus should be on the couple. You should really exercise your clinical judgment, considering factors such as the age of the child/ children, their emotional maturity level, the content being discussed or processed, and how emotionally charged things get at certain points. Your goal is to facilitate a healing environment for the family; however, please understand that there may be times when it may be contraindicated to have young children present in a session or a part of a session.

A Growing Disconnect

Now, back to our session with Josh, Sarah, Amanda, and Tyler.

Sarah breaks the silence.

"I can't stand it anymore, Josh!" she says, with tears brimming in her eyes. " I don't know what to do, how to be, or what to say anymore. Amanda and Tyler are walking on eggshells. It's like we don't even exist in your life anymore. You hardly ever talk. It probably doesn't make any sense to you, but sometimes I feel better when you yell and get mad. At least you are saying something! I think the silence is harder to take." She paused for a minute, and then continued, "Please, Josh. Talk to me. I love you, but I don't know how to handle this. Just talk to me."

Josh didn't respond for some time to Sarah's pleading. He was very collected and rational, almost methodical in his reply: "I'm not sure what to say, Sarah. You want me to make sense of this, but I can't!" His voice began to get louder. He looked her straight in the eyes for the first time since they sat down. "I don't know what the hell is going on! I wish I did! I don't feel like myself! I don't know how to relate to you and the kids. I feel different. Nothing is the same. I don't know what you want from me!" He looked away from her, then down to the floor.

She waited, anticipating something else from him.

He quietly added in a monotone, "I don't know how to be the husband and father you want me to be. I don't know."

You could feel the confusion and desperation on both Josh and Sarah's parts. They both appeared lost, like they were searching for a magical solution but not having any

---

For Your Information: Marital Conflict

It is no surprise that scientists have found biological differences in how men and women deal with conflict in their relationships. Women tend to be more emotionally expressive, whereas men tend to be task-oriented problem solvers (Gottman & Levenson, 1992). Moreover, researchers have found that men are biologically more likely to withdraw from conflicts raised by their wives (Levenson, Carstensen, & Gottman, 1994). They stated that:

> Men and women have different reactions to this heightened arousal. Women have considerable tolerance for physiological arousal and, thus, can maintain high levels of engagement. Men, in contrast, experience this arousal as being highly aversive and act to dissipate it by withdrawing from conflict. (p. 58)

In addition to the increased autonomic arousal that results from PTSD following combat, it is probably necessary to consider the impact of biology on conflict resolution and communication. These points are not raised as judgments or overarching rules. Rather, it may be helpful to take each person's ability to regulate and tolerate arousal into consideration to have a greater understanding of the husband and wife's coping styles in the midst of marital difficulties.

---

luck finding it. They both wanted to make things work for their family. They both knew, as did their children, that things had changed. Now it was a matter of therapeutically joining the family together by helping them understand the world from each other's perspectives.

His Needs, Her Needs

Josh and Sarah have both expressed very significant and real frustrations with one another. Neither feels understood or cared for by the other. On the other hand, both of them want to work on their relationship. They both want their family to be whole again. The problem here is that the needs of family members are not being met. The solution is helping the family to communicate with each other and begin to rediscover what their needs are (see Family Handout Step 2.1).

Helping the family to communicate is an important therapeutic step. Josh and Sarah, and other military families, go through drastic changes in how their individual needs are met as part of the family. Following homecoming after deployment(s), the military family has to recalibrate and readjust. For example, in Josh and Sarah's case, Sarah took on the role of the primary head of the house while Josh was deployed. When Josh came back, this time permanently after discharge, Sarah had to figure out what her place was in the family. Josh, likewise, had to figure out his place after Sarah stepped down from her previous role. In this case, Josh is also injured, so roles may be further complicated or changed, as he cannot work. At this point, I gave Josh and Sarah some exercises to do, to help them learn about each other, as they are today.

Making It Real: Discovering Needs

It is crucial that family members understand what is important to others in the home. Marriages fail because partners stop talking to one another on an intimate and personal level. Families become chaotic or detached when members stop sharing and relating to one another. Before family members begin to inform one another about their own needs, it is important for them to understand what other family members need. This will essentially establish a common ground and help family members connect with each other.

Exercise directions: Please go to Family Handout Step 2.2. Have the family members ask each other these questions.

1. Tell me five words that describe your greatest needs in life, in general.
2. Why are these needs so important to you?
3. Tell me five words that describe what you need most from me.
4. Be completely honest with me. How am I meeting your needs?
5. Help me understand what it means to you for me to meet these needs, or if I haven't met these needs.
6. How do you think your needs have changed since we have been a family?

Talking Points

This last exercise should have been an eye-opening one for the family. In particular, with military families, there is so much change and adaptation that frequently takes place, that spouses and children's needs change considerably as well. What once used to be important to one family member may not take precedence any more.

What Josh Learned

In the case of Josh and Sarah, for example, Josh knew he had not been meeting Sarah's emotional needs since he got back home. Josh was feeling like he could barely contain his own internal stress, more or less, to manage Sarah's or their children's stress. During this exercise, he learned that Sarah needed for him to be physically affectionate with her, for him to take on a family leadership role and make primary decisions, and to share some responsibility in caring for the kids. To Sarah, the fact that he was not doing much of these things meant that he did not emotionally invest himself in their family. Josh thought that he should take a step back since Sarah had been in control while he was gone. He had assumed Sarah wanted it that way. As a result of learning what Sarah needed, Josh committed himself to trying harder and providing these needs for her.

What Sarah Learned

It was also a learning experience for Sarah. She did not realize that Josh needed to be the financial breadwinner of the family, to have more one-on-one time with his children, and to have quiet alone time outside of the home. He didn't want to go out in public around a lot of people because it gave him anxiety. Josh explained that he felt like he had a lot on his mind that he was trying to sort out. He was worried that he might take out his frustrations on his family, so he felt it was better for everyone if he stayed out of the house. Josh explained to Sarah that he would back out of going to the mall with her and the kids because of his anxiety.

This exercise was helpful to start shedding some light for Josh and Sarah, and it can be a good starting point for other military couples and families you work with. A big plus of this exercise is that it clarifies needs and values, which tend to change for people as they get older and go through certain life experiences. You can use this exercise as a talking point. Give the family some time to discuss their responses in detail, to further explore and clarify their needs on a deeper level. It can serve to bond family members together.

Making It Real: A Picture Is Worth a Thousand Words

This exercise is a good follow-up to the last one you did with the family, and it is especially helpful for families with young children. In this exercise, you will take the family to a different level of understanding of each other's needs. As the saying goes, "a picture is worth a thousand words." In this exercise, family members will put a picture together of how they view their family.

Materials needed for this exercise:

Old or used magazines

White or black poster board for each family member

Glue sticks

Scissors

Exercise directions: Please go to Family Handout Step 2.3. Have the family do the following activity together.

1. Have a stack of magazines in your office ready for the family to go through.
2. Tell each family member, "Each of you please go through these magazines. Please cut out the pictures that speak to you on a deep gut level and reflect your vision or view of your family. I'm not going to be more specific because I want you to feel free to go with your gut and not get tied up with whether or not you are doing this right or wrong. Just go with your instinct and pick out all of the pictures that represent your family."

    Have each of the family members look through the magazines and cut out pictures that speak to them and visually represent how they perceive their family. They should go with their initial instincts when they have an emotional connection with the pictures.

3. Have family members glue the pictures they cut out of the magazines onto their individual poster boards.

4. Family members should fill up each of their poster boards like a collage and wait until everyone in the family is finished. Family members should place their poster face down until they present it.

5. As a family exercise, go around one by one to each family member, exploring that individual's poster before moving on to the next person. Start the exploration by asking that family member, "_____, please tell me about your poster so that we can understand how you see your family."

6. Ask the family member, "And what does this mean to you?"

7. Then have each of the other family members ask questions of him or her, to try to understand their point of view better.

8. Repeat this exercise until you have done this same process with all members of the family.

Talking Points

After this exercise, the family should have a little more clarity about how they envision their family. This exercise can stir up feelings of sadness for some families as they realize that their family is not how it used to be, or how they would like it to be. Some families have a rude awakening that their family is not as bonded or as close as before. It is important, however, to reinforce to the family that this exercise is not intended to be used as a point of judgment or criticism among family members. It is a tool that they can and should use positively, to get to know each other better. It is one step among many that will help them grow closer together as their awareness builds.

Amanda's Experience in the Family

For Josh and Sarah's family, the eye-opening moment came for both Josh and Sarah when their 8-year-old daughter, Amanda, showed her collage poster. Amanda had pictures of soldiers, death, a mommy and daddy off away from the family, facing in the other direction and looking rather ill in the picture. When asked about her collage, Amanda responded, "I haven't felt like my daddy has been around for most of my life. I still worry about daddy getting really sick or dying, or leaving us. I feel like daddy doesn't want to be around us, and he misses his military buddies more than he missed us."

This was very difficult for Josh and Sarah to hear. Amanda had and has very real fears, but it was still tough for the family to hear those words said out loud. Understandably, it was especially hard for Josh to hear, and I took the opportunity to explore his feelings in the moment. Here's a snippet of our therapeutic dialogue.

THERAPIST: Josh, I can see that this is very hard for you right now. What was it like for you to hear Amanda say those words?

JOSH:	I heard her say she doesn't feel like I'm around, and that she worries about me leaving or dying.
THERAPIST:	Yes. (I paused, nodding.) And what is that like for you?
JOSH:	How do you think it was?! (looking irritated)

He drew in a long sigh, and then got up out of his seat, turning the other direction, toward the wall. He leaned up against the wall, face downturned to the floor, as if bracing and holding himself up.

At that moment, Amanda looked worried, like her father was angry with her. Sarah equally appeared concerned and began to get up out of her chair. I signaled for her to stay sitting down and give him a minute.

THERAPIST:	Josh, this is harder for you than you want to admit. (I paused.) Isn't it?
JOSH:	Yeah.
THERAPIST:	Josh, can you talk with Amanda and tell her what this is like for you right now?

Josh turned around and approached Amanda, who was still sitting in her chair, looking uncomfortable.

AMANDA:	Daddy, I'm sorry! I'm sorry! I didn't mean to make you mad or sad.
JOSH (knelt down and put his hands on top Amanda's):	Amanda, honey, Daddy is the one who should be sorry. You didn't do anything wrong. (He paused and wiped off her tears.) Daddy is sorry. I know I haven't been there for you. And Daddy is having a rough time right now. You didn't make Daddy sad. Daddy is trying to feel better. And Daddy is not going to leave you, sweetie. I'm not leaving.

The family experienced a big catharsis with this exercise. Several things happened. Josh expressed his feelings and showed his emotions. This was the first time he had cried in years. Amanda expressed herself in a safe environment. Sarah saw a vision of the husband she married. She said this experience started to rekindle the attraction to her husband, as she saw him express his human side, which she hadn't seen in a while. And this takes us to our final exercise for this step, Story Sharing.

Making It Real: Story Sharing

With this exercise, you will help the family to get to an even deeper level of understanding of each other's experiences. The last exercise opened the doors of sharing. With this exercise, you will be taking advantage of the moment when the family is honest, open, and at the level of the heart with each other. It will further solidify the connection that is occurring with the family.

Exercise Directions: Please go to Family Handout Step 2.4. Please have the family do the following.

Have each family member share their story, of how they feel and why.

1. Say to the family: "_____ (say all of their names and make eye contact with each of them), every one of you has had unique experiences over the past several months and years. You are all getting reconnected to each other. To make your relationships stronger, it is important that you all understand what the other has gone through. So now we are going to share stories.

2. Continue: "I'd like to ask each of you to please take a few minutes to share your story with your family. Tell them your experience in your own words. Tell them whatever details you feel you can share right now. Share how you feel and why you feel that way. You will all get to do this for each other. The only rule in this exercise is that no one says anything while the person is sharing. We'll take time to do that after everyone gets a chance to share."

As part of the story sharing, here is a little of what Josh shared with his family.

JOSH: My story . . . I'm not sure what to say. . . . I feel very different inside this time. I went through some things over there this last time that were really hard. I don't really want to talk about that stuff right now. But I am having a hard time sleeping, and I'm having bad dreams. I am having a hard time turning my brain off. I keep remembering things that happened. I am having a rough time being around crowds of people right now. It makes me feel uncomfortable. That's why I don't want to go to the mall or places where it's noisy and crowded. Hopefully that gets easier in the future. I'm not sure why, but I have been having a hard time concentrating, and it's not easy for me to talk to people, including all of you. I don't know why, but it's hard for me to trust people. I know it's not right because you are my family, and I love you all so much. But I don't feel like I can help it. That's why I'm here. . . . That's all I have to say.

Talking Points

After all members of the family have shared their story, please open it up for further sharing on a feeling level. The goal here is to stay at the heart level—at the emotions. Getting back to Josh and Sarah's family, here is how this went for them.

THERAPIST:	Josh, Sarah, Amanda, Tyler, let's take some time for you to share how you are feeling. (Pause.) Who would like to go first?

Sarah lifted a finger and started to talk.

SARAH:	I want to talk with Josh first. (She paused, turning toward him.) Josh, we love you too. And we are always here for you. You can always trust us. We're not going anywhere.
THERAPIST:	Sarah, do you have any questions for Josh?
SARAH:	Yes.

I redirected her to look at Josh and talk with him directly.

SARAH:	Josh, are you happy to be home with us?
JOSH (appears confused and surprised that she asked this):	Of course I'm happy to be home with you guys! (pleading with Sarah) Don't you know I love you guys?
SARAH:	I do. (She paused, looked down, and began to cry.) It's just . . . lately I have wondered because you are off by yourself so much.
JOSH (nodding):	I know, but I do love you. I guess I have figured that if I keep my distance and try to figure this out that I wouldn't hurt you guys. I couldn't bear to hurt you.
SARAH (crying):	I know, Josh, but keeping to yourself and pushing us away hurts too. We can make it together. I am always here for you, Josh. You can talk with me about anything. We need you. And we can handle it, as long as you are with us. That's all that matters.
JOSH:	I didn't know it was harder on you when I kept to myself. I thought I was making it easier on you guys. I'm sorry. (nodding) We're together again. It may not be easy all the time, but it will get better. We can be a strong family again, don't you think?

Sarah, Amanda, and Tyler nodded.
This military family is reconnecting.

Final Thoughts

The key to this exercise and all exercises we provide in this book is not to place blame on any one person in the family. The goal is to increase mutual understanding and to bridge the connection among family members. You want to get family members sharing with each other again.

In the case of Josh and Sarah's family, some progress occurred with these exercises. They informed each other of how they felt and of their worldviews, and they supported each other in the process. The doors of communication have been opened. They are reconnecting. This family is on its way to healing.

Keys to Family Wellness

➤ Sharing in an environment that is emotionally safe and without judgment is healing.

➤ It is important for family members to try to understand others' points of view.

➤ Talking with each other without assigning blame heals and builds trust.

➤ Openness and honesty are necessary foundations for understanding and healing.

➤ Considering any and all factors that can affect how the family sees and feels things is crucial to healing.

➤ Being aware of others' needs, how they see the world, and how they experience it results in empathy, which will lead to healing.

➤ While it can take some time, getting to know each other will heal and strengthen the family, and it will be worth it in the end.

--- **Taking Action** ---

Taking action will help rebuild the family. Please check off each step as the family accomplishes it.

❏ The family should make time during weeknights for a family dinner date. During this time, they should share with each other about the events of their day.

❏ During the family dinner date, family members should each talk for at least a few minutes to get into detail about a positive or negative experience in their day. At the same time, other family members should ask questions to express interest and learn more about why the experience was significant to the person.

❏ The family should make time to practice empathy with their family members this week. This means that they listen without passing judgment and really make an effort to understand their family member's point of view.

3

Discover

Strengthening Coping Skills

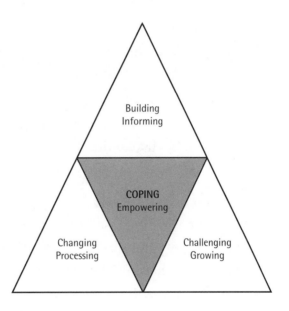

Problems are not the problem; coping is the problem.

—Virginia Satir

Michael and Lisa met when Michael was in the police academy and Lisa was in her last year of college. They married the year after she graduated, and they had a baby girl one year later. After taking a job as a patrol officer in his hometown, Michael joined the Army National Guard to help pay the bills. Shortly thereafter, the country went to war. In the past 10 years, Michael has deployed to Afghanistan, Kuwait, and, most recently, to Iraq. Eight months ago, while driving a lead convoy vehicle near Baghdad, Michael and his assistant were injured during a rocket-propelled grenade (RPG) attack. Michael was medically evacuated to an Army hospital with severe burns to his right leg, arm, and hand. Two months ago, Michael was medically discharged from the Army National Guard and retired from the police force.

Michael has lost much of his ability to use his arm and hand. He continues to suffer from moderate levels of chronic pain, and he has begun receiving treatment for his injuries and pain at the local Veterans Affairs hospital. Lisa, now an elementary school teacher, has done her best to manage her job and their now 12-year-old girl, Abby. This attractive but troubled couple now sits before me. The week, apparently, has not been a good one.

LISA:	*You need to be a father!*
MICHAEL (annoyed):	*I am a father. How am I not a father?*
LISA:	*You never do anything, Michael! Are you going to watch TV all day long for the rest of your life? You spend time alone. You don't talk to me. You don't talk to your daughter! You spend time with your buddies, but not with us (she glares at him).*
MICHAEL:	*Well, my buddies don't interrogate me all the time. My buddies don't snap at me for every little thing. I need a break!*
LISA (sounding incredulous):	A break?! All you do is take breaks! When you're home, you're always watching sports. You're a different person, Michael. I don't even know you anymore!

The family is dealing with multiple changes and numerous demands. When stress demands are high, positive coping methods can go to the wayside. However, at the core of strong families is the consistent use of positive coping. Dealing with stress in a healthy manner means that family members use positive coping both individually and as a family. When families know that they have a variety of tools to help them cope with stress when times are tough, they will be stronger and more resilient in meeting life's challenges.

Setting the Stage

In Step 3 we begin to provide families with coping tools and a roadmap to deal with whatever stressors they face. The purpose of Step 3 is to encourage healthy coping behaviors, which will increase resilience in families. Military families who are suffering from stress are less likely to use tools that will decrease their stress. In this chapter, we introduce coping techniques that will help family members feel useful and capable.

We also provide a variety of positive coping strategies to help the military family manage difficult times and become more resilient for the future. These coping tools will help families become better able to deal with the effects of stressful events.

Managing the Family's Stress

As we previously discussed, service members returning from a difficult combat deployment may go through a period of feeling depressed, anxious, or emotionally numb, and they may not communicate much as they gradually make sense of their war experience within the context of the world stateside. During this readjustment time, it is also common for returnees to feel on edge and to get angry easily. As such, it is important to ensure that the returnee and family members have a variety of positive coping techniques to ease the readjustment stress the family is experiencing. If coping skills are low, then helping the family to gradually try new ways of coping will help them see the positive benefits that healthy coping can bring.

The tools used in this chapter are drawn from cognitive-behavioral theory (e.g., Beck, Rush, Shaw, & Emery, 1979; Lewinsohn, Munoz, Youngren, & Zeiss, 1986) and, if used regularly, can help the family to function better. Military family members who are depressed—or in the case of returnees, suffering from combat injuries—will be less likely to engage in proactive coping. If a returnee is suffering from a physical or psychological injury, take some time to talk with him or her about how coping tools are especially important. Family members should practice these techniques too, so that they can all support each other in their efforts to heal. When individuals take direct action to cope with their problems, they put themselves in a position of power.

The Family's Coping Style

Returning to Michael and Lisa, we see that Michael is trying to adjust to his injuries and to retired living. Michael denies that he is suffering from depressive symptoms or any symptoms of combat stress. However, to cope with readjustment stress, Michael has chosen to become absorbed with the television and, on occasion, to hang out with his former work buddies. With further probing, I find out that Lisa is working 40 hours a week while handling all of the housework and childcare. Due to heavy time constraints, she has completely stopped doing things that are fun or that could release her stress. Both Lisa and Michael need to be validated for the struggles they are facing. However, as I do so, I also need to provide a larger context for the couple while gently shifting their focus toward proactive coping. Here is how the session continued.

THERAPIST: Michael and Lisa, I appreciate how stressful your lives are right now. Michael, I can see that you are adjusting to retired life while having some significant pain. I understand you have faced some pretty big changes. So right now you are dealing with your adjustments mainly by watching TV and spending more time with your buddies. Tell me, what does being with your buddies do for you?

MICHAEL: When I'm with my buddies, I can be myself. I don't know. Half of the guys are in the Guard too. I guess I am different now, but the guys understand that.

THERAPIST: So the "differentness" that you are experiencing makes sense when you're with the guys, and you feel like "yourself." How does it feel at home?

MICHAEL: At home I feel a little out of place. Like I'm a trained soldier in this soft, clean, perfect world. I feel out of sync.

A therapist could probe his feelings further, but the idea at this early stage of therapy is to validate where the couple is at this point and focus on strengthening their resources to cope with their problems. We will probe Michael's feelings deeper in later steps. In this session, we continue on.

THERAPIST: That's a good analogy to help me understand where you are right now. You no longer have the structure that being a cop, or even a soldier, provided for you. It sounds like the structure that you once had in your home is also lacking, so that you feel out of sync in your life.

MICHAEL (looking earnest):   Yeah.

THERAPIST: Lisa, I see that you are struggling with a number of responsibilities and have very little time to relax or enjoy life. It sounds like your life is lacking structure simply due to the overwhelming number of things you take care of in order to keep up.

LISA (quieter now):   Yes.

THERAPIST: You know, everyone has their own way to deal with stress. Where I see you right now is as a couple in the middle of a transition. So many changes have taken place that you haven't been able to keep up.

LISA: I don't even know if I have a chance to breathe, let alone know who I am.

THERAPIST: Well, it's so important that you both were able to recognize the changes and take a step back so you can get back to that place where you *do* know who you are. The work you will do in therapy will take some time, but I know it will be worth it to you. What I would like to do as we get started is to begin to find ways to add positive coping tools to help strengthen your family. Does that sound reasonable?

Lisa and Michael nod.

THERAPIST:	Michael, although your coping tools of watching TV and hanging out with your buddies are working for you at this stage of adjusting to your retired life, it's very important to begin to add some family structure and responsibilities back to your life. Adding structure and responsibilities are very important in helping you begin to feel in sync again. Do you think you can try this?
MICHAEL:	Okay.
THERAPIST:	Lisa, you've been struggling to cope with the transition as well. I see that you love Michael, and want the best for him, but because so many responsibilities are falling on you right now, you find it hard to accept what he may be experiencing.
LISA:	It's just hard to know what I should expect. Yes, Michael's in pain, but does that mean he never has to lift a finger? I'm making all his medical appointments, driving him to the doctor, cooking him dinner, cleaning the house, but he's fine when it comes to going out with his buddies!
THERAPIST:	It is hard to know right now, I think for both of you. So tell me, in the next few weeks, do you think you might be able to adjust your expectations of Michael so that you and he can make changes gradually?
LISA (provides a convincing):	Yes.

Proactive Coping

Proactive coping tools are skills and habits that help us handle stress better now and in the future and that improve our overall health. Proactive coping also includes practicing and mastering skills when we do not immediately need them (e.g., practicing relaxation skills on a daily basis, even when we're already feeling pretty relaxed). In that way we get better and can use the skills when we most need them (and when they are hardest to use).

The Need to Plan Ahead

In order to help military families become stronger, both as individuals and as family members, it is important to help them to regularly incorporate positive coping into their lives. Take time to talk about this, and help them develop a plan to start using positive coping tools on a systematic basis. Some planning for coping techniques should be done individually and some as a family. Helping the family plan ahead will help them actually practice new coping skills. Additionally, let the family know that you will follow up with them during the next session to find out how practicing the coping technique(s) went. Letting them know they will need to be accountable to you will help them take more responsibility to engage in new, positive behaviors.

Proactive Coping Activities

Here is a list of positive or proactive coping activities that family members may want to try:

- Exercising or getting outdoors to enjoy nature.
- Playing a game.
- Playing with a pet.
- Praying or going to church or another place of worship.
- Going out with a friend (playing golf, going bowling, to a movie, or out to dinner).
- Gardening or making home repairs.
- Singing or dancing.
- Attending a social club.
- Inviting someone over for coffee or cards.
- Playing a team sport.
- Going to a party.
- Making new friends.
- Volunteering to help others, such as at a hospital, nursing home, or homeless shelter.
- Helping friends or family members, visiting someone who is lonely.
- Coaching a team.
- Making love to your spouse.
- Creating something: Draw a picture, paint a painting, write or play music, make crafts, garden, or improve your house.
- Trying a new hobby: Build a model, take up photography, learn martial arts, read a book, collect baseball cards, or explore something that is meaningful to you.
- Doing something fun as a family: Go boating, hiking, camping, or swimming, toss a ball or Frisbee, play chess, checkers, or a board or video game, go shopping, plan a trip, take a drive, go fishing or to a concert, a fair, the zoo, a restaurant, a park, a museum, or the beach.
- Writing or journaling: Writing letters, stories, poetry, or writing in a journal can help improve well-being and lower people's risk for disease. Writing 10–15 minutes a day about stress in your life can lower your stress level quite a bit.
- Being spiritual: Pray, meditate, or talk with others about religion or spirituality. Go to a religious service, read sacred works, listen to a sermon, or participate in faith-based groups.

➤ Finding support: Support groups, such as Alcoholics Anonymous, Ala-non, and Ala-teen 12-step groups, provide family members with the opportunity to share about their challenges with people who are experiencing the same type of problems.

➤ Relaxing: Go somewhere that makes you feel peaceful, take a walk, go to the woods, daydream, watch a sunset, go to the library, listen to the radio, or to the sound of the ocean or a running brook.

➤ Practicing mindfulness activities: Mindfulness activities help relax the mind and are often combined with body-centered relaxation exercises. They include:

  ➤ Autogenic training, self-hypnosis, and meditation (including mindfulness meditation) focus your attention on feeling calm and having a clear awareness about your life.

  ➤ Guided imagery (visualization) is a method of using your imagination to help you relax and release tension caused by stress.

➤ Practicing body-centered exercises: Body-centered relaxation skills that help the body relax are useful for those who experience mainly physical symptoms of stress. These are especially good techniques for individuals who hold their stress or tension in their bodies. These skills include:

  ➤ Breathing exercises.

  ➤ Progressive muscle relaxation, which reduces muscle tension by relaxing individual muscle groups.

  ➤ Massage, such as a shoulder and neck massage.

  ➤ Aromatherapy, which uses the aroma-producing oils (essential oils) from plants to promote relaxation.

  ➤ Yoga, tai chi, and Qi gong, which are forms of exercise and meditation. They generally require initial instruction to learn how to practice safely and effectively.

The Family That Plays Together, Stays Together

Everyone and every family is different. Some families like walking in the woods, whereas others like social events with lots of people. Some families like doing projects together, such as working on engines or making dinner with each other. Others like physical activities, such as playing basketball, baseball, or tennis. When it comes to healing and readapting to being home, the best healthy coping behavior is the one that the family can make a commitment to doing on a regular basis. This next exercise will help the family to start using positive coping in their daily lives.

Making It Real: Practicing Positive Coping

The goal of this exercise is to help family members develop a plan to practice positive coping. If family members have a hard time coming up with activities, you can have one family member read the proactive coping activities from their handout. After it is read, have each member choose activities that they enjoy from the list.

Exercise directions: Please go to Family Handout Step 3.1.

➤ "I'd like you to develop a plan of action to help you cope proactively with the stress in your lives. You may not feel interested in the kinds of activities that used to help you relax or have fun. We have talked about a bunch of different coping tools, but we need to find some ways that work for each of you both individually and as a family."

➤ Then ask these questions:

1. What are each family member's favorite types of activities?
2. Which type of activities do you think you would like to do as a family?
3. Can you decide on at least one individual and one family activity to do in the week ahead?
4. Discuss when the family may be able to do each activity they choose during the coming week. In making a commitment to try a new positive coping behavior, it is important that the choice be realistic—help the family find activities that suit them in terms of physical capability, availability, and schedule.

    There is a section for writing down and scheduling activities on the handout. Writing down commitments and following up is very important. With no commitment, they are less likely to engage in these activities. For example, one family agreed to commit to playing billiards for at least an hour on Saturdays, to go to church together on Sundays, to walk the dog together on weeknights, and when others are able, to get together with neighbors for a barbeque on Fridays. It is important to be specific, but at the same time, flexible.

Talking Points

It is important for the family to try to manage their stress every day—not just when they are stressed out. You will want to explain to them the importance of breaking these activities down into manageable goals. The more manageable and feasible the goals are for them, the more likely they will be to do the activities. Here is how I reinforced this point to our military family.

THERAPIST: In order to continue to reconnect and increase resiliency as a family, it is vital to spend time doing things that will provide you with the energy to face life's challenges. Deployments throw off schedules and get people out of sync. Injuries and chronic pain keep you from doing the kinds of activities you used to. So, we have to identify new activities and make the time to do something fun every day. What do you think is do-able for your family in the week ahead?

Because Michael and Lisa were both dealing with significant individual struggles, it was important to help them decide upon small changes that they felt they could accomplish.

In this session, Michael and Lisa agreed to, as a family:

➤ Play a game on Sundays
➤ Watch a movie together on Friday nights

THERAPIST: Busy schedules—going to work, taking care of the kids, the house, and yard—can get in the way of taking good care of ourselves and our families. Let's take a few minutes to identify positive coping activities that can be manageable goals for your week.

Because I suspected that Michael was dealing with at least moderate levels of adjustment stress and depression, it was important to remind the couple that our goal is to begin practicing coping activities gradually, because these will promote resilience—including better overall mood and overall health—in the long run. Especially when a family member is suffering from grief and/or depression, let the family know that they may have trouble enjoying the activities at first. However, these coping activities help move them toward a better mood and lower stress levels. This can help create a pattern of healthy improvement, rather than a continuing decline.

Achieving Balance

Balance is achieved when families are able to schedule time to take care of themselves and each other. Balance also means that, in addition to spending time together, family members need to spend time on their own or with their own friends. We recommend that family members try to make time for at least one individual and one family activity per day. The activities they choose do not have to take a lot of time. For example, one spouse chose to spend 10 minutes practicing tai chi every day. Even taking one minute to hug each other per day will help connect family members. Discuss with family members which coping activity ideas (from our list) they think would be fun to do. Allow them to choose the length of time that they engage in the activity. Help them problem solve how they can schedule times for group and individual coping activities.

Caregiver Stress

Caregivers of children, the elderly, or a disabled family member especially need breaks from caregiving in order to renew their energy. It is very important for caregivers to schedule occasional time away from caregiving to prevent themselves from becoming burned out. Discussing the need to take breaks from caregiving can be a delicate matter. However, in our experience, we find that those receiving care tend to understand that caregivers need time to care for themselves. It helps to explore each family member's feelings about the need to take time for recharging oneself.

For Your Information: Combat-Related Injuries

As of 2010, more than 35,500 U.S. service members have been wounded in action in Iraq or Afghanistan (Masi, 2010). Thus, returnees who participate in family therapy may be adjusting to limb loss, catastrophic wounds, severe burns, and/or traumatic brain injury.

Returnees who are adjusting to new combat injuries and/or chronic pain may now be unable to do the kinds of activities they used to enjoy. Newly injured returnees have added challenges to identify new activities that they can do both individually and as a family, and make the time to do something fun every day. If a returnee is suffering from a physical or psychological injury, take some time to talk about how coping tools are especially important.

Taking Care of Herself to Care for Her Family

This was an important point to discuss with Lisa. We wanted to emphasize that in order for her to have the emotional ability to take care of her family, she would need to start taking better care of herself. Here is how we broached that topic with Lisa in session.

> THERAPIST: It is especially important for caregivers to schedule occasional time to prevent themselves from becoming overwhelmed. However, Lisa, you may feel like you are unable to devote time to yourself. It's important to know, if you schedule some time for yourself, that time will help you have more patience and compassion for helping Michael and Abby. Only when you are physically and emotionally healthy can you help others.

Making Time to Destress

At this point, Michael volunteered to play with Abby two other nights a week so that Lisa would have time to practice progressive muscle relaxation in a quiet place. In addition to progressive muscle relaxation, Lisa agreed to write about all of her concerns and feelings in a journal for 10 minutes per day. Research has shown that journaling about stressors helps prevent both psychological and physical illnesses. Journaling can help Lisa to slow down and recharge.

Michael needs to expand his box of proactive coping tools. With probing, Michael was able to recall that working in the yard was a way for him to relax before he deployed. He felt that this was something he still would benefit from. Therefore, Michael agreed to spend some time each day working in the yard as a proactive coping tool to help him keep his stress low.

When Stress Gets Out of Control

Managing stress is not something that *should* be done. It is something that *needs* to be done every day, particularly when individuals have very stressful jobs. This was the case for another one of our military families, Robert and Felicia.

Robert and Felicia's Experiences

Sergeant Robert White and Staff Sergeant Felicia White had a strong 17-year relationship based upon shared beliefs and goals. Because of their leadership positions in the Army, they are seen as role models by the privates in their respective squads. However, in reality, Robert and Felicia were struggling to deal with the impact of multiple deployments.

During the last three years, the stress of deployments, combined with raising two sons, has resulted in a growing friction in their marriage. Additionally, during our initial assessment, Felicia admitted that she had pushed her 10-year-old son Robbie while Robert was deployed. During a recent argument with Robert, she also had become verbally abusive and "out of control." These events were upsetting to her, and she knew she needed help so that such events would not happen again. However, Felicia was highly concerned about being seen in therapy. She was concerned about what others might think and about how her career would be impacted if she went to an Army clinic.

The Need for Reactive Coping Skills

This was the situation that Robert and Felicia were in as well, and they decided to seek help outside of the DOD system. It was apparent that both Felicia and Robert needed better coping skills. Felicia believed her risk of becoming violent or abusive again was low; however, she agreed to seek anger management treatment from a private source if she felt "out of control" in the future. Now, both Felicia and Robert needed to find reactive coping tools to help them deal with escalating stress.

What Is Reactive Coping?

Reactive coping tools are skills and behaviors that we do in response to a problem. Like firefighters responding to a fire in progress, reactive strategies are focused on reducing or removing a problem that is already there. If you are stressed and use meditation to help

---

For Your Information: Stigma and Treatment-Seeking

Stigma continues to be a factor that keeps service members who need help from seeking it. The U.S. Department of Defense has made progress in changing this aspect of military culture in the past several years. However, stigma and job concerns continue to be factors that keep both service members and veterans from seeking care. In surveys evaluating both OEF/OIF veterans and National Guard members, concern about one's career was one of the main reasons that individuals who met screening criteria for PTSD or substance abuse said kept them from seeking mental health care (Whealin et al., 2011). Seeking mental health services is a particularly touchy subject for individuals who require security clearances. However, service members often go outside of the military to obtain confidential services in the community.

calm yourself down, you are using a reactive coping tool. Several reactive coping tools can help reduce stress and restore the ability to think during stressful times (please go to Family Handout 3.2).

Examples of Reactive Coping

Some examples include:

> Laughing and crying: These are natural ways to relieve stress and release tension. They are both part of the emotional healing process. Tell a joke, laugh at a comedy, or cry during sad movies. All of these can be excellent ways to release stress. Even though we often think that we should not cry, or that it is a sign of weakness, the reality is that crying is an important and natural part of the overall grieving process, and it can be part of getting better.
> Listening to positive music.
> Counting or repeating a positive affirmation.
> Practicing deep breathing, meditation, or progressive muscle relaxation.
> Taking a relaxing bath or shower.
> If you can do so without becoming angry, discussing situations with each other.
> Discussing situations with a close friend, clergy member, a counselor, parent, or other relative.
> Praying or going to a house of worship.
> Writing or journaling.
> Relaxing.

During times of stress, encourage families to continue to do things that are good for them. If possible, help family members continue to stick to their routines and activities. However, when stress levels get high, a third type of coping skill becomes important. This skill is known as "downshifting."

Downshifting

An important reactive coping skill for families to develop is to know when and how to downshift. Downshifting literally refers to shifting a car's transmission into a lower gear. When driving a car, sometimes the road can get steep. When facing the challenges of sharp rises, a car can falter. Imagine starting up a hilly driveway in your car, and the feeling of your car as it begins to hesitate. When your car is facing a challenging hill, it is time to downshift to a lower gear. When downshifting, the car's transmission works more slowly. However, this slower action allows the car to have the power needed to surmount the hill.

How to Downshift During Stress

It is important to discuss ways that the family can cope when they are feeling overwhelmed. As their stress levels build, they can use these five steps to cope better and downshift (please see Family Handout Step 3.3):

> ➤ **Step 1:** Recognize that problems are becoming overwhelming. Recognize that it is time to give yourself and each other a break.
> ➤ **Step 2:** Let others know you need to downshift.
> ➤ **Step 3:** Slow down and breathe. Just like downshifting a car to a lower gear allows the car to have the power to surmount a hill, slowing down and breathing will help us have the strength and wherewithal to cope.
> ➤ **Step 4:** Decide which reactive coping tool to use.
> ➤ **Step 5:** Focus on one task at a time.

Making It Real: Practicing Reactive Coping Skills

The goal of this exercise is to help family members recognize future times when problems are building and help them plan ahead to cope with the situation.

Instructions: Please refer to Family Handout Step 3.4.

Which reactive coping strategies can each of you use when needed?

How will you know when you need to step back from a situation and downshift?

Can you give me an example of a time you may need to downshift, and how you would go through the steps?

Talking Points

Using the analogy of downshifting can be very helpful in teaching families when to slow down. When problems become challenging, it is easy to become overwhelmed. However, it is very important for family members to identify when problems begin to overwhelm them. Reactive coping tools are particularly helpful at this time.

Returnees with postdeployment stress reactions often feel irritated or angry, which can lead some of them to act impulsively. To prevent problems associated with irritability and impulsivity, it is important to help clients become aware of cues that show that their anger may be increasing, and to encourage them to use reactive coping tools. When returnees find themselves in a situation where they are feeling very angry or stressed, they must detach from the situation quickly and use a tool to help them calm down.

Felicia and Robert were both religious and believed that prayer would be a helpful tool to use when they felt their stress levels rising. They agreed to let each other know when they needed time to downshift and detach from a situation. Felicia agreed to notice when she felt frustrated with her boys, or when she started to raise her voice. She walked through the situation that led to her pushing her son Robbie when Robert was deployed. She was able to identify the cues that led to her acting out. She agreed to participate in daily proactive coping activities before her sons returned from school. She identified that, when her stress level was rising, she would pray and repeat a positive affirmation to herself consistent with her spiritual beliefs: "God will guide and protect my family and I." Finally, she agreed to speak to her chaplain when she felt anger toward her husband or children.

Negative Coping

While positive coping methods are helpful, *other coping methods are harmful and can make the problems much worse.* For example, an individual who chooses to do some deep breathing and meditation will gain a sense of calmness, peace, and decreased anxiety. On the other hand, someone who chooses to keep going over his or her worries will become more anxious, uptight, and helpless.

When People Use Negative Coping

Even though family members might be engaging in negative coping activities to try to feel better, the reality is that people who use negative ways of coping usually feel worse. They usually feel angrier, more upset, and more depressed. Plus, they interfere with doing the types of activities that will decrease their stress and build resilience over time.

Examples of Negative Coping

Here are some examples of negative coping (please see Family Handout Step 3.5):

➤ Driving too fast in your car.
➤ Becoming aggressive or violent (hitting someone, throwing, or kicking something).
➤ Eating too much or too little, or drinking a lot of caffeinated beverages.
➤ Smoking or chewing tobacco.
➤ Drinking alcohol or taking recreational drugs.
➤ Taking more medication than your doctor prescribed.
➤ Ruminating about problems.
➤ Criticizing yourself (negative self-talk).
➤ Yelling at or physically attacking your spouse or partner, children, co-workers, or friends.
➤ Avoiding social contact.
➤ Dropping out of recreational activities.
➤ Working long hours to avoid thoughts or people.
➤ Playing video games for hours to avoid thoughts or people.

It is important to evaluate whether the family or a family member is using mainly positive or negative coping strategies. If they are utilizing negative coping, do not reinforce this behavior. Instead, point out that they have done the best they have been able to do up to this point, and that now they may be able to develop better ways to deal with stress in the future.

The Benefits of Negative Coping?

Are there any benefits to using negative coping? Actually, family members tend to engage in negative coping because they perceive a benefit. Negative coping strategies have allure for those who engage in them. Because they are rewarding in some way, it is important to help family members replace negative coping behaviors with positive coping behaviors. It may also be important to address some of the obvious, as well as the more subtle, problems that these behaviors can cause. For example, some veterans may say that driving recklessly—as well as other reckless, thrill-seeking, or adrenaline-seeking behaviors—are the only ways that they "feel alive."

The Dangers of Negative Coping

Combat returnees in particular, when deployed, have to adjust to an environment of constant stress and potential danger. Returning to the normal world may be boring in many ways. However, continuing to seek the adrenaline rush in destructive ways—in addition to the obvious dangers—can also prevent one's body and mind from readapting to normal circumstances. On the other hand, many returnees may avoid social contacts or other recreational activities because they do not feel safe or comfortable in these contexts.

Similarly, children may be using negative coping responses to deal with stress. In older children, negative coping responses include changes in sleeping behavior, changes in eating habits or appetite, complaints of physical problems, problems with authority, persistent anger or depression, or substance abuse. In younger children, negative coping responses can include changes in school performance, persistent disobedience or temper tantrums, refusing to go to school, and hyperactivity. These behaviors are a clue that the child is under stress and a sign that better coping skills are needed.

We now head into our last Making It Real exercise with our families, which will help family members to differentiate among their coping styles.

Making It Real: Positive or Negative Coping?

This exercise will help the military family to become more aware of their normal coping style. In addition, if family members are engaging primarily in negative coping skills, this exercise will help them to transition into using more positive coping tools.

Instructions: Please see Family Handout 3.6.

➤ Ask the family members which coping style they primarily use in their family.

➤ Discuss the impact of using these coping mechanisms.

➤ If you find that a family member is using a negative coping response, see if he or she will negotiate to trade that activity with a positive one. And, go back to the positive coping exercise and mark the activities into the coping activities schedule. This will solidify the use of positive coping tools.

Final Thoughts

Military families in transition that positively cope with their problems become more empowered. As Michael and Lisa identify and regularly use healthy coping techniques, they will be able to regain a sense of control over their lives. Robert and Felicia, too, in practicing positive coping and utilizing reactive coping as needed, will be more prepared to deal with stressful situations as they arise. When military family members regularly practice positive coping, they become psychologically healthier individuals. When they practice positive coping as a family, they grow closer together and become a stronger, more empowered family unit.

Keys to Family Wellness

➤ The key to healing and becoming stronger, both as individuals and as families, is to use proactive coping on a regular basis.

➤ Negative coping causes problems to get worse.

➤ Resilient families can identify and acknowledge when problems become too difficult.

➤ When stressors surmount, resilient families have a plan in place to use reactive coping activities to adapt and adjust accordingly.

─────────── **Taking Action** ───────────

Taking action will help rebuild the family. Please check off each step as the family accomplishes it.

❑ The family should pick one or two proactive coping techniques that they can use as individuals and as a family during the upcoming week.

❑ The family should pick one or two reactive coping techniques and practice downshifting this week during periods of stress.

❑ The family should do at least one family activity together this week.

STEP

4

Empower

Focusing on Strengths

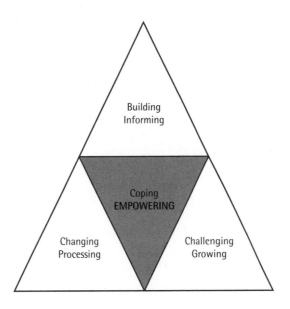

Communication. It's the first thing we really learn in life. Funny thing is, once we grow up, learn our words and really start talking, the harder it becomes to know what to say, or how to ask for what we really need.

—Grey's Anatomy Television Series, Shonda Rhimes
Second Season, "Something to Talk About"

Michael and Lisa are back in my office one week later with their 12-year-old daughter, Abby. This is the first session that Abby has attended, so I spend some time introducing myself. Because she has never been in family therapy, and in order to make her feel comfortable, I also take a few minutes to explain to Abby what her parents and I do when we meet together. I let her know that she can join in today's conversation if she likes, and that I look forward to hearing her input. Then I turn the focus to reviewing Michael and Lisa's week with them. In order to help the family understand the importance of homework, it helps for you to hold the family members accountable every week for following through on it. Last week, Michael had agreed to spend some time every day working in the yard to destress. Lisa agreed to practice progressive muscle relaxation and to write about all of her concerns and feelings in a journal for 10 minutes a day.

THERAPIST:	*So, how did your homework go? Did you practice your coping activities for the week?*
LISA *(with an acerbic tone):*	*Well, one of us did.*
THERAPIST:	*How so? (I am careful not to collude with Lisa's sarcastic tone.)*
LISA:	*I did my homework every night.*
THERAPIST:	*How was that for you?*
LISA:	*It was such a break! I cannot believe how taking just a 10-minute break could recharge me.*
THERAPIST:	*You are seeing the benefits of coping proactively. I'm really glad you were able to take the time to do that, Lisa.*
LISA *(smiling):*	*Thanks. I only wish that Michael would do better.*
THERAPIST *(I pause and look at Michael):*	*Michael, how did your homework go?*
MICHAEL *(looking somewhere in the distance out the window):*	*Okay.*
THERAPIST:	*Tell me about it.*
MICHAEL:	*Well, I spent time with Abby when she (Lisa) was relaxing. But I guess I never made it out to the garden to get any work done.*
THERAPIST:	*Good! I'm glad to hear you spent time with Abby.*
LISA *(folds her arms):*	*You were supposed to do something with Abby, to interact with her. I don't call watching sports interacting.*
THERAPIST:	*(I wait for Michael.)*
Michael *(growling, as he looks back out the window):*	*Here we go again.*

Setting the Stage

When deployments involve high levels of chronic stress and/or traumatic events, returnees may be experiencing bereavement, posttraumatic stress, or depression. When there has been a physical injury, returnees as well as family members need time to psychologically adjust to the disability or associated difficulties, such as chronic pain. In the first few weeks following deployment, the family may need to be guided to give the returnee extra space in order to readjust. However, over time, it is important for returnees to address any problems that linger. With time, service members can resume their role as a spouse or partner and, if children are involved, their role as a parent.

Many returnees experienced the harsh realities of war. They may have witnessed suffering and death, destruction, or atrocities. Many have to come to terms with killing people during war. Many returnees have difficulty dealing with some of those realities. Some may have horrific memories that they frequently reexperience. They may need time to grieve and to come to terms with moral injustices that they may have witnessed. All of these experiences often result in changes in the military family.

One of the key issues that come into play following disabling injuries is the shift in roles and responsibilities between partners. Even when physical or psychological injuries are not an issue, deployment-related shifts in roles and responsibilities require attention. When the changes lead to new patterns of behavior, a family must flexibly adapt to those changes. However, if family members do not communicate what they are experiencing, what they are feeling, or how they have been impacted by change, other family members can feel confused, angry, and resentful.

In Step 4, we help family members communicate on a deeper level, so they feel more connected as a unit. In doing so, we help family members strengthen their trust in each other. In this step, you will learn ways to facilitate open communication

---

For Your Information: Social Isolation, Mental Health, and Social Sharing

As mentioned previously, when a returnee is suffering from symptoms of posttraumatic stress disorder (PTSD) or depression, his or her symptoms can directly and indirectly compromise social relationships within a family. Both disorders are associated with social isolation and emotional numbing, which can make people less likely to seek out and engage in relationships with others. Service members and veterans who have PTSD, in particular, have been shown to socially withdraw from others over time, compared to those without PTSD (Keane, Scott, Chavoya, Lamparaski, & Fairbanks, 1985; King, Taft, King, Hammond, & Stone, 2006). In fact, the more severe the PTSD, the more they lose relationships with nonveteran acquaintances (Laffaye, Cavella, Drescher, & Rosen, 2008).

Ironically, most scholars agree that one must process thoughts and feelings about traumatic events with others in order to overcome the impact of the event (e.g., Foa & Kozak, 1986; Lepore, Silver, Wortman, & Wayment, 1996). However, the response from the listener is very important. When someone shares about trauma and receives negative reactions to the sharing from others, they are more likely to continue to have severe symptoms of PTSD (Ullman, 2003), as well as other psychological and physical difficulties (Ullman, 2003; Ullman & Filipas, 2001). Thus, the role of the family and friends in supporting each other following stressful events is very important.

among the family members. Family members will learn to go beyond their feelings of vulnerability with one another and to focus on each other's strengths. As part of this step, family members will be able to face and express their feelings of sadness and anger to their loved ones.

Identifying and Sharing Emotions

In earlier steps, family members began to share their needs and wants with one another. These earlier steps can give you an indication about each family member's ability to share and trust other members of their family. In Step 4, we continue to build the family's ability and willingness to share by delving more deeply into emotions. Many families will transition well to this stage, but some family members may be reluctant to share what they are going through or may have difficulty identifying emotions.

If family members do not feel supported by one another, they will need to develop trust in order to become resilient as a family unit. Some family members may not possess the communication skills or know how to show support toward others. Some family members prefer not to share feelings because they fear being judged or misunderstood. Some family members may have difficulty being empathetic, or they may feel uncomfortable when others are sharing their feelings. As a clinician, you may need to coach family members on how to "hear" negative emotions. Empathy is the ability to sense other's feelings and attitudes. If families are to thrive, each member must have the capacity to listen to and accept how others feel.

Making It Real: Identifying Feelings

We begin with a simple exercise to see how willing and able each member is to identify and share feelings with each other.

Exercise Directions: Please go to Family Handout 4.1. Please have the family do the following.

➤ Say to the family: "_____ (say all of their names and make eye contact with each of them), many people find it uncomfortable to listen to others who are feeling negative emotions. It can be difficult to listen to someone who is suffering. Often, our first inclination is to change the subject. Sometimes we may feel compelled to try and fix the problem. Either approach can invalidate that person's feelings."

➤ Then lead a discussion around the following questions:
  1. What feelings are you experiencing right now?
  2. Did you experience any other feelings in the last week?
  3. If someone else in your family is feeling very bad, does it make you feel uncomfortable?
  4. When you feel bad, what can others around you do to support you?

Talking Points

Back to Michael and Lisa. Earlier, Lisa shared that she was feeling frustrated that Michael has not shared much about his experiences during deployment. When returnees have experienced dangerous and potentially traumatic events, it can be difficult to weed through their experiences and know what to share with their families. However, in suppressing his emotions, Michael has become less responsive to the needs of his wife, Lisa, and daughter, Abby. Michael is in a Catch-22 situation, like many other returnees. He is bearing his burdens of war, which makes him feel disconnected from his family. And his family, Lisa and Abby, sense his detachment and feel like Michael doesn't trust them or love them the same anymore.

During this exercise, Michael denied that he was having any feelings, and he shared that his emotions had been "numb" since he returned from deployment. However, Michael also said that he feels very uncomfortable when others express sadness, fear, and other negative emotions. He said that, when he feels bad, he prefers that others "leave him alone." Abby, on the other hand, was able to identify her feelings. She said that she was feeling "sad" at the moment and had been feeling "angry and sad" in the previous week. Like her father, Abby feels uncomfortable when others express negative emotions. Unlike Michael, however, she said that she would like others to "listen to her" to show their support when she feels bad. Furthermore, Lisa shared that she, too, had

---

For Your Information: Stigma About Mental Health

Despite military-wide education programs designed to decrease stigma about mental health problems, stigma continues to prevent people from seeking appropriate care. Research shows that concerns about stigma are particularly salient for those who currently suffer from emotional problems (compared to those without problems). Active-duty, reservist, and National Guard OEF/OIF returnees who screen positive for mental health problems consistently report high levels of stigma (e.g., Hoge et al., 2004; Pietrzak et al., 2009).

Many of the stigma-related beliefs held by veterans and active-duty service members reflect concerns about discrimination by others for having mental health problems. For example, active-duty soldiers and Marines returning from Iraq or Afghanistan were concerned, should they seek mental health care, that "My unit leadership might treat me differently" (36.5%), "I would be seen as weak" (35.4%), "Members of my unit might have less confidence in me" (34.2%), or "It would harm my career" (27.0%, Hoge et al., 2004).

Additionally, emerging research shows that OEF/OIF returnees who screen positive for mental health problems have concerns about stigma. For example, recent research shows that some returnees fear that family members would have less confidence in them if they "knew" they had a mental health problem, and they would see them as weak (Whealin et al., 2011). When family members view mental health problems as a sign of weakness, such family members (and peers) may covertly and overtly discourage returnees from talking about their problems (Lorber & Garcia, 2010). In other cases, however, returnees may overestimate the amount of stigma-related beliefs that family members hold and keep symptoms to themselves. In either case, returnees experience shame or guilt for having such symptoms, which only compounds the problem.

been feeling angry and sad. She said that she felt somewhat comfortable having others share negative emotions with her. Additionally, she said that when she shares negative emotions, she would like others to listen to her and give her a hug.

Family Beliefs About Sharing

When someone suffering from emotional problems holds stigma-related beliefs about mental health, they commonly avoid sharing negative emotions for a variety of reasons. For example, some people may equate having emotions, such as fear or sadness, with weakness. Alternatively, others may not want to burden family members with their troubles. Still others may feel that if they share their feelings, they will "lose control." It will be important for you to take some time in the session to explore the family's beliefs about mental health and sharing of experiences.

Helping the Family to Share

In therapy, take time to encourage family members to listen without judging others in the family, especially when they are expressing painful emotions or their fears about expressing emotions. As mentioned earlier, some returnees may have trouble identifying or sharing their emotions. Many returnees believe that expressing their feelings is a sign of weakness. In cases like this, you can emphasize that sharing emotions does not weaken a person. It can be helpful to point out that sharing emotions makes the emotions less intense.

Sharing emotions can also help connect people and make them feel less isolated from others. Reinforce that the avoidance of sharing emotions and problems usually just makes the problems worse and can lead to physical and emotional health problems. Normalize the expression of emotion and validate family members' emotions. This can make the process of sharing easier (please see Family Handout Step 4.2).

The Problem of "Sucking it Up"

In the case of Michael, Lisa, and Abby, it was important to address Michael's discomfort about others expressing negative emotions. Michael said that he believes that expressing sadness and other negative emotions is a sign of weakness. Earlier in our session, Michael had said he had a "suck it up" attitude; that no matter what happens, a service member should be able to "suck it up."

With a client such as Michael, it is important to find out what he or she might be thinking when others share emotions with him or her. Michael said that when Lisa shares negative emotions with him, he feels "helpless" when she is distressed. Lisa explained to Michael that he doesn't need to solve her problems when she is distressed. Rather, she just wants to share part of who she is with him. Last, I discussed with the family that emotions such as sadness are normal reactions to witnessing highly stressful and, at times, morally incomprehensible events. I talked about how "sucking it up" can be protective during war, but stuffing emotions is no longer adaptive once a service member returns home.

Improving Listening Skills

Some family members will have no problem attending to the needs of others in their family, but some family members will need more guidance to understand others' points of view. Michael had mentioned that sometimes it was difficult for him to listen to others. Lisa had specifically voiced concerns that Michael does not listen to their daughter, Abby, when she is feeling upset. You may need to help a family member(s) understand that empathy is essential for healthy communication and, ultimately, for healthy relationships with those whom they love.

Making It Real: Deepening Communication

In this exercise, we get to a deeper level of communication and trust among family members. Open the exercise by addressing the various types of sharing styles that each family member has. It is ideal that family members share with each other in a conversational style during this exercise. Also, it may be necessary to help family members keep in mind that their experience may be very different from that of others in their family. It is vital for family members to value others' right to their feelings and opinions. Even if a family member cannot relate to another family member's feelings and/or opinions, he or she should still be guided to respect their opinions.

Exercise Directions: Please go to Family Handout Step 4.3.

➤ In this exercise, we follow up on the feelings that were expressed earlier. Guide the family to share more about how they are feeling. You may start out by saying:

➤ "I would like you to share more about the feelings you expressed earlier. However, when one person shares, it's important for the other family members not to interrupt, but just to listen. We can use the stress ball as a reminder that one person has the floor. Here are some guidelines for listening to others when they are expressing how they feel:

1. First, take time to provide the person with your full attention.
2. When your family member shares, just listen. Focus on what the other person is communicating. Do not interrupt or think about what you want to say next. Try to put aside any need to rescue the person.
3. Simply let the person know that you support them and are there for them by nodding or encouraging them to share more.
4. Last, ask the person if there is anything you can do to help.

Talking Points

This exercise was a good opportunity for Michael to practice his listening skills. In our previous session, we had identified his need to begin to communicate more effectively with his daughter, Abby. Here is how things went for our family.

THERAPIST:	Who would like to go first?
MICHAEL:	Abby, I'd like to know why you feel sad and angry.
ABBY:	You don't even want to be my father.
MICHAEL:	That's not true, Abby. (sounding calm but surprised at this bit of information) Where did you get that idea?
THERAPIST:	Michael, remember that your role is to listen and support how Abby feels.
MICHAEL:	I'm sorry, Abby, I'd like to hear more about why you think I don't want to be your father.
ABBY:	Well, you never want to be with me. When I showed you the mug I made for you last week, you didn't even look at it!
MICHAEL:	Is there anything else?
ABBY:	When I won the school spelling bee last winter, you didn't even say anything!
MICHAEL:	What can I do to help you, Abby?
ABBY (earnestly):	I don't know. I guess I just want you to listen to me.
MICHAEL (gets down on his knees next to Abby):	Abby, I had no idea. . . . Daddy's just . . . Daddy's just not feeling well right now. It has nothing to do with you. I will do my best to listen to you.

After all members of the family have had a chance to share and listen, please open it up for further sharing on a feeling level. The goal here is to stay at the heart level—at the emotions.

THERAPIST:	Lisa, Michael, Abby, let's take some time to open the floor, for each of you to share with each other how you are feeling. (Pause) Michael, would you like to share your reactions first?
MICHAEL:	Well, first I want to say that I am proud of the accomplishments that Abby and Lisa have made in the last year. I know it wasn't easy with me being so isolated. I didn't know that Abby was angry. I feel like a shit.

Lisa and Abby seem to not know what to say, so after a moment, I jump in.

THERAPIST:	Tell us more.
MICHAEL:	Well, I feel so ashamed. I cannot support you two anymore. I feel like a failure as a husband and father. I let down Frank (the private who was killed during an attack) and I let down you.
LISA:	Anything else?
MICHAEL:	I guess I've been feeling sad. I haven't been able to push through it. I've been feeling sad and that's why I've pushed you two away.

Because Michael seems finished with his sharing, I nod to Lisa.

LISA:	What would you like from us?
MICHAEL (puts his head in his hands then looks at each of them):	I would like you to forgive me for letting you down.
LISA:	I never felt that you let me down, Michael. I am so proud of you. I am proud to be your wife. Thank you so much for sharing how you feel with me.
ABBY:	I'm proud of you, Dad. I think I have the strongest Dad in the world.

How the Ice Got Broken

This last exercise broke the ice for Michael. Up to this point, he had not been able to shed his military identity to even recognize the sadness that he was experiencing. With some extra support, Michael was able to share a little about the attack he experienced when his truck encountered an IED. He told us that, although he was hurt himself, it was even more difficult for him to see Frank, the private who worked for him, get seriously injured. He said that he still thinks about the event. Sharing his experience (even without the gory details) provided Michael with emotional support and helped his family to know that they are important enough to share this part of his life with them.

This exercise helped bridge the gap that was keeping this family detached from one another. The key to healing the military family is to enable family members to risk being vulnerable by sharing, to focus and hone in on each other's strengths, and to help family members begin to build each other up.

Parenting

As a result of all of the adjustments in the family, military children are often affected. When roles and responsibilities change, with one parent coming and going from the family, it can create a confusing situation for some children. So, many military children try to test their parent (returnee) to see if they can get their way now. As in any family, children can act out. However, beyond this, in military families, children lose one of their parents to deployment, sometimes for long periods. Without very clear boundaries in place, children can act out badly and take advantage of the changes in the family structure to get what they want.

Setting Boundaries

Boundary setting is crucial for reestablishing the balance in the military family. One of the main components of family resilience is to have clear rules governing the family's hierarchy (Haley, 2007). Many returnees feel unable to relate to their children (Gottman, Gottman, & Atkins, 2011). Others who are physically or emotionally disabled may develop a pattern of letting the other parent make all of the decisions. In this case, you can help the returnee to step back into the parent role and to define a clear family hierarchy. A first step is to rebuild a "strong parental coalition" between parents.

In the case of Lisa and Michael, both parents have to be and stay in charge. The parent who has been away on deployment may need to learn to take their position back in the parental role. Many returning service members feel guilty for missing parts of their children's lives, and there may be times when they cave in to their kids' requests to get back into their good graces. You can reinforce that being away on deployments does not forfeit their parenting rights. Assert that the best way to help their children adjust is to set boundaries and stick to them. This can be accomplished by having the parents ease back into making decisions together.

Bonding Activities

Michael has struggled with having physical and psychological injuries, and this has left him feeling out of sync with his family. His daughter, Abby, has also been feeling disconnected from her father. One way to help them reconnect is by giving them ways to bond again.

Using Behavior Modification on Adults Too

Behavior modification is often associated with helping children behave better. However, it can also help adults to incorporate more positive behaviors into their lives. In addition, we can use behavior modification to help military parents rebond with their children.

The How-To of Behavior Modification

Behavior modification techniques help clients directly alter their behavior in order to minimize unhealthy coping behavior—such as watching TV for 5 hours a day—and maximize healthy behavior—such as exercising or spending time with children. An effective behavior modification method is to pair a new, healthy coping behavior with a behavior the client already does on a regular basis. The activity a person does on a regular basis serves as reinforcement, thus making them more likely to implement the new coping behavior.

For example, Greg, a young Air Force Airman who recently returned from Afghanistan, was spending most of his time playing video games in the evening. His 18-year-old fiancé, Beth, felt ignored and unappreciated by Greg. In session, I negotiated with Greg to spend at least an hour with Beth per night doing something together as a couple. Together, Greg and Beth came up with activities they both could enjoy, such as playing cards, going to the gym, or watching a TV show. Once he did this, Greg could "reward" himself by playing video games. Soon, the new coping activities and couple time became habit. Behavior modification can help an individual and the family's ability to develop and maintain adaptive coping.

Making Time for Family Time

Time that the family spends together does not "just happen" (Stinnett, 1979). Resilient families make time together happen by scheduling it into their lives. To reinforce the family hierarchy and parental coalition, Michael and Lisa need to start doing things as a family, rather than simply accommodating Michael's isolation. Similarly, Michael should now be pushed to expand his activities, so that his isolating does not become a pattern. However, it is important to make changes gradually, so that the family has a higher likelihood for success when trying their new activities together. Here's how family time was negotiated in session with Michael and Lisa.

THERAPIST: Michael, your coping habits, watching TV, spending time with your buddies, works for you now. However, it's very important to begin to push yourself a little to pick up more of the habits you had before you deployed. Do you remember how you felt before deployment?

MICHAEL: Yeah, I had a lot more energy, and also a lot more patience. I used to spend a lot more time with Lisa and Abby, and to do things like work around the house and in the yard.

THERAPIST: Has your pain made it more difficult to work around the house and in the yard?

MICHAEL: Yeah, I try to ignore the pain, but I guess it is one reason why I don't enjoy working in the yard anymore.

THERAPIST: What might be important for you then is to find a new activity that you do enjoy, that helps get your mind off your pain, while you also enjoy time with your family.

MICHAEL: Well, in my pain management program, they recommended that I begin building models again. That's something I did when I was a kid.

THERAPIST: Okay, great idea, Michael. Maybe you can consider putting a model together with Abby, so that you can spend some quality time together. What do you think about that?

MICHAEL: Yeah, we can try that. I think she'd enjoy it too. A bonding activity. That's good.

Family Rituals

Family rituals are basically a regular bonding activity that family members do together. In the case of Michael and Abby, they would begin to share some usual, quality time putting models together. Rituals can be as simple as this family's repeated activities, or they can be more complicated for very special, marked occasions.

What Is a Ritual?

A ritual is a symbolic form of communication that is performed systematically over time. Rituals can help families bond and grow closer together. Rituals can help establish, clarify, and stabilize via expected roles, boundaries, and rules so that all members know that

---

For Your Information: Family Rituals for Today's Families

Family celebrations include the ways a family celebrates annual events (Christmas, Passover, Thanksgiving, etc.) or rites of passage (weddings, baptisms, bar mitzvahs, etc.). The celebration involves the rituals, which affirm or honor that particular occasion. Celebrations may include family traditions, special food and drink, and gifts. Celebrations help define the family, as well as mark the family's development phase (Wolin & Bennett, 1984, p. 404).

Families today, compared to those in the past, rarely connect with a family story. Piecing together the story(ies) of family members to other members of the family can help create cohesion and a sense of stability. Even when all family members are not explicitly a part of the family story, they benefit from knowing about and participating in the telling of the story. Here are some examples of content areas that help families create a common story:

- How grandpa and grandma came to the United States
- How Mom and Dad met
- How Mom and Dad got engaged
- What Mom and/or Dad did on their deployment
- How Dad came home from deployment when junior was born
- How the family celebrated when Dad came home from deployment
- How big brother took care of his little sister when Mom was deployed

"this is the way our family is" (Wolin & Bennett, 1984, p. 401). Rituals can help facilitate change or transition, while maintaining order.

Robert and Felicia's Family Rituals

Robert and Felicia are the career soldiers we introduced in Step 3. During Robert's last deployment, the couple's two boys, ages 10 and 13, had begun defying Felicia's authority, leading her to act out and actually push their young son, Robbie. When Robert returned from deployment, the boys continued to be defiant and have outbursts of anger. Although Felicia had made significant progress in dealing with her stress, the boys seemed to continue to act out when they felt stressed. In the past month, the older brother, John, had been suspended from school for cutting classes with his friends. Family dinners were a particular issue. In our session, we recognized that dinners had become an opportunity for Felicia to criticize the boys. Often, peaceful dinners only took place when the TV was turned on.

The dysfunction in this family had become a pattern that would take time and effort to overcome. With exploration, we identified that the boys felt resented and resentful. It became clear that, because of the family's lack of communication, John and Robbie were not getting the guidance they needed to help them cope with their stress and navigate life choices.

Talking Points

In our session, Robert and Felicia became aware that the boys needed more structure, as well as guidance and affirmation from both of them. As a family, they decided to begin a ritual—their family would eat dinner together every night, *without* TV. During dinner, the parents asked their sons about what they had learned in school that day and listened to various aspects of their daily experiences. This discussion allowed Robert and Felicia to learn more about the challenges the boys were facing.

By managing her stress, Felicia was able to refrain from criticizing the boys. Instead, she used the time to help the boys explore ways that they could solve problems. Importantly, both parents focused on finding an opportunity to praise their sons for making positive choices. Robert was planning to continue this ritual during Felicia's upcoming deployment, thus providing an element of stability and order in the family.

Final Thoughts

Shifts in roles and responsibilities between partners are common with repeated deployments. However, a family can flexibly adapt to those changes. Families can learn to communicate what they are experiencing and feeling. They can support each other and build each other up. They can spend time together as a unit and create or continue family rituals. Additionally, family members can use reactive coping when their problems or anger become overwhelming. All of these positive efforts will lead to a family that not only has the parents being parents again but that also becomes a more bonded, closer family unit—and that means healing for the military family.

Keys to Family Wellness

> ➤ Sharing emotions helps connect people with others, and so can help people feel less isolated from others.
> ➤ Sharing emotions is associated with better physical and emotional health.
> ➤ Families can learn to communicate what they are experiencing and feeling.
> ➤ It is important for family members to learn to listen to one another and validate each other's feelings.
> ➤ Families can spend time together as a unit and create or continue family rituals.

─── Taking Action ───

Taking action will help rebuild the family. Please check off each step as the family accomplishes it.

❑ The family should practice identifying and expressing their feelings to one another this week.

❑ During family time this week, family members should take turns asking questions about the others' week, how it was for them, and how they felt about different things that happened. Family members should practice listening and validating each other.

❑ The family should come up with a family ritual together, which they can do together this week.

5

Improve

Changing Negative Thoughts

A little kingdom I possess, where thoughts and feelings dwell; and very hard the task I find of governing it well.

—Louisa May Alcott.

Dan and Kate met when they were in college. Dan is an active-duty Army captain, serving as an emergency room physician; Kate is on active duty as a First Lieutenant in the Army, serving as a nurse. Dan and Kate have been together for 14 years and have two children, a 6-year-old son (Todd) and an 8-year-old daughter (Dina). They have been stationed in California for two years. In the past, Dan served a 13-month tour in Iraq and for 8 months at the Army hospital in Germany. Kate served in Iraq for a one-year tour, three years ago. So they have rotated care of their two children. This is really the first time they are all living in the same place as a family. Theoretically, it seems like it should be a great experience, but it has not been without its problems. The children have been adjusting surprisingly well to all of the changes in their lives, but Dan and Kate have been having some difficulties in their relationship. This forty-something couple sits in my office.

Changes in the Military Family

When faced with the brutal realities of war, soldiers are frequently forced to stuff their emotions so that they can remain focused. In war, it is important for soldiers to be functional in order to survive. In addition, when one spouse is off to war, they often suppress their own feelings in order to protect the other from worry while they are away from each other.

After deployment, the family must recalibrate and adjust on many levels, ranging from changing roles in the household, to relearning how to communicate with one another, to getting used to being around each other in the house again, to feeling comfortable and secure in themselves in their sexual relationship. Many military couples struggle in this process, as it can be difficult to pick up emotionally where they left off before deployment.

How does a military couple continually manage to trust when they are frequently apart from one another? How would it feel to be a spouse who is reunited with their partner after being separated for more than a year? What would they talk about that first day together? How would it feel to have the spouse take away all of the roles and responsibilities that were the other spouses for a year? What kind of thoughts would be going through their minds? How confident would they feel as individuals, spouses, lovers, and members of their family?

As one might assume, there are challenges involved in continually being separated and reunited. In order to survive, military families need to successfully adjust to their changed environment, and they need to trust each other throughout that process. In order for any relationship to exist, there must be trust. For an intimate relationship to exist, that trust must be deep. But how can military spouses continue to build up that trust when they are continually apart from each other? And how do they psychologically grow as individuals within that relationship if they have been separated? This can be another challenge for the family, as some spouses may feel insecure or inadequate as their partner evolves, while they remain in what they feel is the same place in life.

Setting the Stage

These are some of the difficulties of military families. In Step 5, we will use the example of Dan and Kate, which exemplifies the underlying issues of intimacy and trust. We will guide you through the process of helping families like that of Dan and Kate, to openly and honestly communicate their deepest needs, wants, thoughts, feelings, and experiences. Because it is a very common problem in many military families, we will focus this step on not only intimacy but also sexual intimacy. We will demonstrate how to address the faulty thoughts that have caused problems at this deep level of intimacy in the family. And, we will help to create positive thoughts and patterns, which will repair the damaged trust and strengthen the bonds of sexual intimacy in the military relationship.

Not Just a Problem With Sex

Dan starts the conversation . . .

DAN:	She needs help. I don't know what's wrong with her.

He pauses for a second. Kate is glaring at him, but clearly biting her tongue.

DAN:	We've been together for 14 years. Despite all of the adjustments we have all had to make, things have worked out (pause). Until now. The main problem has to do with the intimacy and sex in our relationship. First of all, we used to have sex a few times a week. Now it's maybe once a week or every other week. Kate's not interested, and she avoids any attempts on my part to have sex. Maybe it's 'cause I'm a guy, but I need it more often.
	Second thing is that Kate has been freaking out lately when we're having sex. We're going along and everything is great, then all of a sudden, she tells me to stop and rolls over. She starts crying or emotionally shuts down. She won't talk to me or tell me what is wrong. She'll just lie there until morning (pauses). We used to cuddle and hold hands . . . it's like she's not there. I don't know where her mind is. I don't think she is happy with me anymore. I don't know. (Looks down at the floor and becomes silent.)
THERAPIST (breaking the stiffening silence):	Kate, why have you come here?
KATE (stares at the artwork on the wall for a little while):	It's not exactly fair . . . what Dan is saying. Some of it is true. I have been different while we are being intimate. I'm having some difficulties right now. . . (She looks away, tears beginning to brim in her eyes.)

After a few minutes, Kate shares that while she was on tour in Iraq, her commanding officer raped her one evening, then threatened that if she ever told anyone, he would kill her partner and her children. She had never told anyone in the military before, out of terror. She also shared that a few months ago, she was taking care of a patient at the hospital who bore a striking resemblance to the officer who had assaulted her. He was also very rude to her and inappropriate. This experience triggered all of the memories of the rape that had been tucked away. Now she found herself on high alert, anxious, having flashbacks, and feeling overwhelmed while she and her partner were being intimate. She had told Dan about being raped and the threats, but more recently, she never told him why she was emotionally distant during sex.

KATE: But it's not that I don't love Dan or want to be with him. I just feel uncomfortable. He has changed. It's like his desire for sex is insatiable. I can't please him, no matter how hard I try. He used to be gentle. Now he's aggressive and wants things differently than before. It brings everything up for me. . . . I'm sorry, but it's just not fun or pleasurable for me anymore. I feel pressured to be someone I'm not. It doesn't feel like intimacy. It makes me feel like I'm not enough for him. And it makes me feel dirty inside. I don't know who he is anymore, honestly. And I'm not sure I like it. I don't know if his last tour changed him. I don't know if he has someone else. . . .

DAN (interrupts): WHAT? Kate, how can you say that? There's no one else but you!

Kate doesn't look convinced, and she stops him from interrupting her again and continues, looking at me instead of at him.

KATE: It's just that he expects me to be someone I'm not. He spends a lot of time on the computer these days. When I get home, he is on the computer. I've caught him looking at porn videos. There have been several times where he has gotten fully worked up. I walk in the door and catch him on there, then he wants to have sex right then and there. Well, I'm sorry, but I'm tired after working all day. And I can't be like that for him. . . . I don't like it that way. . . . I just want to know why I'm not enough for him anymore. Maybe I can't give him what he wants or needs. It's why I feel he has someone else, or like he wants someone else.

Kate appeared hurt and confused, as well as miffed.

KATE (adds in): I'm not perfect either. I have my share of issues. And I know it hasn't been easy. I know we all change over time. We've both changed. But I just want things the way they used to be. I feel so alone in our relationship, and like I'm just not enough for him. I don't know if after all of these years together, he is bored with me, if he is desiring a younger model, or if he just doesn't want to be with me anymore. I'm here because I want my Dan back.

Eroding Trust in the Family

Clearly, a couple of major issues exist in this military family: sexual compulsion in one partner and a history of military sexual assault in the other. When combined, these issues

---

For Your Information: Military Sexual Trauma, PTSD, and Sexual Experience

In the U.S. Department of Defense Annual Report on Sexual Assault in the Military (2011, March), it was reported that in 2010, 4.4% of active-duty women and 0.9% of active-duty men had experienced unwanted sexual contact in the previous 12 months. In a study of nearly 126,000 veterans who returned from Iraq and Afghanistan, researchers found that 15.1% of the women and 0.7% of the men reported military sexual trauma (Kimerling et al., 2010). Within the Department of Defense study, the report of sexual trauma was said to be as high as 20% (DoD, 2011; 2010 WGRA). Yet, it is believed that many men and women do not report sexual traumas, and underreporting of sexual assault occurs in the military as it does in the civilian world.

Whether reported or not, men and women who experience military sexual trauma (MST) are more vulnerable to long-term negative consequences, such as PTSD, suicide, and substance abuse (DHHS, 2009a, 2009b). Indeed, past hallmark studies have shown that between one-third and one-half of rape victims have experienced sexual difficulties, including decreased sexual satisfaction, decreased arousal, or decreased desire (Becker, Skinner, Abel, & Treacy, 1982; Norris & Feldman-Summers, 1981). In another older study, sexual assault victims were found to experience significantly less sexual satisfaction up to 18 months after their attack (Feldman-Summers, Gordon, & Meagher, 1979; Orlando & Koss, 1983). These past findings have been supported by more recent studies. In fact, researchers emphasize the importance of screening victims of MST, "for adverse sexual effects in all domains of sexual satisfaction: emotional, physical including gynecological, and relational" (McCall-Hosenfeld, Liebschultz, Spiro, & Seaver, 2009).

---

create complexities in treatment. However, broken down to a more fundamental level, this active-duty military family is struggling with the underlying foundation of intimacy and trust. Neither partner trusts the other right now.

As is frequently the case, as the trust erodes in one area of the relationship, it leads to erosion of trust in all areas of the relationship. When family members stop talking with one another, they tend to start imagining the worst and concocting what they think are plausible explanations in their minds. In this example of Dan and Kate, both partners are expressing that they wonder if the other wants to get out of the relationship or find someone else.

Issues in Sexual Intimacy

In the case of Dan and Kate, as with other military families, trust issues are present in the relationship. As you will find from reading on in this chapter, the trust is further affected by Dan's compulsive sexual behavior. However, as commonly occurs, a chicken-and-egg scenario arises, where one partner in the relationship may have a sexual dysfunction, which adversely affects the other partner. This may correlate with sexual compulsivity, which can increase sexual dysfunction in the other partner, and so on.

Considerations During Treatment

Fundamental to healing the relationship is addressing the trust that is broken, as we have been saying throughout this book. From a clinical standpoint, if you are working with the military family, it may become necessary or be beneficial to refer to other therapists who can work one-on-one with each of the partners to address their unique issues. As with most issues, there is no black-and-white answer or cookbook recipe. The key is to attempt to figure out the underlying source of the problems, which are merely symptoms of the deeper problem.

In this case, it will be important to consider if Kate may benefit from individual psychotherapy to help her work through the pain of the rape. And it can be equally as helpful to have a therapist work with Dan individually to address the underlying contributors to his sexual addiction. Simply addressing the outward problems will not have a positive long-term effect on the relationship. There may be cases where it will become necessary to go to the deeper roots of the problem. Taking the family through these steps will help, especially in the short-term, but without healing and insight into the root of the pain for each partner in the relationship, the trust will continue to erode over time.

Intimacy Issues With Dan and Kate

Kate, like many women and men who have been sexually assaulted or raped, has been having difficulties since her attack. Not only has her level of desire gone down, but in addition, when she and Dan have sex, she relives her trauma and emotionally shuts down. Rape victims struggle with a sense of trust and safety after being violated. It is also very common and normal for her to feel less sexually aroused during intercourse.

In our example, Kate expressed frustrations because Dan has been hypersexual (that is, wanting frequent sex), often modeled after things he observes in porn. This results in Kate feeling pressured to be someone she is not. Because her trust is broken from being raped, and she feels unsafe, these changes only add another layer of insecurity for her. As such, her desire for sex has decreased. And when she has sex, Kate has been consistently experiencing flashbacks, followed by a panic attack, then emotional numbing. As Kate has this negative outcome more and more, it becomes increasingly difficult for her to want sex. In the times when she does have sex, Kate finds she can handle making love to her partner and feel some pleasure, until she is overcome by past images of the rape, then she emotionally withdraws, stops responding sexually, and turns away.

Sexual Intimacy and Communication

In military families such as those like Dan and Kate, it is common to encounter problems with trust. As we discussed in earlier chapters, families often have a breakdown in communication. If communication does not improve, it will lead to problems in other areas of the relationship. Consequently, when families do not communicate well with one another on an emotional level, there will be problems communicating on a sexual level as well. This will lead to sexual dysfunction in the relationship, because it takes a deeper trust and willingness to be vulnerable with someone during sex. If an individual feels unsafe or insecure on a physical, mental, emotional, or spiritual level with their partner, they will be less willing to engage in sexual intimacy. Or, they will be more likely to experience sexual difficulties, including (but not limited to) decreased libido, pain during intercourse, decreased arousal, or inability to orgasm.

Self–Disclosure

Up to this point in the book, we have talked about the importance of improving communication. While self-disclosure is the foundation upon which a healthy relationship is built, we will now assist the military family to self-disclose on a more intimate, vulnerable, and personal level. The process of self-disclosure can be a very therapeutic, empowering exercise, which helps individuals to feel more grounded and self-confident. That being said, individuals will only feel empowered if they are sharing in an environment that is nonjudgmental and nonevaluative.

When family members feel like they were heard and understood, as well as unconditionally accepted by others, then healing will occur in the relationship. Conversely, if the other person acts judgmental or self-righteous, that will inevitably result in feelings of hurt and distrust. In short, the family member who is disclosing will feel ashamed, angry, or hurt, and they will tend to become emotionally defensive, emotionally withdrawn, or shut down altogether. In the future, they would choose not to self-disclose, which would further break down the relationship. No relationship can survive without healthy communication.

Taking Sides

When working with the military family, you will be helping them in this process. One task is to ensure that each person feels emotionally safe in their attempts to share and disclose. It will also be important to refrain from colluding with other family members, if they were to look to you for agreement of their opinions or try to use you as an expert to prove that their position is right. The goal is to help all family members share their experience, at an emotionally open, honest, and vulnerable level, without being judged. The goal is to assist family members to really listen to each other, and to communicate unconditional positive regard or acceptance of each other.

Important Precautions

As we continue on in Step 5, toward improving the relationship through correcting faulty thoughts and beliefs, we will be focused on Dan and Kate's problems with intimacy. Please keep in mind that the purpose of this step is *not* to process traumatic memories or heal past traumas, nor is it to focus treatment on sexual compulsions or sexual addiction(s).

Do Not Process Trauma!

Trauma processing should not be done until a few key tasks have been accomplished. First, significant rapport and trust must be built. With any traumatic event, but in particular the trauma of rape or sexual assault, an individual's sense of safety in the world and with people has been deeply affected, so it is imperative that the individual feel safe and trust you. This means that they know you have the knowledge and skills to assist them, but also that you are capable of supporting them and pulling them out of their pain when they face their demons. No trauma processing or deep exploration should ever occur without trust, as doing so would only further violate and traumatize the individual.

Second, along with rapport, the individual should feel secure in her own abilities to self-soothe. Once trauma processing begins, she may be triggered and experience a lot of strong emotions and pain. This can happen in session, but it most likely will occur outside the safety of your office. So, it is crucial that she know how to ground herself and use various prepracticed techniques and skills to calm herself down.

Third, you should educate and validate the individual's reactions and experiences. Many times, people who have gone through traumatic events feel like their reactions are abnormal or crazy. It is important for them to understand that their reactions are normal, considering what they have been through. In addition, it can be very comforting for someone to hear that others have had similar experiences as they have. When you normalize their experience, you also reduce their shame, and this promotes healing in the individual. As far as your work with the military family, healing the individual also helps that family member share their pain and vulnerability, and this helps heal the pain of the family.

Consider Adjunctive Treatments

We do recommend discussing other treatment options with the family. As mentioned earlier, it may be beneficial or necessary to refer family members to another therapist for individual psychotherapy to address specific treatment concerns. In particular, if you find that a family member emotionally regresses or has difficulty coping with their experiences, it would be helpful for them to also have individual therapy to work toward healing.

Starting Self–Disclosure: Kate's Perspective

But now back to Dan and Kate. In our session, I begin this process of self-disclosure with Kate. Again, I do not ask for specific details about her trauma here. Instead, I ask a very open-ended question that helps Kate begin to share her intimate experience with Dan. You will notice that I do not delineate the course of Kate's sharing. I want her to feel empowered to begin to share whatever is most important to her. It's important that the person, in this case Kate, can freely disclose without being interrupted by you or the other person so he or she can feel in control of this process.

THERAPIST: Kate, you and Dan shared some of what you are feeling, some of your frustrations. A very important part of this process for both of you is to begin to really understand what the other thinks, feels, and believes. Kate, you talked about your difficulties with things you see as being different in Dan. You shared about being raped when you were in Iraq. And you talked about wanting things back to the way they were. I'm wondering if you would be willing to share more about what all of this has been like for you?

KATE: Okay. I have just been feeling very frustrated and hurt lately. And confused, I guess. Like I said before, I know we all change. God knows, I have changed. Sometimes I wonder if I will ever be the person I was before. (Pause) It's just that I feel like I have struggled with intimacy since the rape. I have felt scared and unsure of myself. I feel scarred (tears brimming). I don't know if Dan finds me attractive anymore. I don't feel attractive. Sometimes I feel dirty inside. Then when I find him on porn sites watching these women . . . it pisses me off. And it hurts like hell. Because then it just makes me feel even worse about myself. I wonder if he blames me. I wonder if he even wants to be with me. When we are together and having sex, I wonder if he is really feeling good about being with me, the way I am now since the attack, or if he is fantasizing about one of the women from the porn (long pause, Kate looks away).

THERAPIST: Please go on, Kate. What else have you been feeling and thinking?

KATE: I just . . . I don't get it! (now getting angry) I don't get how he can even look at porn when we've been together for so long. Doesn't he see anything wrong with that? If that's not bad enough, he tries to push me into it. I already have a hard time feeling comfortable having sex. But then being pressured into doing stuff I wouldn't do! I'm NOT those women! I don't know WHO I am anymore! But I know I'm not comfortable being that for him.

THERAPIST: What's it like for you when you have to be like those women, Kate? Can you talk more about that?

KATE: I HATE IT! It makes me feel disgusting! It makes me hate sex even more. I have a hard enough time feeling safe. It's not that I'm afraid of Dan. I just feel uncomfortable. It's like my body remembers everything. When Dan and I are together, and he wants me to be a different person, I don't know where he's going to take it. And sometimes he gets aggressive. He doesn't hit me or force me, but I just feel uneasy and uncomfortable. A lot of times he wants it rough. Then I don't respond to him. I can't get aroused. Then he gets frustrated because I want to stop before he's done (looks down to the floor, crying). I feel used, like it can be anyone besides me that would make him happier and satisfied (pauses, still looking down). I feel like I'm being raped over and over again by that bastard!

THERAPIST: Anything else, Kate?

For Your Information: Sexually Compulsive Behavior, PTSD, and Sexual Experience

Sexually compulsive behavior is very common with trauma, including military trauma. This is because the individual utilizes behaviors, in this case sexually based, as a means of escaping their painful emotions and memories. Other methods of escape can include using alcohol or drugs, addictions to gambling, spending, pornography, work, and eating. Howard (2007) added,

> It can include viewing and sometimes masturbating to pornography online. It can also include such behaviors as voyeurism, exhibitionism, mutual masturbation, sexualized chatting, and paying for sex, to name just a few. It includes all of the person's problematic sexual behaviors. (p. 87)

Really, the behaviors can include any that result in avoidance or distraction from the emotional pain someone has inside. Sometimes the stronger and more salient the disturbing images or feelings, the stronger the compulsive behaviors are as well.

Marriage expert Dr. John Gottman (Gottman et al., 2011) recently stated in an *American Psychologist* article,

> Internet pornography for the immediate masturbatory gratification of the soldier as well as an array of actual sexual opportunities on the Internet for the deployed soldier also constitute a major issue for partners back at home . . . trust and betrayal are the issues soldiers and partners fight about most. (p. 53)

U.S. Navy Chaplain Howard (2007) significantly pointed out,

> The spouse or partner of the addict will typically experience significant distress as a result of the addict's behavior. Further complicating matters, in the case of military families who have recently experienced separation due to combat, is the stress from the deployment, subsequent reintegration, as well as symptoms of PTSD that the service member is experiencing and the rest of the family has been exposed to. The spouse or partner will feel betrayed by the addict. Trust, regardless of its previous level, is likely to be destroyed. This person will also experience feelings of low self-esteem or self-worth as he or she perceives that the addict preferred another person or even an image to them. (p. 90)

KATE:	It just feels like my spirit is being sucked out of me repeatedly, but this time it's not the prick that raped me. (Looks up at Dan.) It's you taking pieces of me away. (Sighs deeply, looks away, crying.)
THERAPIST (added therapeutic pause and silence):	Kate, that took a lot of courage. Thank you for being so honest in about what you are thinking and feeling. Is there anything you need from Dan right now?
KATE (shrugs her shoulders, looks at Dan):	I need you to understand what this is like for me, Dan. I need you to love me. But I think what I need most from you is your understanding, and for my needs to matter too.
THERAPIST:	Kate, maybe you can continue to talk with Dan, and tell him what you specifically need from him.
KATE:	I guess I need to hear you say that I am enough for you, Dan. I haven't felt that in awhile. I need you to take my needs into consideration. I need you to stop coercing me into being someone I am not when we are having sex. I want to make love, not feel like it's just an act. That's what I have been feeling—like it's just to get your rocks off instead of loving me, and me loving you. I want us to figure this out and be okay again. I want the real you back, Dan. I miss you.
THERAPIST:	Is there anything else you need from Dan?
KATE (nods):	No, that's mainly it.

As a result of Kate sharing her side of things, a couple of things happened. One, Kate was able to share her experience without being interrupted or judged by her partner. Two, Dan was able to listen to her and take in her side. This is a very important part of the process, of opening the floor up for honest and real communication. The first step to fixing a problem is to understand its source. This dialogue created an open forum, without judgment or criticism.

Going Beneath the Surface

This was the case for Dan and Kate, as well as thousands of other military families. There will be a slow erosion of trust that occurs over time if the problem is not addressed. From a clinical standpoint, it is paramount that you go deeper than the surface manifestations of the compulsive behaviors. For healing to occur, you must work on healing the underlying trauma and pain that is resulting in the avoidance vis-à-vis sexual compulsiveness. That is the only way to truly help the returnee and to heal the trust in the relationship.

Starting Self-Disclosure: Dan's Perspective

Back to our session with Dan and Kate, I continue to facilitate open communication between them. This time, I open the floor up to Dan, where he can do two things: (1) share his thoughts and feelings about what Kate said, and (2) share his own experience.

THERAPIST: Dan, would you be willing to first of all share how you feel about what Kate shared with you?

DAN: Okay. I get where Kate is coming from. I can see why she'd feel pissed and hurt. She always has been pretty conservative as far as the sex part of our relationship. I can see how me asking her to do stuff she normally wouldn't do would make her feel upset. I was hoping we could try different things and be a little more creative. We are both so busy and stressed out, it'd be nice to be able to let loose more when we are having sex. I don't see a problem with the porn. Just because I look at it, doesn't mean I want Kate less. I think she's still as sexy, if not sexier, than the day we first met. I love her with all my heart. I just want to destress and be freer in doing it.

THERAPIST (to encourage more sharing):   Dan, can you talk more about your sexual experience with Kate and how you have been feeling?

DAN: I'm just frustrated. I feel stifled. Like I said, I feel like we are both so wound tight and stressed out, that I just want to be able to have fun. Sometimes I want to go outside the box. Kate's not like that. She never has been since I've known her, but lately it's been worse. I was hoping she could learn to let go more. I don't want her to be someone she's not. . . . I just want her to let go and loosen up.

THERAPIST: Dan, can you talk about what you need from Kate? Can you be more specific?

DAN: I need her to want sex more. We don't do it enough anymore. I need her to be willing to try new things—to initiate more, to take the lead, to try to enjoy herself.

THERAPIST: Anything else, Dan?

DAN: Yeah, I need for her to let go for God's sake. Just frickin' let loose! It's not fun for me anymore either. It's like, because she is miserable, I have to be too. I want the old Kate back. I can't stand this anymore. I don't want to be with anyone else, but it's too much (looks at Kate). I need more than this. That's why I watch porn. Because it makes me feel free inside, and it helps me destress. I like the way it makes me feel—like a man. . . . I haven't felt like that in awhile with you, Kate.

The Gist of the Matter

Essentially, in this dialogue, Dan made it clear that he needs more from Kate sexually. For Kate, sex has become very difficult. It has become emotionally charged and painful, reopening her old wounds of being raped. Her trust has been rebroken, and when Dan looks at porn and wants her to "let loose," it is causing her to feel even more hurt and rejected inside. From Dan's point of view, he expresses feeling frustrated, saying that porn is a way to let go and destress. And by Kate not wanting to go along with it, he says it leaves him feeling more frustrated and driven to seek out sexual fulfillment from porn.

So, while both Kate and Dan were able to openly communicate their own experiences without judging the other person, there are some clear differences in how they are viewing the intimacy in their relationship. It is like they are traveling down different paths or in totally different directions. Our next task is to help them find a common ground, by reframing each of their experiences into healthier ones. If their relationship is to heal, they will both need to change some of their thoughts and beliefs about each other, as related to their sex life. That leads us to using some exercises to try to accomplish this goal.

Making It Real: Intimacy, Sex, Thoughts, and Feelings

In this exercise, we begin to delve deeper into the thoughts and feelings of our military family. In it, we explore what their specific thoughts are, and how they are subsequently feeling about their relationship. The questions in this exercise should be used to help family members openly disclose some of their most intimate feelings and thoughts.

Exercise directions:

1. Please go to Family Handout Step 5.1.
2. Take about 15 to 20 minutes to have each family member (on their own) go through and write out detailed, honest responses to all of the statements.
3. Tell the family members: "We're going to spend about 15 to 20 minutes right now doing this exercise. I'd like to ask each of you to silently to go over the next seven statements. Start at number one and move down the list. Please complete each statement and write any other thoughts, feelings, or reactions you might have. When you are writing these out, the rule is: please be very open and honest. Go with your gut reaction—your first instinct. Don't sit and think about your answers. And don't censor. Just write down how you truly think and feel."
4. After family members have finished, take about 5 to 10 minutes for each family member to share their answers out loud.
5. Then take around 15 to 20 minutes to process this with the family.

THOUGHTS AND FEELINGS ABOUT INTIMACY:

➤ When my partner and I are intimate, I feel . . .

➤ After we have sex, I feel . . .

➤ As far as our love life, lately I have been wondering . . .

➤ When it comes to sex these days, I would describe myself as . . .

➤ I would describe my partner as . . .

➤ When it comes to our sex life and level of intimacy in our relationship, I am concerned that . . .

➤ Sometimes I think . . .

Talking Points

This exercise helps reveal family members' deeper thoughts and feelings. Sometimes, a family member can hold back their true emotions or thoughts when they are saying them out loud. This can happen because the person is afraid of hurting his or her loved one's feelings. Or, they might be afraid that the other person will judge them. For many people, it can be easier to write their feelings down. Beyond this, when we write our thoughts and feelings down without censoring, we access our deeper, underlying reactions, which we may not be willing to say aloud. This exercise would only be partially helpful if we stopped there. True understanding and deeper intimacy comes when family members can share their reactions at the end. Exploring family members' experience after they hear what the other person wrote down is crucial.

When working with Dan and Kate, this exercise further broke the ice and helped them become more aware of each other's issues, as well as reasons why the other person was feeling so frustrated. Take a look at some of Dan and Kate's reactions during this exercise.

Some of Dan's Responses:

➤ When my partner and I are intimate, I feel . . . dissatisfied, like my needs don't matter sometimes.

➤ After we have sex, I feel . . . frustrated and left wanting more.

➤ As far as our love life, lately I have been wondering . . . if things will ever get better, or if it's always going to be like this.

➤ When it comes to sex these days, I would describe myself as . . . needy. I need it bad and a lot, more than Kate can give me.

➤ I would describe my partner as . . . fragile when it comes to sex, but strong in other areas.

➤ When it comes to our sex life and level of intimacy in our relationship, I am concerned that . . . we have turned into different people. I don't know if we can ever feel the same again.

➤ Sometimes I think. . . . I don't know what to think. Maybe I'm being a selfish bastard. Or maybe Kate's being unfair. I don't know.

Some of Kate's Responses:

➤ When my partner and I are intimate, I feel . . . confused. Betrayed. Uncomfortable. Pressured to be someone I am not.

➤ After we have sex, I feel . . . dirty and used. Like I was just an object to help someone else get what they wanted. And I feel lonely and misunderstood.

➤ As far as our love life, lately I have been wondering . . . Will it ever get better? Sometimes I don't think so.

➤ When it comes to sex these days, I would describe myself as . . . very reserved and withdrawn, and scared.

➤ I would describe my partner as . . . horny and needy, like his needs are insatiable.

➤ When it comes to our sex life and level of intimacy in our relationship, I am concerned that . . . sex is just sex. It's not making love anymore. I don't feel like we connect on an intimate level anymore.

➤ Sometimes I think . . . how can this ever get better when we are so different?

As you can see, Dan and Kate have drastically different experiences. However, they have both been wondering if things will ever work out in their relationship. One of the dynamics occurring in this family is that Dan, in his need for sexual pleasure and fulfillment, has requested and acted on his fantasies stemming from porn. Subsequently, Kate has felt pressured to conform, but when she does, it brings up traumatic memories for her and results in her feeling more ashamed and distrustful. This is a very important point for both Dan and Kate to understand. More will be revealed about their feelings as we head into the next exercise.

Making It Real: Defining Intimacy in the Relationship

This exercise can be used to help spouses or partners become very clear about how each of them defines intimacy in their relationship. It also helps partners to clarify expectations they have for one another specific to intimacy and sexuality.

Exercise Directions:

1. Give each family member a copy of Family Handout Step 5.2.
2. Similar to the last exercise, take about 15 to 20 minutes to have each family member (on their own) go through and write out detailed, honest responses to all of the statements.
3. Tell the family members: "Like we did in the last exercise, we're going to spend about 15 to 20 minutes to do this exercise. Please go through these six statements now and complete them. The same rules apply in this exercise. Please be totally honest and don't hold back. Go with your gut reaction, and don't censor how you feel."
4. After family members have finished, take about 5 to 10 minutes for each family member to share their answers out loud.
5. Then take around 15 to 20 minutes to process this with the family.

DEFINING INTIMACY:

➤ To me, intimacy means . . .

➤ As far as our relationship, my idea of what sex should be like is . . .

➤ My expectations for myself in our relationship are . . .

➤ My expectations for my partner in our relationship are . . .

➤ In my ideal fantasy, I would be . . .

➤ In my ideal fantasy, my partner would be . . .

Talking Points

By using this exercise, your military family members will hopefully learn more about each other. When there is conflict in the relationship, invariably there is also a difference of opinion about what each person expects from the other. And if they don't communicate about it or express their frustrations, it will lead to problems down the road. This is especially true for the sexual part of their relationship.

That is exactly what we found in working with our couple, Dan and Kate. When I opened up the discussion and asked Dan and Kate for their reactions, what I heard was not very surprising. Dan expected more sex in their relationship, which he wanted to be spontaneous and exciting. Kate expected that if they were to have sex, it would involve a lack of pressure or demands. In the next exercise, we will go deeper into the couple's perceptions of intimacy.

Making It Real: Breaking it Down

This exercise is very important because it will bring out the family's underlying fears and perceptions about intimacy. We are now going even deeper and getting to the heart of each individual's feelings. We explore not only how each family member feels about the relationship, but also how they feel about themselves while being in the relationship. You will want to have the family complete these statements, like they did in the last two exercises. Then discuss and process their experiences to help them make better sense of their reactions. (Please use Family Handout Step 5.3.) Here are the statements for this exercise:

➤ I realize my biggest fear(s) is/are . . .

➤ In our relationship, on a deep level, I feel . . .

➤ The experience with my partner where I felt closest to him/her and good about myself was (describe it). I felt this way because . . .

➤ The experience with my partner where I felt furthest from him/her and bad about myself was (describe it). I felt this way because . . .

Talking Points

As you go through this exercise with your military families, they will become more aware of the deeper feelings they carry. From these feelings, you can connect the related thoughts and explore their beliefs. Given that the family is struggling and having difficulties, it is safe for you to assume that there will be some foundational beliefs that are not healthy ones. By using this exercise with the family, you can bring these beliefs out and start to correct them. With our military family, we learned of key feelings that revealed core dysfunctional beliefs. Take a look at some of the responses that Dan and Kate provided.

A COUPLE OF DAN'S RESPONSES:

➤ I realize my biggest fear(s) is/are . . . of losing Kate and the kids and being all alone in the world. I've given everything to them.

➤ In our relationship, on a deep level, I feel . . . like I have been losing myself, like I don't know who I am sometimes. I wonder if I am even a good husband anymore.

A COUPLE OF KATE'S RESPONSES:

➤ I realize my biggest fear(s) is/are . . . of losing control, of getting hurt again, of ever feeling like I did when I was attacked. I'm also afraid that Dan will leave me for another woman who will satisfy him more.

➤ In our relationship, on a deep level, I feel . . . inadequate. I feel like I'm not enough to make Dan happy anymore. I think I used to be, but I'm not anymore.

As you can see, there is a common ground for Dan and Kate. Both of them fear that the other one will leave. It is pretty normal for fears of abandonment or rejection to creep up when the family is experiencing problems. It's also common to hear fears come out about being alone. The longer a couple is together, they will mutually have fears about having lost a big chunk of time in their lives, which they devoted to that person. Similarly, many couples devote all of their time to each other for years, sometimes isolating themselves from friends and family. They "put all of their eggs in one basket." Then if they split up, they fear having no one and being alone.

Using Socratic Questioning to Help Kate

Specific to Kate's experiences with a history of sexual trauma, Socratic Questioning is commonly used by leading trauma specialists, including Drs. Edna Foa and Barbara Rothbaum. In their book, *Treating the Trauma of Rape: Cognitive-Behavioral Therapy for PTSD*, Foa and Rothbaum (1998) advised that clinicians use the Socratic Questioning technique to help clients gain more insight. They stated,

> It is not the same as "the power of positive thinking." The purpose is not to trade negative thoughts for positive ones. Rather, the goal of challenging negative

thoughts or beliefs is to recognize the errors in one's logic and thinking that cause distress. These errors need to be corrected and exchanged for beliefs that are more objective and reasonable, and that reflect reality more accurately. (p. 187–188)

The How-To of Socratic Questioning

The entire point of using Socratic Questioning is to increase clients' level of insight. You will help them become more aware of what their specific thoughts are, what thinking patterns tend to prevail for them, and how their thoughts affect their feelings and behaviors. You will be playing devil's advocate with them by challenging their logic. You will be doing a reality check, to help them see whether or not their thought processes are realistic. Socratic Questioning can be a very powerful tool, which helps build insight. It can serve as the springboard from which more realistic, empowering thought processes arise. And when clients think, feel, and behave from a realistic and empowered vantage point, they will be more likely to feel content and be successful in their lives.

For Your Information: Socratic Questioning

The father of cognitive therapy, Dr. Aaron Beck, devised 10 principles that evolved around what he called the Socratic Method (Beck & Emery, 1985). Beck postulated that questions helped clients to become more aware of their thoughts, to observe and examine them, to choose better thought processes, and to plan how to do so. Within this Socratic Method the therapist asks specific questions to challenge the client's thinking processes. In her book, *The Art of the Question: A Guide to Short-Term Question-Centered Therapy*, Dr. Marilee Goldberg (1998) included some very detailed examples of Socratic Questions, such as:

- What is the evidence for or against this idea?
- Where is the logic?
- Are you oversimplifying a causal relationship?
- Are you confusing a habit with a fact?
- Are your interpretations of the situation too far from reality to be accurate?
- Are you confusing your version of the facts with the facts as they are?
- Are you thinking in all-or-none terms?
- Are you using words or phrases that are extreme or exaggerated?
- Are you taking selected examples out of context?
- Are you using cognitive defense mechanisms?
- Is your source of information reliable?
- Are you thinking in terms of certainties rather than probabilities?
- Are you confusing a low probability with a high probability?
- Are your judgments based on feelings instead of facts?
- Are you overfocusing on irrelevant factors? (Goldberg, 1998, p. 50)

We are now going to take you right into the next Making It Real exercise, which will involve challenging these negative beliefs that are creating dissonance in the family. In this exercise, we demonstrate how you can apply Socratic Questioning to correct faulty thinking processes. It is imperative that they be challenged and corrected to help the family heal on an intimate level.

Making It Real: Challenging and Correcting

In this exercise, we will identify, challenge, and modify the negative thoughts, feelings, and beliefs of our family. We will include some key clinical dialogue to illustrate how to do this so that you can go through the same process with other military families (please see Family Handout Step 5.4).

THERAPIST: Dan and Kate, we have talked a lot about finding the common ground in your relationship. Can both of you see that you both have fears about the other leaving? (Both nod.) However, the reasons behind your fears are different. If it's all right, I would like for us to start out with you, Kate? (She nods.) Kate, you shared that you feel inadequate and like you are not enough for Dan in your relationship. Can you say more about what you mean?"

KATE: I do feel inadequate sometimes. I especially feel that way whenever we are having sex. I talked a lot about that already, but I don't feel like I am the person that Dan wants when we are being intimate. I feel afraid sometimes because I don't know where he will take things. I don't think he means to make me feel this way, but I feel objectified. It makes me feel out of control.

THERAPIST: Kate, can you please say more about your feeling out of control?

KATE: First of all, I feel powerless when all of the memories come back to haunt me. There are times when they just overtake me, and I can't stop them. On top of that, there are times when I feel like Dan is not Dan anymore when we are having sex. I feel afraid that he is going to hurt me sometimes.

THERAPIST: Kate, you said that in those moments, "Dan is not Dan anymore." Who is he?

KATE: He becomes my commanding officer, the bastard who raped me while I was in Iraq.

THERAPIST: And what do you feel physically and emotionally in those moments, Kate?

KATE: I can feel my heart pounding in my chest; I have a hard time breathing; I feel panic inside; I feel overwhelmed and afraid.

THERAPIST:	And is there anything specific that you can pinpoint that triggers those memories and feelings in you?
KATE:	It's when Dan gets rougher … when he takes his hands and pins my arms down and is on top of me, it brings everything back for me. Then I am not with Dan anymore, and I feel the terror come back.
THERAPIST:	Kate, had you ever shared that with Dan before?
KATE:	No, I hadn't ever shared anything with Dan about it.
THERAPIST:	Dan, now that you know this, how can it help you when you and Kate are together?
DAN:	Kate, I would never hurt you. And it kills me that the son-of-a-bitch hurt you the way he did. But I am not your C.O. I would never hurt you. But I don't see how me looking at porn is going to make you fear me. That doesn't make any sense.
KATE (looks put-off and irritated):	Dan, I wish you could stop being so stubborn and selfish!
THERAPIST:	Kate, is there anything else that you would like Dan to know, that you feel could help him understand where you are coming from?
KATE:	Just that it makes me feel really shitty about myself (looks down at the floor).
THERAPIST:	Can you say more about that, Kate?
KATE:	It makes me feel ashamed, like I am a worthless piece of shit.
THERAPIST:	Please go on, Kate. What do you think about yourself when you look in the mirror afterward?
KATE:	I can't even look myself in the eye for days after. It's like I don't even recognize the person looking back at me. I just think I'm different. I'm messed up and defective so that Dan would not want me for who I am anymore . . . so that must be why he tries to get me to be someone I am not.
THERAPIST:	So you feel ashamed, and your belief is that you are defective and unworthy. Is that right?
KATE (nods):	Yes.
THERAPIST:	What evidence do you have for this belief, Kate?
KATE:	That Dan wants for me to be someone I'm not.
THERAPIST:	Okay. Dan, can you tell Kate what you think and if this is true for you?

DAN:	Of course it's not true! My God, Kate! I love you! I want you to be you! I don't want you to be anyone else for me.
KATE:	Then why the hell do you make me act like someone else when we are having sex, Dan? I hate that I can't even call it making love. But that's not what it's been for me in a long time.
DAN (silent for a minute):	I guess I didn't realize I was doing that, Kate. My intention was never to make you feel shitty about yourself. I didn't know us fooling around in different ways made you feel that bad inside. I see it as us having a good time.
KATE:	Dan, can't you understand or try to understand for a minute that it's not fun for me? How the hell do you think it would make me feel? Seriously?
DAN:	I see your point, Kate. But I swear to you, I never meant to make you feel worthless. And you are not defective! So you are having a hard time! That doesn't mean there's something wrong with you!
KATE:	You mean it, Dan? Or are you just saying that?
DAN:	Kate (sounding more serious), I swear to God it's true. I love you just the way you are.
KATE (sighs, looking frustrated):	As long as I act like a whore to satisfy your needs, right?
DAN:	No, Kate. I love you for you. I'm not asking you to act like a whore. I just want us to let go a little. That's all.
KATE:	But what about the porn, Dan?
DAN:	What about it?
KATE:	Don't you think that's a problem?
DAN:	No, I don't. Like I said, it has nothing to do with loving you less. I just want our sex life to be alive like when we first got together. It's just gotten boring and lifeless.
KATE:	I'm sorry, Dan. I am doing the best I can (sounding annoyed and looking away).
DAN:	Kate, you just need to understand that my wanting to spice things up has nothing to do with you being unworthy or not enough for me. I love you. Period. End of story.
KATE:	Dan, what if I can never act like someone else? Are you always going to feel that I am enough for you? Or will your eyes start to wander?

DAN:	Yes, you will always be the one for me. And no, my eyes are not going to wander. I don't want anyone else. I want you.
THERAPIST:	Kate, let's go back to your beliefs of being defective and worthless. Does the evidence support your beliefs?
KATE:	No, I guess not.
THERAPIST:	Kate, how are you feeling right now?
KATE:	I'm feeling a little freer inside. I still have some doubts, but I feel a little better I guess.
THERAPIST:	How does this help you feel freer inside, Kate?
KATE:	It felt good to hear Dan say what he did. I just needed to hear it for myself. I have been thinking the worst. I didn't know what to think.
THERAPIST:	So now that you know there is no evidence to support your beliefs, Kate, how true is the statement that you are worthless and defective?
KATE:	I still feel it to a degree. But I feel it a lot less now.
THERAPIST:	On a scale of 0 to 100, with 0 being that you don't believe it at all, 100 being that you are fully convinced it's true, where are you now, Kate?
KATE:	I would say at around 40 percent.
THERAPIST:	Okay, so it is better than before. Right?
KATE:	Yes, I felt it almost 100% of the time before.
THERAPIST:	Okay, that's good progress then. What is the evidence that still keeps you feeling defective and worthless 40% of the time?
KATE:	Huh?
THERAPIST:	Well, we feel what we feel for a reason. What evidence do you hold onto that keeps you feeling defective and worthless? Another way of thinking about it, Kate, is: if we were in a courtroom, what evidence would you present to support your beliefs?
KATE (pauses for some time):	I guess I don't have any evidence.
THERAPIST:	None?
KATE:	I guess not. Dan said that all of that was untrue.
THERAPIST:	So then where do you think those beliefs came from, Kate?
KATE:	I guess from a lot of my insecurities about myself. I don't know.
THERAPIST:	That's good insight, Kate. So rather than telling yourself you are worthless and defective, what can you begin to tell yourself from now on?

KATE:	I don't know.
THERAPIST:	Maybe you can get some feedback from Dan?
KATE:	Okay . . . Dan, what do you think?
DAN:	I would say you tell yourself that you are perfect just the way you are. You are beautiful and smart and sexy. There's nothing wrong with you, Kate.
KATE:	Thank you, Dan.
THERAPIST:	Kate, what do you think?
KATE:	I guess I start telling myself I am okay. And when I try to tell myself I'm not, I remind myself of this moment.
THERAPIST:	Excellent, Kate! It is always a good idea to check the source. So, if Dan or someone else were not the one putting you down, the source would be?
KATE:	It would be me.
THERAPIST:	That's right. We need to be aware of where our thoughts are coming from. The more we repeat a negative thought, it becomes a belief, which can cause a lot of emotional pain. The thing to keep in mind is, if there is no evidence to support that belief, then we are causing ourselves a lot of unnecessary hurt and pain. Essentially, we are telling ourselves lies about ourselves. Right? Once we have gone through the process of challenging a negative belief and refuting it, the next step is to change it into something positive. Just like you did, Kate!

Final Thoughts

Dan and Kate made some progress here. By using Socratic Questioning, we helped Kate realize that there was no evidence to support her negative thoughts, feelings, and beliefs about herself. This exercise healed some of Kate's hurt and shame, which had only kept her bound emotionally and doubting her partner's love for her. This was a positive step toward healing this military family.

By the same token, Dan remained stuck in his beliefs that looking at porn online was harmless to their relationship. This is an area that we will need to get into further in the couple's therapy process. In this situation, Dan did reach a point several sessions later where he realized that he needed more help to deal with his sexual addiction. So we referred him out for additional help from a sex therapist and provided options for a 12-step program. If you encounter this situation with any of your couples, you will need to exercise clinical judgment in deciding whether additional help will be necessary.

As a result of going through this step, our military family was making some gains and healing their intimate bonds. Once the family has reconnected on this deeper level, they will be more ready to move on to the next step: processing. And that is where we head in the next chapter.

Keys to Family Wellness

➤ Help family members to share their experiences, at an emotionally open, honest, and vulnerable level, without being judged in any way, shape, or form.

➤ Help family members to really listen to each other and to communicate unconditional positive regard or acceptance of each other.

➤ Explore the negative thoughts, feelings, and beliefs that exist in members of the family. From there, examine the evidence for them, challenge them, and then guide the family members to change them on their own.

➤ When family members come up with healthy beliefs of themselves and each other, it heals their pain.

➤ It makes them stronger to be able to process and face their challenges and makes them more resilient as a family.

─── Taking Action ───

Taking action will help rebuild the family. Please check off each step as the family accomplishes it.

❏ The family should keep a log during the week of any negative statements or beliefs that come out on an individual or collective level. This will build awareness of the messages that are perpetuating within their family.

❏ The family should take the log and spend an hour at the end of the week going through the log and challenging those negative beliefs. They should work together to state any evidence that supports the beliefs. They should switch off and use Socratic Questioning to name off any and all pieces of evidence that may have perpetuated the beliefs.

❏ The family should spend another hour on the weekend to take the body of evidence, weigh it out and decide if it holds true or not, then replace those negative beliefs with positive, healthy ones that will build up their family.

6

Process

Taking a Deeper Look

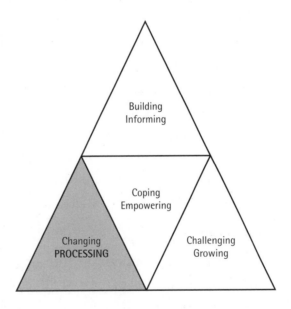

The most important thing in life is to learn how to give out love, and to let it come in.
—Morrie Schwartz

Robert and Felicia, who we introduced in Step 2, had been growing apart over the past several years. The stress of deployments, combined with raising two teenage boys, had resulted in a growing friction and sense of dissatisfaction with each other. Although they had made significant progress in the previous sessions, Robert and Felicia still lacked the connection and communication that is necessary for a deeply fulfilling relationship. In our sessions, it became apparent that the couple did not openly share emotions or even let down their guard with one another.

Robert and Felicia had taken considerable steps to strengthen their family. They had worked to interact better with their sons. However, Robert and Felicia still struggled with being able to open up to each other. The closeness that this couple had years ago had eroded over time. They needed to learn how to change the hurtful and dysfunctional communication patterns that were driving them apart.

Setting the Stage

When service members like Robert and Felicia hold leadership positions, or are hoping to advance in their careers, they may feel a constant pressure on themselves to set an example for others. In the course of being "strong" role models, they can develop a tendency to be "in control" all of the time. When the couple has to cope with the effects of trauma, they can become disconnected from their emotions. Their relationship can suffer as a result of being unable to share with each other.

In Step 6, we work through the key issues of trust and unconditional acceptance with our military families. At this stage, returnees may be reluctant to open up about deployment or war-related experiences. Family members may have fears of rejection or abandonment. In this step, we help family members to let go of their need for control, so that they can reconnect with their loved ones.

While family members began to address intimate trust in Step 5, now we will take it to a deeper level. In Step 6, returnees will be able to share their painful or traumatic experiences, as their family members positively react by giving them unconditional love and acceptance. This step will further empower family members to overcome greater challenges as a family unit, with the knowledge that they are there for each other no matter what.

Why People Stuff Their Emotions

When family members stuff their emotions, including grief, this can create problems in the family. Returnees and their loved ones may have difficulties sharing their feelings and stuff them to protect themselves. Here are some common reasons why people stuff their emotions.

"They Can Handle It on Their Own"

Many people are raised with the idea that people simply shouldn't talk about their problems or express negative emotions. Instead of talking about their problems, some individuals believe that they should handle problems on their own. In addition, certain cultures may hold beliefs that family members should restrain their emotions. Some individuals feel that sharing their feelings can burden or impose on others.

"It's a Sign of Weakness"

As we mentioned in previous chapters, stigma related to mental health prevents many individuals from being willing to share their feelings or admit to having any psychological "weaknesses." Many people believe that sharing their feelings or problems is a sign of weakness, so they stuff their emotions instead. Some family members may believe that when someone is struggling on an emotional level, they are "weak" or "crazy." On a related note, many families hold to the belief that it brings shame to their family if a member discusses their family problems with outsiders.

"I Will Get Hurt if I Open Up"

Some individuals think that other people will not understand what they are going through. Some might fear that others will minimize their problems or feelings, whereas other people may fear being put down or criticized for feeling the way they do. Many individuals refuse to be vulnerable because they remember being hurt before when they shared with someone. As a result, they don't share because they would rather not risk getting hurt again.

"I Wouldn't Know Where to Begin"

Some people will not share because it feels uncomfortable to them. Also, some people might lack basic communication skills when it comes to talking about or listening to others' sensitive feelings.

"They Will Make Fun of Me"

Like the individuals who don't share because of their fears of being hurt, there are people who do not share because they are afraid others will make fun of them or laugh at them. Many people don't know how to appropriately handle sensitive topics. For some, the only way that they know to react when someone is emotionally upset or crying is to giggle or laugh, or to make a joke out of that person's experience. There may also be times when individuals might unintentionally laugh. The result of these reactions is that the person who was the brunt of a joke will be a lot less likely to share their feelings with people again in the future.

A Case in Point: Robert and Felicia

In the case of Robert and Felicia, I had noticed in previous sessions that they both had a tendency to make jokes and cutting remarks toward each other. In earlier exercises, they shared on an intellectual level, but they were still emotionally guarded with one another. As I checked in about their week, I probed deeper into their communication style and level of trust in each other.

THERAPIST: Felicia and Robert, tell me about your week.

FELICIA: It wasn't bad. (looking at Robert) We went to our son, Robbie's, baseball game on Saturday and went out to a retirement party on Sunday.

ROBERT (smiling): There was some good food there.

FELICIA (laughing):	Yes, and we ate too much.
ROBERT:	*You* ate too much.
FELICIA:	*You* ate too much, Robert. Your doctor won't like you eating all that cholesterol.
THERAPIST (interjecting):	Tell me more about what it's like going to parties together.
FELICIA:	Well, I enjoy getting dressed up and going out. We wear uniforms to so many events that sometimes I forget what I look like in civilian clothes. I bought a new dress for the party and these great red shoes.
ROBERT:	Yeah, Staff Sergeant White thought she was sexy.
FELICIA:	What is *that* supposed to mean? Are you saying I'm not attractive?
ROBERT:	Yeah, whipping Fobbits into place all day is what I call sexy. ("Fobbits" is a somewhat derogatory term for soldiers who never leave a forward operations base, or FOB.)
FELICIA:	Well, I can say that Sergeants Young and Lopez told me how nice I looked. At least I know they are men!
ROBERT:	You know what, Felicia, you are a Staff Sergeant, and you are a mother. You're not supposed to look sexy.
FELICIA:	You know *what* Robert? I'm a woman too. If you were more of a man, you would see that!
ROBERT:	Oh God. What's the use in all of this?

Discovering Patterns

I stopped this downhill conversation and pointed out to Felicia and Robert that they were making cutting and invalidating remarks to each other, and they admitted that this type of interaction was typical for them. Not surprisingly, Robert and Felicia also avoided sharing vulnerable emotions with each other. Although they had greatly improved in their abilities to listen to, validate, and positively reinforce their children, they needed to transfer these skills to communicating with one another.

I learned that neither Robert nor Felicia was brought up in a family where feelings like sadness or fear were shared. Robert was raised within a military family. His parents did not hug or openly show affection, and he said his parents would berate him if he made mistakes or showed vulnerability. Felicia was raised in a similar environment, where her family did not express their emotions. She came from a big family, which she described as being highly critical. Money was often tight, and her father was physically abusive.

As adults, the military reinforced Robert and Felicia's need to maintain emotional control, but it was damaging their marriage. They needed to become aware of what their patterns were, where they came from, and to learn how to communicate with each other in a safer and more intimate way. And that is exactly where we headed in our first exercise with this family.

Making It Real: Changing Beliefs About Sharing Emotions

In this exercise, each partner answers questions about their beliefs and fears about sharing their innermost thoughts and feelings. The exercise will also help clinicians to identify the family members' beliefs about sharing negative emotions.

Exercise Directions: Please use Family Handout Step 6.1.

Spend at least 15 minutes on this exercise, or more if needed. Have the couple or family write responses on their handouts. The rule is to be as unguarded and honest as possible. Then, open up a dialogue with the couple by having each partner share their responses out loud and discuss their reactions.

The first two questions in this exercise can help the couple understand how they normally share their emotions. When partners identify a person with whom they shared feelings of fear and/or sadness, take note of what that experience was like.

In most cases, sharing emotions is a positive experience associated with feelings of comfort, closeness, or validation. Discuss the importance of sharing such experiences as a couple. If a client had no one with whom to share vulnerable emotions, or had negative experiences when they shared with another person, take time to explore what that was like for the client.

The last question can help reveal whether a family member understands how to respond when someone else shares vulnerable information and communicates his or her needs. Overall, the question can help set the stage for family members to share any inner thoughts or feelings. As the clinician, you can educate the couple or family here about the value of emotional disclosure. Through observation and questioning, address any potential communication barriers. You may need to train family members to share and empathetically receive difficult content, and otherwise help them overcome trust issues and fears of rejection within the relationship. Here are the questions:

> ➤ When you were young, was there someone you talked to when you felt sad or scared?
>> ➤ If no, what did you do instead when you felt that way?
>> ➤ If yes, who was that? What was it like to share with them?
> ➤ Imagine that you talked to your partner about something that made you feel sad or scared. What would that be like for you?
> ➤ If you told your partner about a secret you had never shared with anyone, how would you like your partner to respond and show that they are listening to you?

Talking Points

Robert and Felicia both went through negative experiences in the past after they shared their emotions with someone they had trusted. As a result of the pain they had experienced in the past, both Robert and Felicia believed that the other would betray their trust. They were both afraid to be vulnerable with each other. Take a look at Robert and Felicia's responses to the questions.

Felicia's Responses:

1. Yes, my older sister. It was reassuring to know that I wasn't crazy.
2. Very difficult, but I could do it if he agreed not to tell anyone else.
3. By letting me know that he would never tell anyone else or otherwise use it against me.

Robert's Responses:

1. Yes, my dog. Comforting.
2. Embarrassing.
3. Listening without speaking, nodding her head.

Robert's Past Experiences With Sharing

Felicia felt that Robert just "doesn't open up" to her at all anymore. Robert remembered times when he was ridiculed for being scared. For example, when Robert was a little boy, he was afraid that there were monsters hiding under his bed. His older brothers made fun of Robert because of his fears. Years later, when he was a little older and learned that his parents had been in a car accident, Robert told his brothers that he felt scared. Again, his brothers poked fun at him.

Because of these experiences he had growing up, Robert hesitated when it came to sharing his feelings with others. Felicia pointed out that Robert never cried during sad movies. When one of his friends from childhood and his grandmother died, Robert did not show any emotion at their funerals. Robert acknowledged that his early experiences kept him from sharing emotions and made it difficult for him to admit that he could "have a problem." As a result of doing this exercise, Felicia learned why Robert had such a hard time sharing his feelings. This helped her understand why Robert didn't open up to her about things.

Felicia's Past Experiences With Sharing

When she was a child, Felicia used to share her feelings with her sister. Felicia felt comfortable sharing with her. But that all changed when Felicia found out her sister had betrayed her trust by telling her friends what she had shared in private. Because of this, Felicia came to believe that everyone would betray her trust if she shared her feelings.

In their marriage, Felicia expected Robert to make light of her feelings or to put her down around her friends, so she kept a stiff upper lip and maintained control over her emotions.

Coming to Truce

In the session, Robert promised that if Felicia got upset, he would never share this with anyone else. Robert and Felicia also vowed that if either of them needed to vent about something, that the other would just listen. Through this exercise, Robert and Felicia understood each other better and learned how important it is for family members to be vulnerable with each other. Robert and Felicia could now see how they had slipped into some of the same communication patterns with which they were raised. They both agreed that they wanted their relationship to be a lot better than what their parents had. Also, Felicia expressed that she would appreciate it if Robert would be more openly affectionate toward her.

Opening Up About Traumatic Experiences

When they are deployed, service members go through powerful changes as a result of their experiences. Service members endure profound, life-altering events, such as being in danger, losing their buddies, being physically injured, and killing others. In a war zone, service members need to be able to ignore their emotions and focus only on surviving. They need to channel their anger into the battle so that they can survive. To get through their experiences, service members also need to ignore their feelings when they are involved in or witness grotesque deaths, atrocities, or severe human suffering.

When service members return from combat, they may still be ignoring and stuffing their emotions. They may try to forget about their trauma. It is common for service members to feel numb and like they are in automatic mode. Many service members maintain a tough soldier mentality that can be difficult to break.

For Your Information: Talking About Traumatic Events

For most people, talking about difficult experiences and expressing their emotions helps them feel better. When people do not disclose painful experiences, they can experience adverse physical and mental effects (Pennebaker, 1989; Pennebaker & Beall, 1986). People who do not feel that they can share their traumatic experiences have higher levels of PTSD symptoms over time (Cordova, Ruzek, Benoit, & Brunet, 2003). On the other hand, trauma survivors who disclose their traumatic experience(s) to people who support them have less distress, and they cope better compared to those who do not (Lepore et al., 1996; Pennebaker, 1993). Also, sharing traumatic experiences is linked to lower rates of PTSD in various groups, including veterans (Green, Grace, Lindy, Gleser, & Leonard, 1990).

(continued)

Many scholars believe that processing potentially traumatic events with another person is necessary for overcoming PTSD (e.g., Foa & Kozak, 1986; Rimé, 2007; Stroebe, Hansson, Stroebe, & Shut, 2001). The term "trauma processing" refers to contemplating, confronting, and integrating a highly stressful event into a person's view of himself and the world (Cordova et al., 2003; Foa & Kozak, 1986). In some theories about PTSD, the traumatic event becomes "stuck" as a memory (Monson et al., 2006; Resick & Schnicke, 1993). According to these researchers, talking about a traumatic event triggers the original memory so that it can become "unstuck," and this can reduce a person's psychological distress related to the event.

On the other hand, when trauma survivors share their experience and have someone react negatively to them (e.g., minimizing or invalidating their experience), this can result in greater levels of PTSD than those who had positive reactions from people (Cordova et al., 2003). As such, when a trauma survivor shares their traumatic experiences with a spouse or other family member, it is important that they listen and respond with empathy.

Another factor that makes it difficult for trauma survivors to share is avoidance. When people go through very traumatic events, the brain becomes overreactive to stress. Because certain things will trigger uncomfortable feelings or thoughts of their deployment, service members will instead avoid things that remind them of their experiences. And when they avoid thinking about, feeling, or talking about the war zone, this provides temporary relief from the reexperiencing and hyperarousal symptoms of PTSD. Unfortunately, continual avoidance actually drives or maintains the PTSD.

Avoidance can generalize to other life situations as well. For example, if a returnee feels uncomfortable in a shopping mall, he might avoid going there. If a returnee is triggered by seeing people who look like the enemy, she may begin to avoid being around similar-looking types of people. Some people may start to isolate from others more and more, avoid talking about their traumatic experiences, or stop going to crowded places or events, but avoiding something does not make it go away. By the same token, until an individual stops avoiding the trauma, he or she will not emotionally heal. The PTSD will only continue to get worse. Sharing is essential to healing traumatic experiences.

Feeling Out of Place in the Family

We first met Michael and Lisa in Step 3. Michael was medically discharged from the Army following an injury in which he lost most of his ability to use his arm and hand. In Step 3, Michael mentioned that when he is with his buddies, he could be "himself." He said that at home he feels out of place, "like I'm a trained soldier and cop in this soft, clean, perfect world."

In the exercise earlier in this step, Michael told Lisa and I that when he was younger, he didn't have anyone with whom to share his innermost thoughts and feelings. His father was a police officer and would say that cops are "tough" and "feelings were for sissies." Michael learned to internalize his father's beliefs. Earlier, he had scoffed at the second item in the exercise, where he was asked to share his feelings with Lisa. When we discussed it later on, Michael admitted that it "might be helpful for other guys" to share vulnerable feelings, but that he wouldn't do it himself because of his pride.

Michael's Sharing Process

Michael had previously alluded to seeing some "bad stuff" while he was deployed, including the event that led to his disabilities. In other sessions, Michael denied that he was feeling depressed or having any symptoms of PTSD. I had suspected that he had been downplaying his symptoms, but we made some progress in this session when Michael finally admitted that he felt sad about his assistant, Frank, getting injured in an IED attack. I asked to speak with him alone at the beginning of our next session. Here is an excerpt from our conversation.

THERAPIST: Michael, in the last session you said that it "might be helpful for other guys" to share vulnerable feelings, but that your pride kept you from sharing yourself.

MICHAEL: Yeah, it may be pride, but sometimes talking about the bad stuff is just not necessary.

THERAPIST: And so what is it about pride that tells you not to talk about the bad stuff?

MICHAEL: Well, men aren't babies or sissies. They shouldn't have to talk about that.

THERAPIST: Talking about vulnerable feelings equals being a baby, or a sissy?

MICHAEL: More or less.

THERAPIST: Do you know any men who have talked about feeling sad or scared in-country?

MICHAEL: Yeah, I guess so.

THERAPIST: Can you tell me about them?

MICHAEL: There were guys who broke down in the field. Some guys just become a mess. They can't handle it.

THERAPIST: And how did the unit respond to those guys?

MICHAEL: We just left them alone for a while. Most of them got over it. We had to Medevac a few out, and we never saw them again.

THERAPIST: What about some of the guys who stayed? Did you see them as sissies?

MICHAEL: No, but I'm sure they were pretty ashamed at the time.

THERAPIST: What makes you think so?

MICHAEL: They broke down and cried. That's pretty embarrassing.

THERAPIST: What happened to the guys after they broke down?

MICHAEL: They got over it. I saw my sergeant with his face in his hands bawling once. He got over it.

THERAPIST: And is he a sissy?

MICHAEL: No . . . he's not . . . he was back in the field two hours later.

THERAPIST: Remember how I mentioned that holding in emotions is related to having more bad memories and other PTSD symptoms?

MICHAEL: Yeah.

THERAPIST: In addition to those short-term problems, holding in emotions is also related to chronic health problems. So, actually the guys who went ahead and cried are going to be healthier in the long run.

MICHAEL: Even if they looked like babies?

THERAPIST: Sometimes the strongest thing to do is realize that pride isn't helping you, and it isn't even making you look better. Sometimes the strong thing to do is realize you're not fooling anyone. The strong soldiers purge the bad stuff.

The Turnaround Point for Michael

I told Michael that I could see that, on some level, things were not going as well for him as he let on. Michael admitted he had been denying symptoms, to himself as well as to his family and loved ones. He said he was dealing with reminders of what had happened during the IED incident. He was particularly troubled by images of his buddy Frank before he died. However, he didn't want his family to know how bad his symptoms were.

We explored what was behind his need to conceal his symptoms. Michael didn't want his family to worry about him. He also said he was concerned that, if he opened up about what happened and ended up being vulnerable, he might appear to be "less of a man" in Lisa's eyes. But Michael wanted to save his marriage. I told him that I thought Lisa would actually think *more* of him for sharing something so important from his life.

Once Lisa came back into the room, the three of us discussed the fact that many service members have a natural tendency to try to ignore and forget about the "bad stuff" that they have seen. We talked about how family members who do not share their experiences with each other actually grow further apart. Lisa said she would really like to hear about Michael's experiences. Michael, with some hesitancy, said he thought he was ready to talk about it.

For Your Information: Trauma-Related Thoughts and Emotions

The sudden and/or violent death of a significant other in combat is often shocking and horrifying and can be difficult to accept. Service members who go to combat are trained to watch out for their buddies or fellow unit members. They are able to fight because they know their buddy has their back. When service members lose a peer or subordinate they were supposed to look out for, they may feel a profound sense of failure.

It is also common for surviving service members to blame themselves for the loss. When returnees have killed or harmed others, they may feel disgust or guilt about their actions. Even if they had been following orders, they may blame themselves. Some may consider themselves to be an "animal" or, in one returnee's words, "the devil." Other times, service members will blame their unit leader for making a strategic error that led to the deaths. Finally, service members may experience survivor guilt. That is, they may strongly regret surviving because they feel like they don't deserve to live as much as the person who died.

Service members' guilt or blame (toward self or others) can essentially serve as a way to "undo" the events (Resick & Schnicke, 1993). When service members obsess about changing the events leading up to the loss, they avoid coming to terms with and grieving the loss. People suffering from traumatic grief may also feel that if they accept the trauma, or even stop suffering the effects of the trauma, it means they are no longer honoring a person who has died. It may even feel like a betrayal to let go of the event.

In general, trauma survivors who suffer from PTSD have persistent and exaggerated negative thoughts about one's self, others, and/or the world. Here are some examples:

- "Because I was a part of the mission that resulted in deaths of innocent people, I am bad."
- "Because I was assaulted, no one can be trusted."
- "Because so many people died, the world is completely dangerous."
- "Because I have seen human beings torturing innocent people, human beings are completely depraved."
- "Because I was raped, I am permanently ruined."
- "Because I didn't save more people, I do not deserve to live."
- "Because I could have performed that procedure more quickly, I am to blame for the loss of other service members' lives."

These beliefs prevent people from resolving their traumas and have been identified as risk factors for PTSD (Brewin, Andrews, & Valentine, 2000). When trauma survivors share their stories, you can help to identify and gently challenge maladaptive beliefs they might be having associated with fear, guilt, anger, and sadness. For example, a returnee shared that having killed an enemy soldier in a battle now makes him a "murderer." In this case, the clinician might highlight the differences between killing in war and murder. When the trauma survivor shares their experience and is loved and accepted by others, this will help the person have more accurate interpretations of what happened. In essence, they will consider different ways of looking at the trauma (Lepore et al., 1996).

The Need to Grieve

When service members continue to suffer in silence, it can be very therapeutic for them to share their experience and grieve with their loved ones. As the clinician, you can assist in two very important ways during the sharing process. First, you can encourage family members to be unconditionally loving and supportive. Second, you can guide the service member to stay in the moment and feel their emotional pain. With these two elements present, the returnee will be able to heal from these experiences, and it will bond family members closer together.

Some More Precautions Before Processing Trauma

As we have shared throughout this book, trauma processing is not something to be lightly treaded upon. As such, we would like to review a few very important points for you to consider as you proceed in this step with your military families.

> ➤ Prior to sharing, you may need to normalize the service member's fears about sharing upsetting content with their spouse or other family member(s).
> ➤ The person sharing the trauma needs to be in control over what he or she shares.
> ➤ Do *not* include children in this stage.
> ➤ Ensure that the survivor does not share in a manner that harms him or his partner or other family member(s).
> ➤ When the survivor shares his or her experiences, it is important for the family to respond with empathy. For more suggestions on this, Exercise 6.1 will have provided the family member with some clues on how to respond.
> ➤ If necessary, work with the family members beforehand, on how they can respond after their loved one has shared their experience.
> ➤ As a special note, if either partner is suffering from a mental illness that is affecting his or her ability to function, we recommend that he or she first address severe mental health issues in individual therapy. For example, if a service member is experiencing severe PTSD or has active suicidal ideation, we recommend that he or she also be in individual therapy, and that the family therapist coordinate care with the individual therapist.

Making It Real: Honoring the Loss

This exercise will help family members make sense of and begin their healing from trauma. It involves sharing the details of what happened and its impact on one's family member(s) or spouse/partner.

Instructions: Please go to Family Handout Step 6.2.

We recommend first having the trauma survivor write out the event using the Step 6.2 handout "Honoring the Loss." Any loss can be discussed, whether it's an event, a particular person, a group of people, the loss of physical health, or of becoming disabled. However, we recommend that the loss be discrete enough to be able to discuss as one impression. For example, if a service member lost several unit members over the course of a year deployment, ask him to choose one person who he was particularly close to or who might particularly stand out to represent the rest. Please have the family member who has survived trauma respond to these questions.

1. What is it or who was it that you lost?
2. What was important to you about that person, thing, or event?

3. When did the loss occur?
4. How did the loss occur? What took place?
5. What were your thoughts when the loss occurred?
6. What are your thoughts now about the loss?
7. How exactly did having the person, place, or thing in your life change your life?
8. What can you do to honor the person, thing, or event?

Talking Points

With his family's support, Michael was able to share about his loss, which he identified as "Losing Frank and being helpless to counterattack." Michael shared some funny stories about when he first met Frank, and then told us about the day when his truck encountered an IED. He shared that, although he was hurt himself, it was even harder for him to see his close buddy Frank suffer from severe injuries and then die. He told Lisa that he thinks about the event several times a day. His thoughts focused on what he "should have done" and his belief that he was "responsible for" Frank's death.

When I saw him grimacing and holding back tears, I gently reminded Michael to sit for a moment with his feelings and just breathe. Michael began to cry and exclaimed, "Damn it, Frank, damn it! Why'd you have to go?"

After Michael spent a few minutes experiencing his grief, I thanked Michael and let him know how much courage I thought he had to share his story with us. We discussed his difficulty accepting the loss of his buddy Frank. He said he had been obsessed with thoughts such as "I could have saved Frank" and "I should have known that we were going to hit an IED," while he was at home watching TV or in bed at night. So we addressed these thoughts and briefly utilized cognitive processing therapy with Michael to address his guilt and self-blame for his friend's death. Here is a little snapshot of this process.

THERAPIST: Michael, how do you know that you really could have saved Frank?

MICHAEL: "If I had acted more quickly, I may have been able to save Frank. It took me a few minutes to shake off the impact and move. By the time I put on the tourniquet, half of the blood was gone from his body.

THERAPIST: And so the IED should not have impacted you too?

MICHAEL: No.

THERAPIST: You were under attack and hit by an IED. How did the blast affect you?

MICHAEL: Well . . . my arm and hand were shattered, and I was bleeding from my face wounds (touching his injured arm with his other hand).

THERAPIST (gently):   Michael, Frank's death was not in your control. He was killed by the enemy. There was no way for you to prevent that from happening. Can you see that?

MICHAEL (looks at Lisa and me with new tears in his eyes):   I just want that kid back.

After Michael allowed himself a few more minutes to grieve, I let him know that I thought Frank was lucky to have such a loyal and caring friend and leader. Lisa nodded in agreement and put her hand on Michael's leg. He put his arm around Lisa and thanked her for "putting up with him." Lisa told him that she actually felt relieved because now she understood what was going on with him, and she wished she had known earlier. Michael told Lisa that he was afraid of burdening her and Abby with his war experiences. She told him that sharing his deepest experiences with her was a gift, and thanked him for doing so.

A Load Off of His Shoulders

Sharing his experience in detail provided Michael with a chance to unload the weight he had been carrying around alone. Opening up about his military experiences to his wife also helped Lisa better understand and feel closer to Michael. Furthermore, Michael allowed himself to let down his guard and be vulnerable with Lisa. This experience helped strengthen the bond between the couple.

In later sessions, Michael seemed like a different man, without a heavy weight on his shoulders. Now, rather than feeling like a stranger or an imposter, Michael sees his home as a sanctuary away from his role as a soldier/cop. Michael can call on those roles if he chooses, but he can also "hang up that hat."

Traumatic Grief

People suffering from trauma sometimes feel that if they accept the trauma, or even stop suffering the effects of the trauma, it means they are no longer respecting the person or event. It may even feel like a betrayal to let go of the loss. Helping your clients find meaning in their losses can help them let go in a healthy manner.

Sometimes a trauma survivor will need to undergo more intensive and specialized psychotherapy for PTSD before experiencing relief from their symptoms. If problems with PTSD symptoms persist, specialized treatment by an appropriately trained clinician with experience in prolonged exposure therapy (PE) and cognitive processing therapy (CPT) is recommended. Most of these, such as prolonged exposure and cognitive processing therapy (e.g., Monson et al., 2006), are individually based interventions, although cognitive processing for couples is also available.

In some treatments, clients are asked to write about the impact and content of the traumatic memory, and this is read aloud during the sessions. Such treatments directly target PTSD, as well as associated problems, such as depression, guilt, and anger. More information about these interventions is available on the National Center for PTSD website, http://www.ptsd.va.gov/professional/index.asp.

Making It Real: Meaning Making

This exercise focuses on helping trauma survivors honor the person, thing, or event that they lost through meaningful rituals or activities. You will help the trauma survivors to identify an activity or ritual that they can do with the support of their spouse or other family members.

Instructions: Please go to Family Handout Steps 6.3. and 6.4.

➤ Have the family read through Family Handout Step 6.3.

➤ Then go to Family Handout Step 6.4.

➤ Using this handout, please have the family member who has survived trauma answer the questions. They will be writing about what they can do to make meaning out of the experience.

➤ Spend some time helping the family to plan out when they can do this activity together during the week ahead.

For Your Information: Traumatic Grief

Grief involves sad and painful emotions and other reactions to a major loss, such as the death of a loved one. Traumatic grief, however, is a different process that can interfere with the normal grieving process (Resick & Schnicke, 1993). Traumatic grief occurs when someone anguishes over a loss for an extended period. It often includes unwanted, invasive thoughts and a powerful need to reconnect to the person or object of the loss (Lichtenthal, Cruess, & Prigerson, 2004; Prigerson et al., 1995).

People suffering from traumatic grief may have:

- Difficulty accepting their loss
- Avoidance of reminders of the loss
- Difficulties with trusting others
- Bitterness or anger surrounding the loss
- Difficulty moving on
- Numbness and shock
- Confusion about one's role in life
- A sense that life is meaningless (Lichtenthal et al., 2004; Prigerson et al., 1997; Prigerson et al., 1999)

Approximately 15% of people who are suffering from bereavement related to the loss of a loved one experience prolonged traumatic grief following the loss (Prigerson et al., 1999).

Talking Points

When we did this exercise, Michael immediately thought of an activity to honor his friend. Frank had often talked about his younger brother, who was mentally disabled. Because Frank was no longer around to support his brother, Michael decided to devote time volunteering with the Special Olympics. Due to the distance, Michael was unable to physically be there for Frank's brother; however, he could support Frank by supporting a cause that was meaningful to his lost friend. Michael also created a new ritual to do with his family. He and his family would attend the yearly Special Olympics meets.

Letting Love Come In

As human beings, we all need to give love and be loved. To love unconditionally means that we love someone regardless of their qualities or actions. Humanistic psychologists such as Drs. Alfred Adler and Abraham Maslow considered unconditional love to be essential to a person's sense of well-being. They believed that all people, even the most stoic or jaded, longed for intimacy and closeness. All people have an innate need to be loved and accepted. When family members receive unconditional love, they can be vulnerable enough to present their real selves because they know their family members are on "their side." This last Making It Real exercise for this step will help family members to give and receive unconditional love and acceptance.

Making It Real: Unconditional Support and Acceptance

This exercise can be done with couples or family members. In this exercise, family members take turns making commitments to give unconditional love, support, and acceptance toward their loved ones. Family members make vows to be there for each other no matter what and learn how to give out love and to let it come in.

Exercise directions: Please go to Family Handout Step 6.5.

➤ Explain to the family that when we tell the truth about ourselves to other people, especially about our flaws and fears, we let others see our true selves. Sharing our true selves allows our family to accept us and give unconditional love and acceptance. When we let others know our innermost secrets, and others don't feel disappointed in us, we are experiencing unconditional love.

➤ Have family members make statements or vows to promise to unconditionally love and accept one another. Some examples might include:
  ➤ I will love you forever.
  ➤ I promise to be there for you no matter what.
  ➤ I love you and am proud to be your (husband/wife/father/mother/daughter/son, etc.).

➤ You are a beautiful person and I feel very lucky to be your (husband/wife).

➤ You are an amazing person and I fully commit myself to you.

➤ Ask each person to come up with a statement for each of their family members. Once the family member has chosen their statement, have them stand and face one family member. Have the dyad look into each other's eyes (similar to how couples stand when they make wedding vows). The person making the statement should say the receiving family member's name and make the statement. Have the recipient show that they have heard and received by acknowledging the statement. They can do this by repeating the statement, for example, "Michael, you think I am a beautiful person and feel very lucky to be my husband." Alternatively, you may have them simply say thank you while continuing to make eye contact and then take their turn.

Talking Points

This last exercise was a turning point for Michael and Lisa's relationship. Here were Michael and Lisa's vows to each other.

Michael's Vows

"Lisa, I don't know how you have put up with me since I got back. I know I am hard to handle. From this moment on, I vow to open myself up to you. I will trust you with my thoughts, feelings, and pain. I will share myself with you and stop shutting you out. I vow to do my best to get closer to you, and to stop driving you away. You are the most important person in my life. And I love you so much."

Lisa's Vows

"Michael, I didn't realize everything that you went through. I didn't understand where you were coming from. I want to be there for you like you have never known before. I vow to be there for you, to listen, validate, and support you in any way you need me to. I vow to love you with all of my heart, regardless of what you are thinking or feeling. You are my heart, and I vow to always be there for you."

When Michael and Lisa held hands and exchanged their vows, they couldn't contain their feelings. You could see and feel all of the love this couple had for each other. This exercise helped to deeply strengthen Michael and Lisa's relationship. They both came to understand more about each other, and they unconditionally loved and accepted one another.

Final Thoughts

Michael and Lisa shared their flaws and mistakes with each other. Michael was able to share his traumatic war experiences with Lisa, who was able to support her husband.

This helped both Michael and Lisa to feel a deep sense of trust that they hadn't felt in awhile. By giving and letting love come in, this family has grown closer together.

In your work with military families, we can't emphasize enough how important it is to foster this unconditional support among family members. When family members know that they can be who they are, and still be loved in return, this will promote a more loving, trusting, accepting home. The family will learn to feel more at peace and at home with themselves and with each other. Their relationship bonds will be tighter, and they will be ready to move forward in life, to set new goals and face challenges together as a fortified military family.

Keys to Family Wellness

➤ Helping family members to share their experiences, at an emotionally open, honest, and vulnerable level, without being judged in any way, shape, or form strengthens the bonds of commitment among family members.

➤ Sharing vulnerable emotions and previously undisclosed experiences helps couples deeply connect with one another.

➤ Helping family members to really listen to each other, and to communicate unconditional positive regard or acceptance of each other, makes them feel closer to each other and more deeply committed to one another.

➤ Taking risks and being vulnerable with each other makes for a more resilient military family.

— Taking Action —

Taking action will help rebuild the family. Please check off each step as the family accomplishes it.

❑ The family should engage in a meaningful activity or ritual related to the trauma.

❑ The family should continue to practice taking time to listen, support, and validate each other.

❑ The family should take time to review their vows and demonstrate unconditional positive regard to their loved ones this week.

STEP **7**

Challenge

Setting Higher Life Goals

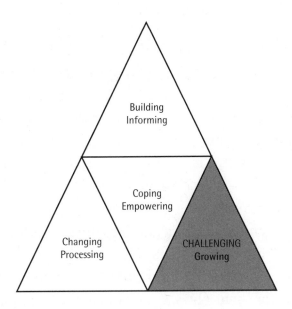

I have a dream . . .

—Martin Luther King, Jr.

As you can recall from the story of John and Amy, John had just returned from deployment to Iraq. Amy was feeling like John did not understand where she was coming from. Amy expressed feeling very disconnected from her husband, and she did not feel like he was making much of an effort to strengthen their relationship. The couple has struggled with several issues, including intimacy, as did Dan and Kate, and they have different goals for their relationship and for their lives in general.

Key Issues for John and Amy

John, having returned from deployment, wants to focus on his work and spending some time with his buddies. Amy, however, wants to spend her time with John in activities that build up their relationship. Amy's personal goals involve wanting to go back to college and get back into her career, but she has been feeling torn between achieving the things that are important to her and those that are important to her husband. The key issue for Amy is that she has based her self-esteem upon being married to John and taking care of their daughter, but now she is unsure how to move forward in life with her dreams and visions for herself. On the other hand, John is content with simply "being" and is not concerned with the same things as Amy. This couple needs help with being able to understand and respect each other's differences in goals and coming up with a reasonable middle ground or compromise in the meantime.

Setting the Stage

As military couples and family members go through multiple deployments and redeployments, they may find themselves feeling emotionally disconnected from their loved ones, wondering how they came to be in different places in their lives. Similarly, when military families also adjust to the returnee being injured or disabled, or dealing with chronic pain or a traumatic brain injury, this often causes a major shift in not only family member's priorities, but it may also lead to family members reevaluating their life goals. You will see that this is the case with our military families. We will be sharing their experiences in this chapter.

Up to this point, family members have strengthened their level of trust in each other and have built up their relationships. However, in Step 7, we will take each family member where they are presently at in their lives and help the family to set individual and collective goals for themselves. As you take the family through the process of goal setting, family members will find even stronger trust in each other, and this will heal the family.

For Your Information: Maslow's Hierarchy of Needs and Goal Setting

We've talked a lot in this chapter about "needs." One of the most widely accepted theories of human needs is that of Abraham Maslow (1970), who devised a Hierarchy of Needs. In this theory, Maslow postulated that there were five levels of human needs. As you may recall, the first-level needs were physiological, which included our basic human needs such as food, water, and air. Maslow felt that without meeting these basic human needs, individuals would not be able to reach the second level of the hierarchy pyramid, which included safety and security needs.

The next level, safety and security needs, includes things such as having a safe living environment, savings, adequate shelter, and just feeling physically safe in general. In situations where individuals feel that their safety is in jeopardy, they may never be able to reach the third rung of the ladder.

Should they reach the third level, individuals' needs will be those of love and belonging. At this level, their primary needs are of having meaningful relationships with other people, being accepted by others, gaining approval, and just feeling like they belong in social relationships.

Next on the hierarchy are needs for esteem. When individuals get to this point and have their physiological, safety and security, and love and belonging needs met, they will be able to have self-confidence and self-esteem. As human beings, when we possess a healthy self-esteem, then and only then are we psychologically capable of reaching the final step on the hierarchy: self-actualization needs. Self-actualization essentially means that a person fulfills oneself as a creative and unique individual. Maslow believed that few individuals would be capable of achieving self-actualization in their lifetime.

To put Maslow's hierarchy in perspective and apply it to the present day, one might hypothesize that the reason few individuals achieve self-actualization is because of all of the external forces that prevent a person from moving on in life. For example, in today's world, some 40 years after Maslow came up with his hierarchy, millions of individuals have been affected by job loss, millions of others have lost their homes, and many others have lost their livelihoods because of the recession. Beyond this, millions of individuals suffer from psychiatric and physical illnesses, which according to Maslow will keep them stuck at the basic levels of human need.

You will see that the military families we portray will struggle with being able to set goals for themselves. Family members often differ in terms of what is important to each of them at a particular time in their lives. Similarly, they will struggle with cognitive dissonance. That is, they may come to a point where their visions and goals for themselves differ from where they are in life. Or, they may feel unsure that they can realistically achieve those visions for themselves. As clinicians, we can help military family members to set realistic, healthy goals as individuals and as a family. Connecting this back to Maslow, you will help your family members to move up the ladder toward greater psychological health, healing, success, and happiness.

Assessing Needs and Personal Life Values

John and Amy have made significant progress in their relationship. They were learning to communicate in a healthier manner. They were both making valiant efforts at trying to understand the other's point of view. In fact, John and Amy were beginning to express that they didn't feel that they needed psychotherapy anymore because they felt like they were doing so well—up until now. . . .

John had continued to spend what Amy described as "inordinate" amounts of time with his buddies, playing golf and hanging out at the local bar for drinks a few nights a week after work. Amy shared that she felt insulted and ignored, like she was left at home to take care of their daughter when her husband could go out whenever he felt like it to "goof off." In addition, Amy had been feeling strong urges to resume her career, to finish her Bachelor's degree and go on for her Master's. Amy shared that she felt angry that the responsibilities for all of the childcare were hers alone. Of course, she didn't mind taking care of their daughter, Ashley. She was her life. She had put off her career for her. She would do anything for her. But she vented that it didn't seem fair since there were two parents at home now—at least there were supposed to be. And so we pick up where we left off with John and Amy. Our goal was to assess the couple's individual and joint needs.

I interrupted the silence.

THERAPIST:	John and Amy, you have both done a great job at working on your relationship. You are communicating better with each other. It seems like you are in a better place than when we first started. How do you feel like things are going?
AMY (jumps right in without hesitation):	We are doing better, and we almost felt like we could stop with therapy. But it's too soon. We have a ways to go. I'm frustrated. (long pause) Sometimes I feel like I resent John. (Pauses again, as if choosing her words very carefully.)
THERAPIST:	Go on, Amy. Can you say more about that to John?
AMY (looks at John):	I am finding myself getting pissed off a lot, John. This is the first time you have been back for a long time from deployment. And we never see you. You work all day, and then you go and hang out until late at night. You don't spend time with Ashley. You don't spend any time with me. (stops talking)
THERAPIST (encouraging her to express herself):	Amy, maybe you can tell John why you feel pissed.
AMY:	It isn't just that we don't see you or spend time together. I guess I'm kind of used to that since you are deployed most of the time anyway (sounding a little sarcastic). What burns me up is that you are gone for most of the year, and now you are actually home and you are never home! We are both parents to our daughter, John. I am a single parent while you are gone. Now that you are here, I would think you would want to be with Ashley and help out. I still feel like a single parent, even though you are here. And I feel like I never get a break! I need to get away sometimes too! I'd like to go hang out with my girlfriends. I'd like to get some "me" time too! Don't you think I could use some? It just really pisses me off! I feel like I resent you, John, because you get to do whatever the hell you want, and I don't. I feel like I am the grown-up in the family.

John looked like he was getting angry, but he was clearly biting his tongue.

THERAPIST: John, what did you hear Amy say?

JOHN: I get it. She wants time for herself.

THERAPIST: John, please tell Amy how you feel about what she said.

JOHN: I heard you say that you need time for yourself, that you feel like you never get a break. You said you don't see me that much. That you feel like a single parent. (Pauses, looks at the floor, and contemplates for a minute.) I work all day, and I need a break afterwards, Amy. I don't think that's unreasonable. I want to see my buddies. I just want to chill for a little while before I come home.

AMY (stops John):   John, the problem is not you "chilling," it's that you only spend a few minutes with Ashley before she goes to bed. And you and I don't get time at all. How are we supposed to build our relationship if we don't talk to each other?

JOHN: Amy, I'm not going to apologize because I didn't do anything wrong!

AMY: On top of going to the bar, you get to golf on the weekend for four to five hours too! What the *hell*?! When do *I* get to go out with my girlfriends? I can't even remember the last time that I got to go out for four hours! What a luxury! I don't think you can appreciate that, John. (Pauses for a moment.) You know what eats me up, too, John? (Doesn't wait for a response.)

John is looking kind of dumbfounded at this point.

AMY: What gets me is that all of these years, since we got married, I have spent my life devoted to you. I have moved around the world for your career. I have played single parent because of your career. I have raised our daughter on my own. I have taken care of the house, the finances . . . everything—without so much as a thank you. I had dreams and plans for my life, just like you did, John. You went into the military and planned on spending your career in the service. I had planned on becoming a teacher. I stopped my education after the first year we met. That was it for my dreams. Now I'm a decade older and what do I have to show for it? What about things that matter to me, John? When do I get to focus a little on my goals?

John sat for a couple of minutes processing what just took place. He looked like a deer in the headlights, shocked that his wife had held these feelings in and never said anything about them. Now they just came out like an explosion.

Setting Aside Dreams

This occurrence is not unusual. In fact, this is a common theme that plays out in many military families. Often, one individual sets her or his dreams aside for years, while focusing on the partner's military career. They make personal sacrifices for their loved one. For some, they feel like their purpose is to support their military partner. Their career is to be a military husband or military wife of an active-duty service member. For many others, however, it is a little more complicated.

Many partners may carry an underlying sense of regret or resentment for putting all of their needs on the backburner for years of their life. Some reach a point where they begin to reassess their own needs and realize that they don't know who they are because they have put so much into their partner's career and ambitions, while laying aside their own. This is the case with John and Amy, and it is likely the case with military families whom you may work with. Where do you begin? You start with helping to assess the needs of both partners. That takes us into our first Making It Real exercise for this family.

Making It Real: Assessing Needs and Clarifying Values

In this exercise, you will assist the military family to talk with one another and discover their unfulfilled needs and values.

Exercise directions: Please use Family Handout Step 7.1.

Have the family members ask each other these questions and share their deepest, most honest thoughts and feelings to every question.

1. Please share with me one of the most important, peak experiences you have had in your personal or professional life. This experience would have made you feel on top of the world, enthusiastic, driven, and fulfilled at a deep level inside. It is one of the most important experiences in your life. Please tell me about it in detail, sharing everything you remember about it.
2. Don't be humble: What would you say you value the most about yourself? What are some other things you value about yourself?
3. What do you see as being your most important strengths? And how do you think these strengths relate to your most peak experience(s)?
4. How do you feel your relationship has helped or hurt your abilities to have more peak experiences like the one you shared in this exercise?

Talking Points

As you may recall, back in Step 2, we showed you an exercise to assist military family members to clarify their individual needs and values. With this last exercise, we also clarified values and needs; however, we now take it to a much deeper level. When family members have reached a place where they can respect one another's deepest thoughts and feelings, they can now also accept the importance of what matters most to their partner and other family members.

When family members recall and share their peak experiences aloud, it can be a very moving and salient experience for them. Many people forget those key experiences that happened in their lives. However, when they start to remember how they felt, it can stir up feelings of passion for something, which made them feel more connected and alive in life. These key or peak experiences also stand out as being crucial or pivotal, having a major effect on the person. And when you work with the family members and highlight not only these key experiences but also their deepest core values, it can be an eye-opening "A-ha!" experience for them. With John and Amy, this is exactly what happened.

John's Experience

John went first and shared that his peak experience was when he went on his first mission as a Marine years ago. He shared the details of this experience, where they successfully took out the enemy in an ambush that they had planned out for weeks. He excitedly talked about how they had gone in and wiped out the enemy without them even suspecting the attack. He expressed feeling proud of his team and their success in the mission. He shared the feeling of camaraderie and closeness he felt with the other men in the squad. He expressed how he felt "stoked" and "out there" with excitement "like nothing could ever hold us back," like "we could conquer anything and everything after this," like "that was when I knew I was making a difference in the world."

With this exercise, John discovered that his core values were success, power, risk-taking, connecting with others to accomplish a task, being driven, and independence. John also realized that his strengths and his core values were quite similar. He listed his strengths as being: focused, driven, competitive, strong, and independent. It made sense to him how the military and being a Marine all of these years reinforced these values on a consistent basis. He understood why he felt like he was doing what he was supposed to in his life. John also realized how much of an impact his wife had in his being able to focus all of his attention on advancing in his career. John had never fully realized that his wife made it possible for him to do what he loved. This exercise helped John to appreciate how important his wife was in his life.

Amy's Experience

For Amy, the experience was a little different. Amy described her peak experience as a time, over 13 years ago, when she was asked by a friend of hers to lead a Vacation Bible School class at her church. Amy recounted that, at first, she wanted to tell her friend "no," but she decided to do it. Amy glowed as she shared how she had put together a presentation for the kids, who were sitting cross-legged in a circle in front of her, leaning forward and hanging onto every word she was saying. She shared how the kids were excited to learn, and that they came up to her afterwards, hugged her, and wanted to hang out with her after class was over.

Amy shared that this was a key experience for her. It was the most alive she had ever felt. She shared how she felt "unbelievable," "on top of the world," "jazzed about being able to do this for a living," and "like I was a piece of the human puzzle." And it was then that she figured out that she wanted to be a teacher. Amy's head fell and her gaze broke as she said that she has not been able to fulfill that dream.

Amy shared that she felt her core values were in caring, her creativity, serving others, her ability to connect, and her love for children and learning. Amy listed her strengths as being a good communicator, patient, calm, caring, and supportive. With this exercise, she realized how her values and strengths were in perfect alignment with her past peak experience and her vision of being a teacher. She realized how easy it would be for her to fill that role in life. Her face had etchings of sadness as she shared these realizations.

Amy courageously shared that she felt that their relationship had held her back from being able to fully realize these parts of herself. She thought that it had prevented her from fulfilling her needs and using her strengths and the things that she valued most in life. Amy added at the end of this exercise, "but I guess in some really small way I do this by teaching our daughter and putting all of my love and attention into her learning and growth. So I guess it's not a loss." At this point, we moved onto our next Making It Real exercise.

Making It Real: Aligning Visions

In this exercise, we take things to the next level. We work with the family to explore what their deepest, most personal wishes, visions, and dreams are for their individual and collective lives. And we help to build insight into how their vision aligns with their reality, as well as their inherent strengths.

Exercise directions: Please use Family Handout Step 7.2.

Have the family members ask each other these questions and share their deepest, most honest thoughts and feelings to every question.

1. If I were a genie and could grant you three wishes in life, what would they be for you? For your family?

2. How does your reality measure up to what your deepest wishes are for yourself? For your family?
3. How can you use your strengths and values to fulfill these wishes and make them a reality?
4. How can we as a family align these visions and make them happen for you? For our family?

Talking Points

Amy began again by asking John these questions. Here were John and Amy's responses and realizations from doing the exercise.

John's Wishes

John's three wishes for himself were:

1. To advance to the top rank in his career
2. Lifelong health
3. To inherit a huge fortune

John's wishes for his family were:

1. That he and his wife will be together forever
2. That their sex life remain amazing through their old age
3. That their daughter becomes wildly successful and finds a great guy who will make her very happy

John realized in doing this exercise that the first and second wishes were probably the ones based in reality. He felt that he was using his strengths well, and that his decisions and actions were helping him get promoted to higher ranks rather quickly. And, he was healthy and in excellent physical condition because of the lifestyle choices he made every day. John believed that his family had already made all of this possible for him, and he expressed his gratitude for all they had done. Next John asked Amy the same questions.

Amy's Wishes

Amy's three wishes for herself were:

1. To become a teacher
2. To be healthy and strong to take care of her family
3. To have a big, beautiful, expensive new house near the beach with lots of land, horses, privacy behind a wrought-iron gate, a personal maid, and gardeners

Amy's wishes for her family were:

1. To always be there for her kids
2. To learn how to balance "family time" with "me time"
3. For all of them to be healthy and happy in their lives

Amy wasn't sure how realistic the last wish would be for them at this phase in their lives, so she focused on her first two wishes. Amy realized that she took "okay" care of herself. She admitted that she didn't exercise as much as she should, and she could probably work on that some more. As far as her first and most important wish, Amy did not feel she was using her strengths or values to make this wish a reality. Amy realized that she used her strengths every single day, with their daughter. She realized that she had been practicing for almost a decade, honing her strengths. As far as how she could use her strengths to make her reality come true, Amy said she did not know how this was possible because she married into the military as well. On the last question, Amy repeated that she felt stuck because of being a military wife. I used this opportunity as a talking point and further explored this with the family.

Helping Family Members Get Unstuck

We would encourage you to do the same when you are hearing from family members that they are "stuck," "trapped," or "resigned into" a place in their lives. This is the perfect opportunity to use this stuck point and help the family members to find solutions they can work on together. By doing so, they can feel more connected and driven toward a common goal. And when they achieve those goals and visions for each other, they will have a greater sense of respect, appreciation, and connection to one another, which will help the family continue to grow. Here's a little excerpt from our session with John and Amy.

AMY: Honestly, I just feel very stuck. Don't get me wrong. I love you guys more than my life itself, but I feel like I have had to resign myself to focusing on what makes you and Ashley happy. I feel like my needs haven't mattered in a really long time.

THERAPIST: John, what are your thoughts about what Amy said?

JOHN: I guess I feel kind of shitty about it. I never really stopped to think about it before. I mean, we both knew that our lives would be that of a military family. We would move, I would get deployed every once in awhile, I would be away from home, and we'd have some adjustments to make. I figured it's just part of the job. It's what we do (pauses). I never really stopped to consider that Amy's needs would be snuffed out in the process.

John looks at Amy with awe.

JOHN:	Amy, honey, I'm so sorry. I've been kind of a selfish bastard. Some stuff I don't have any control over, but some things I can. I want you to be happy too. I didn't realize how much you wanted to be a teacher. I didn't know it was that important to you. I mean, if I didn't have my career, I don't know what I would do. I would feel lost, worthless maybe. Is that how you feel?
AMY:	Thank you, John. No, I don't feel worthless, but I do feel lost sometimes. I just feel like I keep pushing my dreams further and further back inside of me to hold our family together. But I'm getting older, and I haven't made it happen yet. I would like to do it while I still have the energy to go back to school. I know I would feel more fulfilled and happier if I could achieve my dreams too.
JOHN (looking very determined and driven)	Amy, we can do this. I want you to be happy. I never meant for you to give up all of your dreams. Let's figure something out. Let's think about this and figure out how we can make it work. Do you want to do that?
AMY (nods in agreement):	Really? Yes! Oh God, yes!
THERAPIST:	You guys just had a breakthrough! That's fantastic! The goal now is to explore possible solutions that can make this happen.

Connecting the Dots

This military family had a big breakthrough during this session. These exercises can be enlightening to many people. It can be a very powerful and cathartic experience for individuals coming face to face with their innermost passions and visions for themselves. As human beings, when we are unable to achieve those dreams and the standard we set for ourselves, it can cause anxiety, depression, frustration, and regret. A process of cognitive dissonance occurs. That is, when an individual has dreams or visions for herself, which do not coexist in real life, it can cause a tension or dissonance. It is essentially a mental tug-of-war that goes on for a person, and she will not feel at peace or satisfied until those dreams or visions for her life are achieved.

Amy's situation, like that of many other military family members, highlighted her frustrations and sense of helplessness. Amy expressed that she felt very trapped and stuck in her life. If you recall, according to Maslow's hierarchy, Amy would be stuck at safety and security needs. Her self-esteem was suffering because she felt unfulfilled as a person. From this point on in the session, our goal is to help the family explore solutions to make Amy's dreams a reality. As she works toward achieving her goals and fulfilling her needs, her self-esteem will grow. As her self-esteem grows, so will her loyalty and appreciation toward her family. As this occurs, this family will heal further. As they practice exploring positive solutions for problems and respecting each other's feedback, they will begin to feel a collective sense of self-efficacy. That is, they will feel united to stand in the face of adversity and challenges.

For Your Information: Goal Setting and a Coaching Model for Change in the Family

You may say that the focus of most models of psychotherapy is working through one's past. As clinicians, we utilize combinations of psychotherapeutic interventions to help increase an individual's insight and to get to the root causes of present-day problems. However, the first step in helping individuals to move *forward* is goal setting. The focus here is on the present and looking toward the future. In this step, our focus becomes assisting individuals to find their inner purpose and set specific goals so they can achieve it.

Some seminal authors in the fields of positive psychology, life coaching, and business consulting have addressed the topic of goal setting and purpose. It is virtually impossible to include all of the primary figures here. However, what follows are key ideas or concepts that clarify the process of goal setting as it pertains to life purpose.

Richard Leider (2010) has written numerous books about purpose and life calling. He stated, "Nothing shapes our lives as much as the questions we ask, or refuse to ask, throughout our lives" (p. 1). Leider believes that purpose is the "recognition of the presence of the sacred within us and the choice of work that is consistent with that presence" (p. 11). He went on to say, "When you have a good idea of what your gifts are and what moves you, you have the power of purpose. Life and work decisions based on both gifts and passion produce energy, flow, and aliveness" (p. 119). It is this passion and aliveness that we spoke about earlier in this chapter. Individuals feel this energy when they are aligned with their purpose. One can say that it is the basis of peak experiences in life.

According to leading business consultant, Brian Tracy (2010), goal setting begins with an individual realizing that he or she has "virtually unlimited potential to be, have, or do anything you really want in life. The second part of goal setting is for you to accept complete responsibility for your life, and for everything that happens to you, with no blaming, and no excuses" (p. 27).

A few key models used in positive psychology and coaching focus on goal setting. One easy-to-follow and effective model focuses on positive outcomes and what is G.O.O.D. (Auerbach, 2001). In this model, Dr. Jeffrey E. Auerbach, Founder and President of the College of Executive Coaching, helps clients to discover their Goals, Options, Obstacles, and what it takes for them to Do it—to achieve their goals. In the first step, the coach will spend time exploring the client's most important life goals, which should resonate with their peak experiences and passions in life. Next, the coach will explore all of the possible options that are presently available that can help support the individual in making these goals become a reality. The coach will help bring out any and all possible options, no matter how insignificant they may seem at the time. Third, the coach explores what the obstacles might be that could get in the way of achieving these goals. Similar to a SWOT (Strengths, Weaknesses, Opportunities, Threats) analysis in business, this step is important because it helps clients identify potential external forces that would impede their progress. By identifying the obstacles ahead of time, the coach can help the client devise a plan—the Do part of the equation. In this step, the client will, with the support and feedback of the coach, devise a specific, detailed plan of how they will accomplish their goals and plan.

This G.O.O.D. model is a useful tool for assisting clients to bring their innermost dreams and desires to fruition. As the clinician, your task is to help your clients discover what their innermost passion and purpose is, and to help them reconnect with those parts of themselves. To put it in a different way, "We all are called. Everybody has a calling. And your real job in life is to figure out what it is and get about the business of doing it" (Oprah Winfrey, 2011).

A very important piece of the goal-setting equation is that the client has the wisdom inside of him or herself. As in the classic movie, The Wizard of Oz (1939), near the end, Dorothy clicks the heels of her ruby red slippers three times, and Glinda the Good Witch says to her that she "had the power inside of [her] all along." The clients have the inner knowledge and knowing. It is our task as clinicians to assist them in reconnecting with it, rekindling the passion, and bringing this knowing to the forefront so they can begin to work toward manifesting it in their lives.

Goal Setting in John and Amy's Family

We now return to our work with John and Amy. In the last Making It Real exercise, John realized how important Amy's goals were to her and that she had put off her passion to support their family. He realized that Amy made it possible for him to achieve his goals and all that mattered to him in life, but she had not had the chance to realize her dreams.

This was a big breakthrough for John and Amy, but we don't stop there. Now it is time to take that knowledge and wisdom and work with John and Amy to come up with a key action plan and solutions to realize her dreams. So we are going to further explore Amy's passion and goals. Then we will incorporate the G.O.O.D. coaching model for change into this family session, to help the family work together to come up with a plan for achieving Amy's calling or purpose in life.

Making It Real: Enhancing the Vision

In this exercise, we will work with the family to further enhance and clarify the family member's vision for his or her life. In this exercise, you will assist the family member by using guided imagery, to draw out the key underlying elements of their vision in life.

Exercise directions: Please use Family Handout Step 7.3.

Take at least 15 to 20 minutes for this exercise. You will take one family member at a time through a guided imagery exercise. Have them designate a family member to take notes on their responses. Guide them with these phrases and have them answer aloud. Take at least 10 to 15 minutes afterward to process the client's experience, as well as any feedback from their family member(s), and share your own feedback as well about what you noticed as being most salient for the client.

1. Recall your peak experience. Sit with the experience in your mind for the next couple of minutes. Don't answer these questions aloud. Just remember the details and allow yourself to connect with the passion and purpose you felt at that time. Reconnect with what you were seeing, hearing, smelling, tasting, and touching. Who was with you at the time? What were you doing?

2. Ask the client: Please nod your head when you feel connected with your peak experience.

3. I'm going to go through some questions with you, _____(name). Stay connected in your peak experience and how you are feeling right now. Answer these questions.

4. What is the most significant thing you are experiencing in your peak experience right now? Tell me in detail. (Their family member is taking notes, as verbatim as possible.)

5. What is it you feel the most connected with? How does it make you feel right now?

6. Describe yourself while you are in your peak experience.

7. What do you realize are your strengths in this experience?

8. Describe the passion you are feeling right now in your experience.

9. What else do you notice about yourself in your experience, that maybe you didn't realize before?

10. In your peak experience, how did you accomplish all of this? What did it take for you to do it?

Talking Points

When we processed this experience afterward, Amy had what you could describe as a driven, passionate look on her face. She appeared convicted and compelled to move toward her vision. Amy fully reconnected with her peak experience this time, and she realized things about herself that she never had in the past. For example, Amy realized that her caring spirit and love for children guided every word that came out of her mouth. She realized that she has always possessed this caring spirit within her. She had never lost it, she just hadn't used it in the same way as she had wanted to. Amy had been questioning whether she had what it would take to go back to college, study, stay up late and lose sleep, and still run a family, now years later in her life.

With this exercise, Amy realized that she had what it would take to do it. She realized that this caring spirit was a very powerful, driving force for her. It was something she used every day with her daughter. She just had to channel that energy in a different direction. Amy realized she had it in her, and that she could do it. With this resurrected passion inside of her, we *now* take it a step further, to take her vision and set goals to help her accomplish everything she had dreamed of.

Making It Real: Setting Goals for Positive Life Change

In this exercise, we work with the family to help them take their inner knowledge and passion, and to devise a clear, specific plan to make it happen. This exercise incorporates a key, leading coaching model to assist the military family to create positive changes in their lives.

Exercise directions: Please use Family Handout Step 7.4.

Have the family member who wants to work on his or her goals read these questions aloud and voice their responses to their other family member(s). The other family member(s) should provide honest, constructive feedback and add in any additional information that could help in the process. After the family has completed this part, process everything with the family in the session.

1. You realize now that you have what it takes to do anything you want in your life. You can begin to take steps toward your life vision, purpose, and what makes you feel passion. What are your most important goals for your life that will help you realize your vision?
2. What do you see as being all of your options to make your vision a reality?
3. What are all of the possible obstacles that could get in the way?
4. How will you do it? What are the steps you need to take now?

Working Toward the Greater G.O.O.D.

Amy and her husband were moving in the right direction. They were working together as a team, a husband-wife duo that would dynamically achieve all that she had hoped for in her life. We would now like to give you a clearer picture of how to use the G.O.O.D. model to help your military family move toward their goals.

THERAPIST: John and Amy, it is great to see you both joining together to work toward a common goal. That will help strengthen your relationship in a big way. I'd like for us to take some time to come up with a more detailed, specific plan that you and your family can work on, to help Amy achieve her goals. Let's get started. Amy, if you could do anything without any limits, what would it be?

AMY: I would be a teacher.

THERAPIST: What kind of teacher do you envision yourself as being?

AMY: I guess a grade-school teacher. I love younger children.

THERAPIST: And what grade would you like to teach?

AMY:	Probably third grade if I had a choice.
THERAPIST:	Great! Tell me what your specific goals are that you would like to achieve.
AMY (pauses for a moment to think):	I want to finish the last three years of my Bachelor's degree, then do a Master's degree in early education and get that credential.
THERAPIST:	Anything else? It can be anything at all that you have dreamed of.
AMY (looks away):	Well, it has been a dream of mine to write and publish a children's book for younger kids.
JOHN (looking very surprised):	Honey, I didn't know you could write or wanted to write a book! That's so cool!
AMY (looking happy, smiling at John):	I had forgotten about it, John. I've always wanted to do it.
JOHN:	You can do it, Amy. You are the perfect person to do it. Look at how amazing you are as a mother to Ashley. You have so much to offer.
AMY (smiling bigger at her husband):	Thank you, sweetheart. I can't tell you how much I appreciate your encouragement. I didn't know I could do it, honestly.
THERAPIST:	Amy, that's a really great vision. Tell me more about the vision for your book.
AMY:	Well, I see it as a book for young children. I actually see myself as starting with one, but writing a series on different topics that pertain to kids, like dealing with peer pressure, getting motivated in school, believing in themselves, having a plan in life, building positive relationships, doing their best in all they do . . . to name a few. I see lots of books, with colorful illustrations. Maybe it could even be an animated electronic book some day. That'd be cool.
THERAPIST:	Amy, it sounds like writing a book is something that is really important to you. Where do you see this as falling into your life plans and visions?
AMY:	Well, I don't know. I hadn't thought about it. I think realistically, I would have to finish school first and get my teaching credentials. Then I might have time to work on a book.
THERAPIST:	Okay, any other goals?
AMY:	No, those are the most important to me.

THERAPIST:	Okay, so tell me your goals in order of importance for you, Amy.
AMY:	I guess it would be: (1) go back to college and finish my Bachelor's degree, (2) get my Master's, (3) get my teaching certification in early childhood development, and (4) write children's books.
THERAPIST:	Great job! So let's take a look at your first goal, Amy. What is the process you need to go through to accomplish that goal?
AMY:	Well, I need to contact my old college and see if my grades from before are still good, or if my units have expired. Then I would need to get the money to pay for school, sign up for classes, and find the time to do it and study. (Gets a worried look on her face.)
THERAPIST:	Amy, I can see you are looking concerned about this. But let's break this down, okay? (Amy nods.) What are your options, or what do you see as ideas for how you can do this?
AMY:	Um, let's see. Well, I need to get a career counselor I can work with to get things started. And I can get a financial aid counselor at the college.
THERAPIST:	Okay, great ideas, Amy. Anything else?
AMY:	No. I think that's it.
THERAPIST:	Alright. Are there any obstacles that you can see that could get in the way of you achieving your goals?
AMY:	Yes. One thing I hadn't even thought about until now is that some of the classes I took years ago—thirteen to be exact—might be expired or outdated. I might need to take them over. A big obstacle is the money. Another obstacle is having time to study.
THERAPIST:	Anything else, Amy?
AMY (stops and thinks):	I guess John's schedule and outings at night. Because that is when I would have to either be in classes or studying.
JOHN:	Amy, I know how important this is to you now, so we will do whatever it takes to make it happen. Okay?
AMY (looking more assured):	Okay.
THERAPIST:	Amy, I'd like to ask you and John to spend a few minutes together right now exploring ways that you could eliminate these things as obstacles. What are some steps you can take as a family to achieve your goals?

Amy and John discussed this, then we opened the floor back up to continue brainstorming.

THERAPIST: John and Amy, did you come up with some steps you can take?

AMY (nods):   Yes, we did. In talking this out, John said he would be willing to stay home on all nights that I would be studying or in school. He said he could take care of Ashley and put her in bed if I'm not home by then. If I was home studying, John said he would make sure I'd have quiet time in the office so I could concentrate. And he would take care of everything.

THERAPIST: John, how will you do this?

JOHN: I won't go out with my buddies as much. At least I won't go out when Amy needs to study or when she'll be in school. I guess when the time comes, we can come up with a structured schedule and put up a calendar, so that we can plan out what those days are.

THERAPIST: Okay, good. What about the finance issue?

JOHN: We talked about that one too. We will figure something out. But for right now, I bring home enough money and will have at least an extra $1000 per month that we could use toward Amy's tuition.

AMY: I'm also going to talk to the financial aid counselor at school to get more options. I can apply for scholarships. Or maybe we can come up with a payment plan. If I need more money, I can apply for loans. Or, come to think of it, John (looks at her husband), maybe the military offers some kind of financial assistance for spouses?

JOHN: I don't know, but I will look into that.

THERAPIST: You have both done a great job at working together to find solutions. So, Amy, what is your plan to get the ball rolling this week? Tell me three things you can do this week to start working on your goals?

AMY: Well, let's see. First, I will call the college. I will make an appointment to talk to a career counselor, and I will find out about my units from before, to see if they're still good. I will get options for classes and see what the layout looks like for getting the program done. Second, I will call the financial aid counselor and make an appointment to speak with him or her, to get all of our options for financing my education. Third . . . I'm not sure. John? Can you think of something I've left out?

JOHN: Yeah, actually. If you don't have anything, I will do the third one. I will contact my C.O. and see if he knows of any programs to finance education that would apply to spouses.

THERAPIST: Excellent. So we have a session set for next Wednesday at 3:00 p.m. So you both have a week to accomplish these tasks, right? (They both nod.) Can I get a commitment from both of you that you complete these steps this week, by our next appointment together? (They both nod again.) Great! I'm looking forward to hearing all of your progress next time! Before we wrap up, Amy, I am wondering how this feels for you?

AMY: It's an amazing feeling. I actually feel excited and alive inside! I feel motivated and like I have something to look forward to. I know it's not going to be easy, but I can't wait to do what I feel called to do in my life.

THERAPIST: John, how does it feel to work with Amy as a team to accomplish her goals?

JOHN: It feels great. I feel like we both have a common mission. I want to help make this happen for Amy. And I know we can pull it off together.

AMY: And I can't tell you how much this means to me, John. I feel closer to you right now than I have in a long time. I have always loved you. But it feels very special to have you not only pulling for me, but also helping and supporting me in this. I think this process is going to make us stronger as a couple and will help strengthen our family. In fact, if we can pull this off together, there's no reason we can't do anything together in the future. I believe that.

JOHN: I do too. We can do anything when we have a common goal that we work on together. There's no stopping us working together as a family.

THERAPIST: That's a positive ending for our session and a really positive start to your week as you focus on your future together.

Positive Directions for John and Amy

In this session, we used guided imagery and visualization, and then the G.O.O.D. model (Auerbach, 2001), to help this family work together to devise a very specific, achievable plan. The result of these exercises was that not only did Amy feel excited about looking forward to her future, but she also feels unconditionally supported by her husband. They now feel more bonded together. They are exploring options, obstacles, and solutions together; they are coming up with a plan together; and they are working together to make Amy's dreams a reality. Beyond this, because they are collaborating and working on her goals, they become the family's goals as well. And this positive teamwork ultimately leads to a stronger, more focused, bonded family that is unified in purpose.

Revisiting Our Families: Josh, Sarah, Amanda, and Tyler

We would like to revisit a couple of our other military families and see how their experiences fit into the process of goal setting. In the case of Josh, Sarah, Amanda, and Tyler if you recall, Josh was medically discharged for a mild TBI and severe knee injury, and he had PTSD. The ramifications of polytrauma syndrome were causing challenges in Josh and Sarah's relationship. Josh and Sarah were feeling relationally disconnected from one another. Josh had essentially been feeling stuck and unsure of how to negotiate his way since becoming disabled. Josh was isolating himself from his wife and his daughter, Amanda, to try to avoid hurting them. As a result of doing so, their relationship was suffering because they were not able to relate to one another.

Key Issues for This Military Family

Things have fortunately gotten better for this family, as Josh has been spending more time with his wife and daughter. They have come to a different point in their relationship—having different goals for themselves and for their relationship. Josh continues to struggle with adjusting to his TBI and disabilities, which have left him feeling stuck and unable to have the mental strength or emotional energy to figure out where to go from this point on in his life. Josh also feels disconnected from Amanda and Tyler because of his pain and disabilities.

In a similar vein, Sarah has been immersed in taking care of Josh's physical needs and trying to soothe his emotional pain. Additionally, Sarah has been focused on trying to make this adjustment easier for their children. So the difficulty that Sarah is having right now is that she feels stuck like Josh does. In many ways, Sarah has felt trapped and lost, unsure of her place in the world. However, Sarah does know that she wants to focus her attention, for the next several months at least, on helping Josh adjust. She feels incapable of seeing beyond this moment right now.

Goal Setting for Josh and Sarah's Family

The challenge for this family was to help align Josh and Sarah's goals, and help them move beyond feeling stuck, to deepen their sense of love and belonging in their relationship. Sarah, Amanda, and Tyler expressed that they wanted to focus their attention on doing whatever they could to help Josh get physically stronger. In working with the family in their present experience, we took Josh's vision and goals of walking again without an assistive device or wheelchair.

Josh's peak experience was of the time he taught his daughter to ride a bike, and when she succeeded at doing this without training wheels. Josh recalled the feelings while he ran next to her as she struggled to steady the bike, but then squealed with delight when she was able to do it. We worked with this family to explore Josh's strengths and values. We went through the guided imagery exercise with the family, then the G.O.O.D. model for change.

The result? Josh, Sarah, Amanda, and Tyler have set the goals of doing very concentrated physical therapy work with Josh for two hours a day. Sarah would get up an hour early every day, do stretches on his leg, then work with him in their home gym with therapy resistance bands, as his physical therapist had showed them. Then Amanda and Tyler would work with their dad every day after school and on weekends. They would usually go home and swim after school every day anyway. So, they would swim and then work with their dad for an hour in their pool, helping him walk back and forth. Amanda would help him however she could with the water exercises his physical therapist had recommended, and Tyler would cheer his dad on in the process. Their mutual goals as a family were to do this daily, for the next three months, to help Josh be able to walk without a cane to their mailbox at the end of the driveway.

This military family expressed similar feelings like John and Amy's family. They shared how they felt bonded together, like they were finally united on something. They talked about how they hadn't felt this close in quite awhile, at least since Josh had been wounded. They spoke about how they had previously felt disconnected and isolated from one another, like they were roommates who felt awkward being around each other. Now, they felt connected, like they were learning to be a family again.

Revisiting Our Families: Dan and Kate

If you recall, Dan and Kate struggled with their sexual relationship and intimacy. Dan and Kate were in very different places in their lives. Dan is essentially in the place where his self-esteem needs are being met by his position in the military. Yet, he is unable to set goals beyond the present because he so strongly defines who he is based upon his rank, his career, his affiliations, and his material possessions. Kate, on the other hand, often struggles with feeling physically, sexually, and sometimes emotionally unsafe in the world and in her relationship. So for Kate, she has had difficulties moving beyond her safety and security needs and feeling assured in her relationship, which in turn has presented challenges for her to build her self-esteem. Ultimately, this has left Kate feeling stuck at times and unsure of how to move beyond this point to set goals for herself and their relationship.

Key Issues for This Military Family

The challenge for this family was to help align their visions for strengthening their relationship. After our last session with this couple, Dan expressed that he wanted to help Kate to feel sexually safer with him. He wanted her to feel good about herself again, and he wanted to help her feel positive about sex again. Because Kate's past experience with being raped was still affecting her in the present, and because their sex life had had such an impact on their relationship, Kate wanted to focus her attention on their intimacy as well.

Goal Setting for Dan and Kate's Family

So the couple had a joint goal: to work together toward Kate's healing and trust. While they knew that this would not erase the memories of what had happened to Kate, they both felt that it was important that they try to make new, positive memories together.

In our subsequent sessions, we explored Kate's past peak experiences related to her sexuality. We explored her strengths, clarified her values, went through guided imagery together, and culminated the experience with goal-setting exercises to focus their work together. The result? Dan and Kate have decided to make two date nights per week where they can be alone together—one during the work week and the other on the weekend. Dan and Kate mutually set goals to spend at least two hours together by themselves each night. They would do things together like go out to eat and watch a movie. They would both keep gratitude or appreciation journals that they would read over together before bed. They would share things they loved and appreciated about each other. During their dates, they would make time to be sexually intimate. They would work together to make it a positive experience. Dan agreed he would stop asking Kate to experiment sexually in ways that made her feel uncomfortable. In addition, Kate wants to see a clinical psychologist for individual psychotherapy, to work through her past trauma.

Moving Toward Resiliency

Dan and Kate are united in purpose. They both admit that they feel emotionally closer to each other, and they are working toward rekindling the sexual spark in their relationship again. They believe this will help them fall in love again, focus on the positive in each other, and help them to want to take their relationship to a higher level. Dan and Kate are working together to heal and reignite the intimate passion that had been lost for many years—and that is a really good start.

Dan and Kate, like our other military families, are on their way to healing. They are like-minded in purpose, working side-by-side, hand-in-hand, toward their important visions in life. As they help lead each other down these paths, they will find that their relationships get stronger and stronger. They are one step closer to becoming resilient.

Keys to Family Wellness

➤ Recognizing and assessing each family member's innermost needs and clarifying their values in life.

➤ Remembering pivotal, peak experiences in their lives that shaped their visions of the future.

➤ Aligning family member's visions.

➤ Using guided imagery and visualization to help family members see their inherent strengths and abilities to achieve their dreams and visions.

➤ Setting positive goals together, working as a team, to brainstorm solutions and what steps to take to realize their goals.

➤ Bonding together as a unit, with single-minded purpose of meeting their goals as a family.

Taking Action

Taking action will help rebuild the family. Please check off each step as the family accomplishes it.

❑ The family should practice looking for and pointing out each other's strengths every day of the week.

❑ The family should spend 15 minutes at bedtime doing guided imagery, replaying their vision, as if their goals and visions are fulfilled.

❑ The family should work together on their steps (from the G.O.O.D. model), every day this week, striving toward meeting their ultimate mutual goals.

8

Grow

Fostering Lifelong Resilience

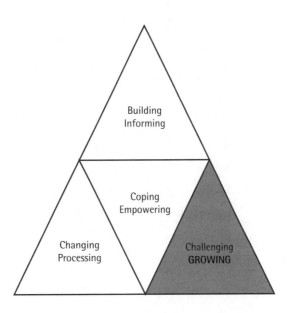

Where we love is home, home that our feet may leave, but not our hearts.

—Oliver Wendell Holmes, Sr.

Michael, the medically retired police officer and Army Guardsman, and his wife Lisa, the school teacher, have put in the effort needed to conquer several challenges in their lives and relationship. Early in their work in therapy, Michael overcame his habit of isolating from his family. He stepped back into the role of father to their daughter by adding to the time that he spent with Abby and with the family. In addition to her devotion to taking care of her family, Lisa became better able to tend to her own needs by putting aside time for herself by practicing relaxation and exercising. This helped her overcome the resentment she felt when Michael spent time with his buddies.

Michael and Lisa are now back in my office on a cold, rainy day. However, the climate between the couple is much sunnier than in the past.

THERAPIST:	*Michael and Lisa, what was your week like?*
MICHAEL:	*It went pretty well. I've gotten into watching the TV channels that feature cooking.*
LISA:	*He's introducing Abby and I to some new cooking techniques.*
MICHAEL:	*And some new dishes.*
LISA (enthusiastically):	*Last night we made baked salmon. It was cooked in parchment paper. It was amazing!*
THERAPIST:	*How nice!*
LISA (sounding excited):	*And I have to tell you . . . I've signed up for a yoga class, believe it or not. It's every Monday and Wednesday night, so now those are Michael's nights with Abby.*
THERAPIST:	*Good job taking care of yourself, Lisa! It sounds like you are doing a lot of proactive coping! Michael, you have found a new hobby to share with your family that you enjoy, and Lisa, you are taking time for yourself!*
LISA:	*It's true. Writing in my journal is a habit now. I look forward to it every night. Meditation has gone okay. It can be a struggle to fit my relaxation exercises in, so sometimes I still forget. I think it will be easier to commit to a whole yoga class, because I will have to be there when it starts.*
THERAPIST:	*And how have Lisa's new changes impacted you, Michael?*
MICHAEL:	*Well, it's nice to see Lisa happier now. She is much more relaxed. And she doesn't give me the silent treatment anymore for hanging out with the guys.*
LISA (sounding surprised):	*What?*
MICHAEL (smiling):	*Yeah, you used to give me the cold shoulder! I can't believe it now. Last Friday I told you I was going over Ben's and you actually said "Have fun, honey."*
LISA:	*I used to give you the cold shoulder?*
MICHAEL:	*Yeah! You used to look like you wanted to kill me when I said I was going over Ben's. Now you have your own life too. So now you're glad that I am doing something that is fun for me.*
THERAPIST:	*Sounds like there have been a lot of positive changes for both of you.*

Michaels nods, and looks at Lisa. Lisa is nodding as well, looking happy.

THERAPIST: How about your time with Abby? How has that been for you?

MICHAEL: I don't know. . . . It's up and down. Abby doesn't seem to like anything I do. I'm not "cool" to her. . . . What do you think, Lisa?

LISA: I think Abby's glad to be spending time with you, even if she doesn't show it. You're not the warmest person in the world either you know!

MICHAEL: Yeah, I know. I've got my own stuff going on.

THERAPIST: Michael, how do you think your "stuff" gets in the way?

MICHAEL: Sometimes I feel like Abby's a stranger. Like, who is this person?

LISA: But you have to spend time finding out more about her. I just wish you would talk to her a little more.

THERAPIST: What do you think, Michael?

MICHAEL: I don't know. I guess I feel like some people are born to be fathers, and the rest of us just have to do our best.

THERAPIST: So, Michael, you think you were not "born" to be a father? I know in the past that you said you felt like an "imposter." Do you still feel like that?

MICHAEL: I guess not so much an imposter now. I feel like . . . I don't know what to say to her . . . so I sometimes feel like I'm not cut out to be a good father.

LISA: You know what, Michael? You just need to continue to practice those basic skills of expressing interest in and listening to Abby. Just *ask* her about herself.

THERAPIST: Michael, remember when you brought Abby to her first therapy session? You did a fine job of listening to her then. How did that session feel?

MICHAEL: Well, on one hand I felt awful because I didn't know that Abby was angry with me.

THERAPIST: What else did you feel?

MICHAEL: Well, I guess I understood her better.

THERAPIST: Did you feel close to her?

MICHAEL: Yeah, I felt close. I felt like a father.

THERAPIST: Do you think you could take some time to ask her more about herself from time to time?

MICHAEL: Sure.

Setting the Stage

Michael and Lisa have made considerable changes in their three months of therapy. Michael began to adjust to his injuries and new role at home in a healthy way. He was able to ease back into his role of parenting Abby and making decisions together with Lisa. The family found ways to spend quality time together, and they also made time to have quality time on their own. By using proactive coping and shifting some of the parenting responsibilities back to Michael, the family became more balanced.

In Step 6, Michael was able to overcome his fears about "burdening" Lisa by sharing his war experiences with her. He also overcame an even bigger challenge—his own stigma-related beliefs about mental health problems. If you recall, Michael believed that, as a man, he "should not" be experiencing any mental health problems, that having these types of problems meant he was weak, and that it was unacceptable to be weak. However, we were informed about military culture and developed a strong, trusting therapeutic rapport with Michael. As such, Michael started to honestly admit to the difficulties he was having. Michael then courageously moved beyond his rigid beliefs about sharing emotions. For the first time, he let his guard down and shared his grief over his war experiences with Lisa. These experiences developed a new trust between Michael and Lisa, which helped them to integrate their new post-deployment roles at home and grow stronger as a couple.

According to some of the founders of the field of family resilience (e.g. McCubbin, McCubbin, Patterson, Cauble, Wilson, & Warwick, 1983; Trivette, Dunst, Deal, & Hamer, 1990) resilient families are those whose relationship patterns, interpersonal skills and competencies, and social and family identities do the following:

1. Promote satisfying interactions among family members.
2. Encourage the development of the potential of the family group and individual family members.
3. Contribute to the family's ability to deal effectively with stress and crisis.

In Step 8, the military family is ready to finalize the stages of growing together and becoming resilient. They are ready to maintain fulfilling relationships with one another that reinforce their individual and collective strengths as a family. They continue to bolster each other's fullest potential and support one another's goals. These military families become resilient and therefore more able to face future challenges in their lives in ways that are positive, healthy, and empowering for everyone.

Overview of the Problem

Michael and Lisa's experiences are typical of those of military families who are in transition. Changes occur—in this case, Michael's injury, chronic pain, posttraumatic stress, and subsequent medical discharge—that can throw off the family balance. Without resilient coping, a spouse who is physically or emotionally injured may embrace a "disabled" role by foregoing their role as a spouse and/or parent. The resilient spouse, on the other hand, readapts to changes by resuming, to the extent that is possible, normal activities, including their responsibilities as parents.

Through open communication, flexibility, and shared decision making, the military couple draws on their own strengths to readjust to changes so that their families can thrive. Michael has made a good effort to overcome his urge to isolate. Because of their time spent apart during his three deployments, Michael has some catching up to do in his relationship with his wife and daughter. Michael still needs to take time to reestablish his relationship with his daughter, Abby. Even though this is difficult for Michael at first, it will lead to a more fulfilling relationship with her.

Promoting Family Cohesion

In Step 8, the family or couple will begin to see themselves as a well-functioning team. In the sports world, coaches know that teams that are able to work together and make the most of each player's individual talents experience the most success. The same can be true for families. The highly functioning family uses the diverse strengths of its members and, at the same time, balances each other's weaknesses.

Acceptance of Each Other's Strengths and Weaknesses

In sports, good coaches know each player's strengths and weaknesses. Basketball coach Sean Glaze (2010), for example, states that,

> Team-building is the ON-GOING process of energizing a group to work together with an appreciation of diversity and talents and commit to their role in achieving the team's chosen goals. Once they identify that shared purpose, GREAT teams take time to learn about and appreciate the background and talents of its members, and bonds together through shared experiences and activities.

Helping families to identify a shared identity and purpose will provide a powerful resilience to enable them to cope with their immediate problems.

Acceptance of Differing Values

Our values are the qualities in life that are most important to us. Even though we all have values that guide the way we live our lives, we rarely take a moment to think about what our values are. Like sports teams, everyone in the family team has diverse strengths and values that they bring to the table. The therapeutic process can be used to help families identify individual and shared strengths and values to increase their sense of cohesion. For example, a family can promote their sense of purpose and commit to a goal by talking and agreeing upon shared values. At the same time, identifying values can be yet another way to promote communication within a family.

For Your Information: Values, Growth, and Meaning Making

When service members first return from combat, they may be focused on the suffering, fear, or anger associated with a deployment (Reivich, Seligman, & McBride, 2011). Early in the transition, returnees may have difficulty in looking beyond some of the blatantly negative experiences that they had or witnessed. However, recognizing positive changes gained through adversity will help service members broaden their outlook on life (Reivich et al., 2011). The same can be true for the spouses left behind. When spouses focus on the negative, it can overshadow positive growth that is taking place. These attitudes often trickle down to the children.

According to Dr. Viktor Frankl (1946), striving to find meaning in one's life is the most powerful and healing force driving human behavior. Frankl, a physician and survivor of Holocaust internment camps, discusses how identifying meaning in stressful or tragic events can be very therapeutic for trauma survivors. In his landmark book, *Man's Search for Meaning* (1946), Frankl shares about his years in Nazi concentration camps during the Holocaust. He observed that the prisoners who had positive attitudes about the future and who were able to make meaning of their present situation were more likely to survive the brutal conditions of the camps. Frankl describes how his personal experience of finding meaning in what could have been an entirely horrific experience helped him to survive his years in the concentration camps.

Finding positive meaning in the face of adversity is associated with long-term resilience (e.g., Southwick, Vythilingam, & Charney, 2005). During stressful deployments, when service members are able to find a broader significance of their role in a mission, they find it easier to justify hardships or sacrifices they make (Litz, Orsillo, Friedman, Ehlich, & Batres, 1997). People who are able to see the positive side to stressful situations and are committed to higher values are much more resilient in stressful life situations (e.g., Tugade & Frederickson, 2004).

Even former prisoners of war (POWs) are able to identify ways in which they grew in some manner from being a POW (Solomon et al., 1999). Despite immeasurable losses, many POWs say that they would not give up having the experience, because being a POW helped give them the values that define who they are today. As a result of their POW experiences, these individuals gained a greater appreciation for freedom and for their family and friends, greater patience and understanding, more optimism about life, as well as the ability to know what's important in life versus what is trivial (Feder et al., 2008; Solomon et al., 1999). Thus, amidst any adverse or even traumatic event, there are ways in which people can grow and improve as a result.

The Shared Values of the Family

Resilient families find meaning, purpose, and connection to something beyond themselves. By seeing themselves as part of something greater, families are able to take a larger view of any problems they may be having, which can lead to a heightened sense of purpose in their lives (Walsh, 2006). One way to promote shared meaning and purpose, while helping family members better understand each other, is by identifying their values both as individuals and as a family.

Dr. Brenda Thames (2008) describes values as a reflection of who we are, of our culture and of our own unique heritage, and of how our experience affects our behavior.

Our values help us prioritize what is important to us. As such, our values guide our decision-making processes. Thames (2008) writes that, as children approach adolescence, they begin to act on the values that have been established by their families. Because peers become more influential during adolescence, it becomes even more critical that children develop positive values. Families become empowered to establish their priorities and make positive decisions when they have clear values. And that is where we are heading with our military families in this step's first Making It Real exercise.

Making It Real: Our Core Values

In this exercise, we help the family identify their individual and shared values. In this exercise, each family member rates how often a variety of values are important to them, then rates how often they think those values are important to their family as a whole. You may wish to have family members complete the handout before the session. Then, in session, they can discuss their answers with one another. As follows, the family develops a list of their most important shared values.

Instructions: Please go to Family Handout Step 8.1.

1. Say to the family: "Our values are the qualities in life that are most important to us. Even though we all have values that guide the way we live our lives, we rarely take a moment to think about what our values are. Although values tend to be enduring, they can change over time and with experience. However, the more aware that we are about our values and the closer we follow our values in our day-to-day lives, the more meaningful our lives can be. In this exercise, I'd like you to think about and identify values—your own and what you think are your family's core values." You can provide them with examples of values, such as:

   ➤ Being at peace
   ➤ Being ethical and honest
   ➤ Freedom of speech
   ➤ Honoring my country
   ➤ Respecting elders
   ➤ Being a loyal friend
   ➤ Being disciplined
   ➤ Being a positive role model
   ➤ Being a good parent, spouse, son or daughter
   ➤ Having close and loving relationships
   ➤ Honoring God
   ➤ Being spiritual
   ➤ Being honest
   ➤ Being the best

> ➤ Gaining financial success
> ➤ Being successful
> ➤ Being powerful
> ➤ Being independent
> ➤ Being creative
> ➤ Being physically attractive
> ➤ Living a healthy lifestyle
> ➤ Commitment to a social cause or causes
> ➤ Being responsible for one's duties
> ➤ Being valued by the community
> ➤ Being a model citizen
> ➤ Working hard
> ➤ Gaining education
> ➤ Intellectual pursuits
> ➤ Being tolerant of differences in others
> ➤ Having fun
> ➤ Learning
> ➤ Being fair
> ➤ Respecting the environment
> ➤ Having compassion for all living things
> ➤ Seeking justice and equality for all
> ➤ Having a sense of humor
> ➤ Helping those who are less fortunate
> ➤ Being adventurous
> ➤ Being famous
> ➤ Being popular
> ➤ Being brave
> ➤ Being happy

2. "On your own, choose five to ten values that are most important to you. Then, as a family, decide which values are most important to your family as a whole. This also might include five or so items."

3. After the family has decided which are their most core values, have each family member provide a recent example of how these values influenced a decision or behavior. Then discuss with them if any of these values have become even more important to them in the last year.

Talking Points

In the case of Michael, Lisa, and Abby, a discussion of core values also served as a useful tool to promote communication and understanding among each other. Michael and Lisa were provided with three copies of Handout 8.1 and asked to have each family member complete the handout individually prior to their next session. In session, we review their responses. Here is some of that dialogue.

THERAPIST: Abby, Lisa, and Michael, first, what did each of you choose as your most important individual values?

ABBY: I have: doing my best job, being happy, being popular, and helping those who are less fortunate as most important. Oh, and having fun.

LISA: For me, being at peace, being a good parent and spouse, being ethical and honest, having close and loving relationships, and being happy are most important.

MICHAEL: I have being ethical and honest, being a good parent and spouse, honoring my country, doing my best job, and helping those who are less fortunate.

THERAPIST: Very good! Now, what values do you think are most core for your family?

LISA: Well, it looks like everyone agrees on helping those who are less fortunate. But I think that being ethical and honest should be one of our most important values. But I guess we are supposed to decide what our values are as a group.

MICHAEL: I would hope that being ethical and honest would be one of our core values.

LISA: But we're supposed to decide what our values really are, not what we think they should be. We have to be honest.

ABBY: Being ethical and honest is an important value to me. I try to be honest all of the time, but sometimes I slip.

THERAPIST: Can you tell us more about that, Abby?

ABBY: Well, if I think about it, compared to being popular, being ethical is probably more important to me. But it's hard sometimes.

THERAPIST: Abby, think about your life. Do you have an example that shows how these values are more important to you?

ABBY: Well, I did something really stupid last month. Everyone was making fun of this girl nobody likes, and I don't know why, but I made fun of her too. She started crying. I wanted to be with the popular crowd, but then I've felt like a jerk ever since. When they did it again last week I just told them to leave her alone.

THERAPIST: It sounds like you made a tough decision.

ABBY: I was afraid that they would start making fun of me, but they didn't.

MICHAEL: Abby, that was very ethical of you. You made the right choice not to give into peer pressure.

LISA: And you were very honest right now to tell us about what happened.

ABBY:	Well, I want to be popular, but sometimes it's more important to be ethical. I should have put that value down too.
MICHAEL:	So, what do you think? Do we all agree that being ethical and honest is one of our core family values?

Everyone agreed.

THERAPIST:	What else?
ABBY:	I think it's important to us to want to do our best job. I want to go to college and to go to a good one. I have to get good grades, so I try to do my best at school. But my Dad says to *always* do your best job, no matter what you're doing. I do that. It just makes me feel good.
LISA:	I agree.
MICHAEL:	So doing our best job is one of our core family values?

Everyone nodded.

THERAPIST:	What else would you suggest?
MICHAEL:	Well, I put down being a good parent and spouse. I may not always be the best parent or husband, but it's becoming more important to me all the time.
THERAPIST:	Can you tell us more about that, Michael?
MICHAEL:	I saw so much suffering while deployed—and losing Frank, being apart from my family—made me value Lisa and Abby.
THERAPIST:	It sounds like you are able to recognize positive changes that have occurred despite all of the losses you went through.
MICHAEL:	It's true. Ironically, my grief almost ruined my relationships with Lisa and Abby. I used to think that moving on with my life was in some way betraying Frank, but I see now that I can honor Frank *and* get on with my life.
LISA:	Thank you for that, Michael. That means so much to me.
MICHAEL (facing Lisa):	Because I lost Frank, I recognize that I need to appreciate you and Abby while I have you in my life.
LISA:	I agree that we all have to appreciate each other. That's kind of why being happy has become more important to me. I realize that life is short. I can't believe it, but Abby is going to be 13 years old next month. Time is going so fast, I want to enjoy my family and appreciate each day.
ABBY:	Can being happy be one of our family values too?
MICHAEL:	I think being happy *should* be one of our core family values.

For Your Information: Negative and Positive Statements

In addition to sharing core values, resilient families recognize the positive side of situations and people in their lives. By recognizing the positive and expressing gratitude to others, military families can put their day-to-day conflicts and annoyances into perspective. This helps family members maintain a larger context in which to view any problems they may be having.

A lack of positive statements between couples damages relationships. In his early research days, Dr. John Gottman videotaped married couples discussing a conflict (e.g., Buehlman, Gottman, & Katz, 1992). He then broke the conversations down into categories of positive, neutral, or negative emotion. Among couples who eventually divorced, the ratio of positive to negative interactions was 0.8 to 1. In stable and happy couples who did not eventually divorce, the ratio of positive to negative interactions was 5 to 1. These ratios predicted eventual divorce in approximately 90% of the cases.

This is not to say that resilient families don't fight or sometimes hurt one another's feelings. However, resilient families talk about fights or hurt feelings in order to repair the relationship. Relationships will have some negativity involved, but healthy relationships are based upon positive interactions, especially when couples are resolving conflicts. Similarly, expressing gratitude appears highly important for successful marriages and long-term resilience.

Children need role models who promote and support positive values. Being aware of what family members believe is important, can give both parents and children a sense of direction and help them develop their strengths. When families have a clear sense of direction, they can act more consistently on their values. In turn, the closer the family follows their values in their day-to-day lives, the more meaningful their lives will be.

By discussing and deciding upon their core values, Lisa, Michael, and Abby showed that they had diverse opinions, but they also shared some common values. This will help Michael, Lisa, and Abby's family to have a stronger sense of meaning, direction, and cohesion. The exercise also allowed Michael to embrace his role as father in the family, while focusing his attention on Lisa and Abby's beliefs and feelings.

Fostering Gratitude in Robert and Felicia's Family

Luckily, experiencing and expressing gratitude is a skill that can be acquired with practice. For some families, the ability to identify and express gratitude may need to be developed. We provide a segment of Felicia and Robert's therapy session to illustrate this point.

THERAPIST:	Felicia and Robert, how was your week?
FELICIA:	It was okay. We had Robbie's baseball game as usual on Saturday and went to church on Sunday, then spent all afternoon cleaning the yard. But that was okay. Work was the same.
ROBERT (rolling his eyes playfully):	Work was work.

FELICIA (laughing):	Yes, work was work!
ROBERT (smiling):	Felicia is dealing with a new Commander. I don't think that guy knows what he's doing yet.
FELICIA (looking annoyed):	I know he doesn't know what he's doing.
ROBERT:	Well, it's not the first time you whipped a new boss into shape.
FELICIA:	Well, I got your butt in shape this week.
ROBERT (laughing):	Yeah you did! I had my final written training exam, and Felicia helped me study for it. I probably wouldn't have passed otherwise.
THERAPIST:	Sounds like there's a compliment in there somewhere, Robert.
ROBERT (smiling):	Nah!

For Your Information: Gratitude

Gratitude is the quality of being thankful. In addition, gratitude implies a readiness to show appreciation for and to return kindness. Emmons & Crumpler (2000) describe gratitude as an emotional state and an attitude toward life that is a source of human strength to enhance personal and relational well-being. Research that examines individual differences in gratitude has recently shown that gratitude is uniquely and strongly related to well-being. People who habitually recognize the positive sides of situations and people, and who express gratitude toward others, have better health and even sleep better (Wood, Froh, & Geraghty, 2010).

Interventions designed to increase gratitude appear to also increase well-being. Training people to habitually focus on and appreciate the positive aspects of life has been shown to increase their well-being (Wood et al., 2010). For example, research participants in one study were randomly assigned to one of three experimental conditions: (1) writing about hassles, (2) gratitude listing, or (3) listing either neutral life events or social comparison on a daily basis (Emmons & McCullough, 2003). Those who were instructed to list things they were grateful for reported a better mood, healthier behaviors, and more positive overall life appraisals compared to the people in the other two groups.

In a second study, persons with neuromuscular disease were randomly assigned to either the gratitude writing condition or to a control writing condition. Compared to the control group, the gratitude group developed a more positive affect. The authors conclude that a conscious focus on gratitude likely has both emotional and interpersonal benefits (Emmons & McCullough, 2003).

Family members who are stuck in negative thoughts will benefit from assistance with identifying the positive in other people and events. With practice, people can begin to habitually recognize the positive sides of situations and people in their lives. Furthermore, to enhance family relationships, family members can be trained to become aware of and express gratitude toward others.

Helping families identify the positive can be particularly important following stressful deployments. At this time, service members often benefit from identifying things related to their service that they can be grateful for, such as positive characteristics they have gained through their time in the military. For example, even though many combat-related skills may not be useful in other contexts, many positive characteristics can develop (e.g., maturity, leadership skills, and the ability to quickly synthesize information and make difficult decisions). By appreciating what they are gaining from their hardships, individuals' outlooks can be more balanced.

Also following deployments, helping family members identify things they are grateful for in each other will help increase cohesion. Too often, family members only focus on the negatives in each other. Parents may forget to focus on their children's good behavior and end up only paying attention to them when they are bad. Additionally, certain cultural groups believe that making positive statements to children "spoils" them. We know from the research on positive reinforcement by parents, however, that identifying positives in others leads to more positive behavior. In the next Making It Real exercise, we help our military families develop their attitude of gratitude for each other.

Making It Real: Communicating Gratitude

The goal of the following exercise is to help family members continue practicing healthy communication, and also to build resilience by showing gratitude toward one another. The first component is a warm-up.

Instructions: Please go to Family Handout Step 8.2.

➤ Bring up the concept of gratitude to the family and discuss the benefits of feeling and expressing gratitude.

➤ Then tell the family, "This exercise is designed to help family members communicate gratitude. I am going to pass the stress ball to each family member, which as you know, signifies that the person holding the ball is going to share and everyone else is going to listen. We're going to go around in a circle and have everyone repeat and finish the following statement:

Three things I am most grateful about my family are . . .

➤ In the second component of this exercise, each family member shares at least three things that they are grateful for about each family member present using the sentence stems that follow. Again, the speaker holds the ball. Once they are finished, they give the ball to the person who they were just expressing gratitude to. When that listener gets the ball, they first need to summarize what they heard the other person say about them. Then they choose someone to share gratitude with. The process is repeated until all members have shared something that they are grateful for about all family members present. Please have them use the following sentence stems from Handout 8.2:

I am most grateful for you, _____, because . . .

I admire that you . . .

I am thankful for your . . .

Talking Points

Here's what Felicia and Robert had to say during this last exercise:

> FELICIA: Three things I am most grateful about my family are that they are good people, that we support each other, and that . . . they put up with me!"

The couple laughs.

> ROBERT: Okay, three things I am most grateful for about my family are that they are intelligent, fun, and they put up with Felicia!
>
> FELICIA: Hey!
>
> ROBERT   I'm just joking. I am grateful that my family is intelligent, fun, and has
> (laughing):   strong moral values.
>
> THERAPIST: Very nice, you two!

I explain Part Two of the exercise to them. Additionally, to encourage Robert and Felicia to move past their defenses, I encourage them to be genuine.

> THERAPIST: Okay, next I'd like you to share at least three things that you are grateful for about each other using the sentence stems on Part Two of this handout. Now, remember, this part is serious. The reason you are here in therapy is to be honest and authentic with one another. This exercise is a chance to be authentic. Are you ready to give it a go?

They both agree.

> THERAPIST: Felicia, you have the ball. Would you like to start?
>
> FELICIA: Okay, let's see. Robert, I am most grateful for you because you stuck by me all these years. I admire that you are strong, and that you are such a good role model for the boys. I am thankful for your loyalty, and thankful that I can go home and see you every night.

Robert repeats back the statement. They are both smiling.

> THERAPIST: Nice job, Felicia! Now it's Robert's turn.
>
> ROBERT: Let me think for a second. Okay. I am most grateful for you, Felicia, because you are an amazing woman. I admire that you are beautiful, sexy, intelligent, and strong. I am thankful that you have been so loyal to me, and thankful that I get to be with you every night.

Felicia looks surprised. As she repeats the statements back to Robert, her voice cracks. She looks at him earnestly, and I see that her eyes are brimming with tears.

> THERAPIST: Now just take a minute and let that sink in.

After a minute . . .

FELICIA (still looking at Robert):	Thank you, Robert.
ROBERT:	Thank you, Angel-boo.
FELICIA:	Angel-boo! You haven't called me that in ten years!

Felicia and Robert are laughing but look grounded and connected.

THERAPIST, (after a pause):	Wow! What was that like for you?
ROBERT (obviously touched):	It . . . was good.
FELICIA (grabbing a tissue and wiping her eyes):	Yes.
THERAPIST:	What else?
FELICIA (smiling):	It feels real nice.
ROBERT:	I guess it works.
FELICIA (laughing):	Who would have known?
ROBERT (not taking his eyes off of Felicia):	Yes, and you know what? We used to do this!
THERAPIST:	I want you to *keep* doing it.

Felicia and Robert hadn't shared their gratitude for one another in a long time. They thought that they didn't need to say such things out loud, that the other person should "just know it." However, in reality, the messages they had been sharing with each other conveyed the opposite message. They often cut each other down "jokingly." This is a common pattern among military peers, and that culture had become a part of their relationship with one another. However, successful romantic relationships require intimacy and trust. The cutting messages between them were slowly eating at each person's self esteem and undermining their relationship.

Communicating appreciation for each other deeply touched Robert and Felicia. We discussed together what the couple was like when they first met. Felicia related that they were "in love" and that, when they were dating, Robert used to "sweet talk" to her "all the time." We talked about how positive changes can fuel a healthy relationship and keep trust from eroding. Robert and Felicia agreed to find time to keep telling each other why they are grateful on a regular basis.

Termination: A Resilient Future

In the first session, the therapy timeline should have been discussed, so family members should have an idea of what to expect by the end of therapy. However, especially if termination was not discussed, or if family members do not recall the discussion, family members should be prepared for termination. Ideally, in family counseling, each client who participated in most of the therapy sessions should be involved in termination. However, participation will be less important for children or other parties who were involved in only one or two sessions.

In Dr. John Gottman's couples' therapy, follow-up sessions are planned at 6 months, 12 months, 18 months, and after two years as part of an outcome-evaluation phase. These sessions have been shown through research to significantly decrease the chances of relapse into previous, unhelpful patterns. We suggest having one follow-up session that allows for a little more time between sessions. This session might be one to several months following the termination of regular therapy, based on the needs and situation of the family. In the case of military families, the lapse until the follow-up session often has to be titrated due to deployment or changes of station.

The last session is a good time to review what the family has learned, discuss progress that was made, and talk about any feelings that termination may bring up for the family members. If necessary, you may also discuss what goals were not accomplished in therapy and what the client may do about them. And that leads us to our last Making It Real exercise with all of our military families.

Making It Real: Toward a Resilient Future

The goal of this exercise is to help family members solidify the progress they have made in therapy and develop a plan to maintain their resilience in the future. After recounting their areas of growth, family members plan ahead and imagine themselves implementing their new skills and attitudes when new problems arise.

You may choose to give family members 5 minutes to complete these questions together or, as with previous exercises, have them complete the questions individually on their own.

Instructions: Please go to Family Handout Step 8.3.

Alternatively, it is also valuable to simply ask the family these questions in session. What is important is that each member takes the time to reflect on their progress, to share their own thoughts about the therapy process and plans for a resilient future.

1. What are the most important ways your family has grown through therapy?
2. What do you see as your newfound strengths?
3. What new behaviors or skills have you learned that your family will use to manage challenges in the future?
4. What is the most important thing that has changed about how you act as a family?
5. How do you see yourselves as being more resilient as the result of going through this process?

Talking Points

In this section, we hear from each of our military families. First up are Felicia and Robert. It's our last session together, and I have read question 1 out loud to them.

THERAPIST: Felicia and Robert, you have made so many positive changes in therapy. I'd like you to take some time to think about where you were when you decided to begin therapy and where you are today.

ROBERT: Sure.

THERAPIST: In thinking about these past few months, what do you think are the most important ways your family has grown as a result of your work in therapy?

FELICIA: I feel that the biggest changes had to do with my way of approaching Robert and the boys. I didn't realize how tightly wound up I became when I was in Kabul. Looking back, I see how much my family life became mixed with my professional role and life in Kabul. I had Robert to balance me, but then when he deployed, my attitude just became worse. I've grown by stepping back and reevaluating how we do things.

ROBERT: I agree. I'd say being able to take a broader look at the situation made me see how we got on a downhill path. I didn't realize that I was unhappy in our marriage or that we all had changed so much. I feel like a family again, and feel great about my family.

Michael, Lisa, and Abby

Next is an excerpt from Lisa, Michael, and Abby answering question 2 during their last session.

THERAPIST: Michael and Lisa, since being in therapy, what do you see as your new-found strengths?

LISA: Our family feels much more stable now. I feel like one strength is that we all have a new commitment to appreciating each other. For myself, I've found the strength to put myself first sometimes.

MICHAEL: I love that Lisa woke me up and made me stop sitting around and feeling sorry for myself. When she said she was going to take time to exercise and relax, I have to admit I felt a little panicky. I didn't know if I was going to like it. But her having the strength to take care of herself gave me the determination to do the same.

LISA: And you found the determination to be a great father!

MICHAEL: I feel like I now have the strength of character to be a father. I want to be a role model. I know I'm not the perfect Dad, but I don't have to be perfect.

THERAPIST: Abby, what about you?

ABBY: I think I realized that I care about people a lot. I want to treat others with respect. I also love that my dad and I are getting closer. It's been cool getting to spend time with him every day. We didn't have that before all of this. (looks at her father) You are not a perfect father. Probably no one is, but you are a great Dad to me. I'm glad we get to be friends now.

Michael, Lisa, and Abby all smile in unison.

LISA: I feel like we now have the strength to overcome any challenge. No matter what it is, we can do it.

Dan and Kate

Here is an excerpt from the last session with our couple, Dan and Kate.

THERAPIST: Dan and Kate, what new behaviors or skills have you learned that your family will use to manage challenges in the future?

KATE: I think we have learned a lot of new skills. Probably the biggest for us, I think, is ways that we can communicate better with each other. And for me personally, I can't tell you how much of a relief it was to be open and honest with Dan about how ashamed I felt about the rape, and how his sexual behaviors and needs were making me feel worse. That was a big step for me. And I think it helped our relationship to get it all out in the open. From that point, things seemed to get better.

THERAPIST: That's great, Kate! Taking that a step further, what did you learn that you can use in your married life in the future?

KATE: Well, I would say I learned that it's okay to take risks and be honest. I also realized that secrets in our family just lead to us trying to guess what was bothering the other. So, it's just better to get the truth out and deal with it.

THERAPIST: That's great insight, Kate. Dan, how about you? What did you learn in this process that you can use in your family life?

DAN: I realized how much I need my family. And I guess I would agree with Kate about being honest and open with each other, about anything and everything. A lot of times the secrets get bigger and are worse than the real deal. You know? So, I think we will just continue to be honest with each other and try to not keep things from each other.

John and Amy

Here is a snapshot of our last session with John and Amy.

THERAPIST: Next, I'm curious, what do you both see as the most important thing that has changed about how you behave or act with one another?

JOHN: If I could go first on that one, I think I have changed for the better. I never realized how much I expected from Amy, or how selfish I was being. I take time now to consider Amy's needs too. I ask her what she needs. And I am stoked about helping her get back on track to finish her schooling. For the first time in a long time, I feel really connected to her because I feel like we are on the same page about something important in our lives.

THERAPIST: That's great, John! Amy, how about you? What do you see as the most important thing that has changed about your behavior?

AMY: Well, I do feel supported by John now. I think for me, the biggest change is that I am actually focusing on my needs. I haven't done that in a long time. For the first time in years, I am considering what I need too. I don't feel like I'm being selfish, and I don't feel racked with guilt that I'm a bad wife or mother. That is a huge step of growth for me.

THERAPIST: That's terrific, Amy! And to feel supported in your efforts by John has to feel good. How do you think that has helped strengthen your family as a whole?

AMY: I think I can speak for both John and I when I say that we have grown closer together as a family. When I put all of my needs aside, I would get to the point where I felt resentful, irritable, and stressed out sometimes. Now I let John or our daughter know that I need to have some "me time." That's when I relax and then focus on what's important to me for a half hour or so. I think it actually helps me be an even better wife and mom. We frequently ask each other what we need. And then we support each other. It's made a big difference in our family. I think just that one tool has helped us to grow closer and stronger as a family.

Josh, Sarah, Amanda, and Tyler

Finally, here is a snippet from our last session with Josh, Sarah, Amanda, and Tyler.

THERAPIST: Josh and Sarah, how do you see yourselves as being more resilient as the result of going through this process?

SARAH: I think we have gotten stronger as a family. We have worked together as a family to help Josh. I can't explain it. I just know that we have become closer. We spend focused time together every day. We focus on the positives in each other. We practice appreciation in our family now. All I know is that the arguing has taken a back seat. We like being around each other now.

THERAPIST: That's great news, Sarah. Josh, what do you think?

JOSH: Well, I know none of this has been easy. I was feeling sorry for myself, I guess. I still have days like that. I'm not gonna lie. But, it is awesome that we all work together as a family. I can't say I ever had that with my parents or sisters. It feels good when we do stuff together. When I get frustrated, I try my best not to snap at Sarah or the kids. But if I do, they point it out. Then I remind myself that they are trying to help me, not hurt me. And that we are in it together as a family.

THERAPIST: And how do you feel that your family is more resilient?

SARAH: I would second what Josh said. We work together. It's like we are driven as a family. We are united. And let me give you an example. One thing we have done, just to make sure we stay positive in our family, is to have an appreciation jar. If any of us complains or says anything negative about each other, that person has to put a dollar for every negative comment in the other person's jar. Then the other jokes and says, "Hey, I appreciate it, Dad." Or, "I appreciate it, Mom." Maybe it sounds goofy. But, when you have to put money in someone else's jar, it quickly makes you realize what you're doing. It has helped us to refocus our energy and our thoughts to being positive and expressing appreciation with our mouths, not our wallets (smiles). Somehow, it has bonded us closer together because we just automatically appreciate each other more.

THERAPIST: Amanda, what do you think? How do you think your family has gotten stronger?

AMANDA: I think we work together now. Before, it felt like we were kind of working against each other. Now it feels different. It's like we are all doing stuff together as a family. I like it much better.

THERAPIST: That's great, Amanda! Tyler, what about you?

TYLER: I get to swim in the pool with my Daddy every day now. I love doing things with him. And Mommy seems happier too.

THERAPIST: It sounds like your family has come a long way, everybody! Great work! Anyone have anything else they'd like to say as we wrap it up?

SARAH: I do. I think we all realize we can take on whatever comes because we love each other so much. And it feels like now we are in it together as a family.

Final Thoughts

These families have grown more resilient. That is not to say that they will be without struggles, problems, or difficulties in the future, but they have learned a lot. They have grown a lot. In our work with these military families, we watched them learn to communicate more openly with each other. We witnessed a gradual transformation, from negativity and isolating from one another to family members getting to know each other again and spending time with each other. We shared in their struggles and their joys as they reconnected. We supported them as they gave their pain a voice and honestly expressed it with their loved ones. We guided them to look for the positive in each other and appreciate one another more.

We were honored to play a part in helping these family members to work through these steps together. We were moved as we heard their stories of growth—coming from a place of hurt, pain, isolation, and confusion—to deeper love, connection, unconditional acceptance, strength, and resiliency as a family. Our experiences of success with military families compelled us to share these steps with you. It is our greatest hope that the military family members with whom you work will experience this deep healing as well.

Keys to Family Wellness

➤ The highly functioning family uses the diverse strengths of it members and, at the same time, balances each other's weaknesses.

➤ Family members who are stuck in negative thoughts will benefit from assistance with identifying the positive in other people and events.

➤ Finding positive meaning in the face of adversity is associated with long-term resilience.

➤ Talking about and agreeing on shared values can promote a sense of family purpose and commitment to a greater goal.

➤ The closer the family follows their values in their day-to-day lives, the more meaningful their lives will be.

➤ Training family members to habitually think about and express gratitude will improve their individual and collective well-being.

Taking Action

Taking action will help rebuild the family. Please check off each step as the family accomplishes it.

❑ The family should continue to focus on the positive aspects of their situation.

❑ The family should take time to think about and express gratitude every day.

❑ The family should feel prepared to face the future as a strong and resilient team!

Handouts for Families and Clinicians

Handouts for Military Families

List of Family Handouts

Step 1: Connect

Family Handout Step 1.1: Transition Stress and the Military Family

Family Handout Step 1.2: Communicating to Decrease Transition Stress

Family Handout Step 1.3: Practicing Healthy Communication

Family Handout Step 1.4: Providing Support

Family Handout Step 1.5: Practicing Appreciation

Step 2: Explain

Family Handout Step 2.1: Building Family Awareness

Family Handout Step 2.2: Discovering Needs

Family Handout Step 2.3: A Picture Is Worth a Thousand Words

Family Handout Step 2.4: Story Sharing

Step 3: Discover

Family Handout Step 3.1: Practicing Positive Coping

Family Handout Step 3.2: In an Emergency! Reactive Coping Activities

Family Handout Step 3.3: Reactive Coping Activities—Downshifting

Family Handout Step 3.4: Practicing Reactive Coping Skills

Family Handout Step 3.5: Negative Coping

Family Handout Step 3.6: Positive or Negative Coping?

Step 4: Empower

Family Handout Step 4.1: Identifying Feelings

Family Handout Step 4.2: Sharing Emotions

Family Handout Step 4.3: Deepening Communication

Step 5: Improve

Family Handout Step 5.1: Intimacy, Sex, Thoughts, and Feelings

Family Handout Step 5.2: Defining Intimacy in the Relationship

Family Handout Step 5.3: Breaking It Down

Family Handout Step 5.4: Challenging and Correcting

Step 6: Process

Family Handout Step 6.1: Changing Beliefs About Sharing Emotions

Family Handout Step 6.2: Honoring the Loss

Family Handout Step 6.3: What Is Grief?

Family Handout Step 6.4: Meaning Making

Family Handout Step 6.5: Unconditional Support and Acceptance

Step 7: Challenge

Family Handout Step 7.1: Assessing Needs and Clarifying Values

Family Handout Step 7.2: Aligning Visions

Family Handout Step 7.3: Enhancing the Vision

Family Handout Step 7.4: Setting Goals for Positive Life Change

Step 8: Grow

Family Handout Step 8.1: Our Core Values

Family Handout Step 8.2: Communicating Gratitude

Family Handout Step 8.3: A Resilient Future

Step 1: Connect

Building the Relationship

Family Handout Step 1.1

Transition Stress and the Military Family

Not everyone is able to make the transition back to family life with ease after deployment. The service member has changed, and the family has changed as well. Following are some changes that service members returning from long or dangerous deployments have experienced. Have you noticed any of these in your own life?

- Some service members have felt a loss of interest in activities. This can confuse family and friends and make them feel cut off or left out.
- Some service members have difficulty trusting and feeling close to others. As a result, family and friends may feel hurt and betrayed.
- Some service members may feel like they need to be in control at all times. The service member may have become accustomed to authority and expect their spouse or children to respond to them immediately.
- Some service members may have suppressed their emotions in order to handle emergencies and, in some cases, stay alive. They may not show emotions besides anger, which can hurt their relationships.
- Some service members may have difficulty feeling love and being intimate.
- Some service members may be reluctant to talk about what happened during their deployment, which might make family or friends feel left out or insignificant.

Service members and spouses/partners often report changes in their relationships with their spouse or partner when they return from deployment. Problems commonly come up that can make getting back together as a couple very challenging. Here are some typical problems that you may face as you transition back to being a couple:

- Face-to-face communication may be difficult.
- Intimacy may feel awkward, or it may be difficult to connect like you used to.
- Because of stress or, possibly, physical injuries, returnees may have lost interest in sexual activities, which may lead to their spouse or partner feeling hurt.
- Service members may feel closer to their military buddies and feel like their spouse or partner is a stranger.
- The roles you each used to play for basic household chores may have changed.
- The spouse or partner left at home may be more independent now, or he or she may be involved in activities that don't include the service member.
- You may have changed in your outlook and priorities in life. Or, maybe your spouse or partner's priorities have changed while you were away.
- If you have children, they may have difficulty communicating or feeling close to the returnee.

Family Handout Step 1.2

Communicating to Decrease Transition Stress

Often, the primary source of support for the service member is his or her partner or other family members. For service members who are undergoing deployment-related stressors, family can be extremely important in helping them deal with and overcome transition stress. Family members can help by:

- Providing a sense of companionship to buffer feelings of isolation
- Providing a sense of belonging to increase a sense of safety
- Increasing self-esteem that can help buffer depression
- Offering opportunities to make a positive contribution by helping others
- Giving practical, problem-solving support to better handle difficulties
- Offering emotional support to help in coping with life stressors

Unfortunately, although families can be a source of support, they can also be sources of stress if family members do not communicate or make an effort to reconnect with one another. In order to begin to overcome transition stress, each family member must make an effort to act in a way that makes others feel listened to and respected. Reconnecting by communicating, possibly slowly at first, will eventually help resolve your problems.

Here are some suggestions to help you and your family members reconnect and communicate better:

- Take time to listen to your spouse or partner, children, and other important family members and friends. Make individual time for each person.
- Take time for just you and your spouse or partner.
- Go slowly when reestablishing your place in the family. Roles may have changed and will need to be renegotiated.
- The service member might need to take some breaks by him or herself or with his or her buddies. The spouse or partner may also need some breaks at times because he or she is not used to having the service member there all of the time. It will be an adjustment for both of you, as well as your children.
- Make efforts to explain to your family and friends what you are feeling and what you would like or need from them. It is very helpful to communicate any changes to your family so that they understand why you may be different. Remember that family members may need help understanding how you have changed.
- Keep in mind that your experience was and is very different from that of your family. Be patient and remember that it will take some time for all of you to readjust back to normal life.
- Be prepared to make some adjustments. A family is not a military unit. You may have to renegotiate with them regarding family responsibilities and routines.
- Support and reinforce good things your family has done during the deployment and the positive things they are doing for your family now.

Family Handout Step 1.3

Practicing Healthy Communication

The goal of this exercise is to help your family to listen attentively and communicate better with each other. Please answer each of these questions openly and honestly.

My experience with deployment has been . . .

_____

_____

_____

_____

_____

_____

The most challenging part of deployment for me was . . .

_____

_____

_____

_____

_____

I feel concerned about . . .

_____

_____

_____

_____

_____

Family Handout Step 1.4

Providing Support

The goal of this exercise is to help your family practice healthy communication, and also to practice the art of support for each other. Please answer this question openly and honestly.

Describe in detail a time when you felt most supported by your family members (what did they do or say?).

_____

_____

_____

_____

_____

_____

_____

_____

_____

_____

_____

_____

_____

_____

_____

_____

_____

_____

_____

_____

_____

_____

_____

Family Handout Step 1.5

Practicing Appreciation

The goal of this exercise is to help your family members continue practicing healthy communication, and also to practice the art of appreciation. Please answer the following questions about your family members.

I appreciate how you . . .

_____

_____

_____

_____

_____

I appreciate that you . . .

_____

_____

_____

_____

_____

I appreciate your . . .

_____

_____

_____

_____

_____

Step 2: Explain

Informing of Experiences

Family Handout Step 2.1

Building Family Awareness

Family bonds erode when family members stop communicating with each other. In addition, it is important that family members understand other family member's perspectives at a given time in life. Here are some suggestions for building family members' awareness of each other:

- Ask what your family members need and why that is important to them.
- Ask for specific feedback from members of the family. Ask how you are meeting their needs and what you can do to improve.
- Ask questions like "What is this like for you?" to better understand where other family members are coming from.
- Have your family members share their own personal stories.

Family Handout Step 2.2

Discovering Needs

This exercise will help your family members to connect with each other. Please answer the following questions.

1. Tell me five words that describe your greatest needs in life, in general.

    1._____

    2._____

    3._____

    4._____

    5._____

2. Why are these needs so important to you?

    _____

    _____

    _____

    _____

    _____

    _____

    _____

3. Tell me five words that describe what you need most from me.

    1._____

    2._____

    3._____

    4._____

    5._____

4. Be completely honest with me. How am I meeting your needs?

    _____

    _____

    _____

    _____

    _____

    _____

5. Help me understand what it means to you for me to meet these needs, or if I haven't met these needs.

_____

_____

_____

_____

_____

_____

6. How do you think your needs have changed since we have been a family?

_____

_____

_____

_____

_____

_____

Family Handout Step 2.3

A Picture Is Worth a Thousand Words

This exercise is a good follow-up to the last one you did together as a family. In this exercise, you will learn more about each other and your individual needs. Please answer these questions in open and honest detail.

Please describe what your picture is about and how it relates to your family.

_____

_____

_____

_____

_____

_____

_____

_____

_____

What does your picture or collage mean to you? Please talk about this in detail.

_____

_____

_____

_____

_____

_____

_____

_____

_____

_____

_____

_____

_____

_____

_____

_____

Family Handout Step 2.4

Story Sharing

With this exercise, your family will get to an even deeper level of understanding of each other's experiences.

Please write openly and honestly about your personal story. Write it in great detail, describing your deepest thoughts, feelings, behaviors, and reactions. Write it so that your family can understand your experience on a deep, personal level.

My Story

_____

_____

_____

_____

_____

_____

_____

_____

_____

_____

_____

_____

_____

_____

_____

_____

_____

_____

_____

_____

_____

_____

_____

_____

_____

_____

_____

_____

_____

Step 3: Discover
Strengthening Coping Skills

Family Handout Step 3.1

Practicing Positive Coping

The goal of this exercise is to help your family develop a plan to practice positive coping. Different families enjoy different kinds of activities. Several healthy coping activities are listed as follows:

1. Use the coping activity ideas to identify both individual and family activities that you and your family would enjoy doing.
2. Decide which activities you can do as a family.
3. Use the coping schedule on the next page to write down times when you can do a healthy coping activity.
4. Try to make time for at least one individual and one family activity per day.

Keep the schedule in a place in your home where you will see it often, such as on your refrigerator.

Positive Coping Activities

➤ Exercising or getting outdoors to enjoy nature
➤ Playing a game
➤ Playing with a pet
➤ Praying or going to church
➤ Going out with a friend (playing golf, going bowling, to a movie, or out to dinner)
➤ Gardening or making home repairs
➤ Singing or dancing
➤ Attending a social club
➤ Inviting someone over for coffee or cards
➤ Playing a team sport
➤ Going to a party
➤ Making new friends
➤ Volunteering to help others, such as at a hospital, nursing home, or homeless shelter
➤ Helping friends or family members; visiting someone who is lonely
➤ Coaching a team
➤ Making love to your spouse

➤ Creating something: Draw a picture, paint a painting, write or play music, make crafts, garden, or improve your house

➤ Trying a hobby: Build a model, take up photography, learn martial arts, read a book, collect baseball cards, or something that is meaningful to you

➤ Doing something fun as a family: Go boating, hiking, camping, or swimming, toss a ball or Frisbee, play chess, checkers, or a board or video game, go shopping, plan a trip, take a drive, go fishing or to a concert, a fair, the zoo, a restaurant, a park, a museum, or the beach

➤ Writing or journaling: Writing letters, stories, poetry, or writing in a journal can help improve well-being and lower people's risk for disease. Writing 10 to 15 minutes a day about stress in your life especially can lower your stress level quite a bit.

➤ Being spiritual: Pray, join a house of worship, talk with others about ethics or religion, go to a religious service, read sacred works, listen to a sermon, or participate in church groups

➤ Finding support: Support groups, such as Alcoholics Anonymous, Alanon, and Alateen 12-step groups, provide family members with the opportunity to share about their challenges with people who are experiencing the same type of problems.

➤ Relaxing somewhere that makes you feel peaceful: Take a walk, go to the woods, daydream, watch a sunset, go to the library, listen to the radio or to the sound of the ocean or a running brook

Mindfulness activities: Learn mindfulness activities that help relax the mind and combine body-centered relaxation exercises. They include:

➤ Autogenic, self-hypnosis, and meditation (including mindfulness meditation) training to focus your attention on feeling calm and having a clear awareness about your life.

➤ Guided imagery (visualization): Using your imagination to help you relax and release tension caused by stress.

Body-centered exercises: Learning body-centered relaxation skills is useful for those who experience mainly physical symptoms of stress. These are especially good techniques for individuals who hold their stress or tension in their bodies. These skills may include:

➤ Breathing exercises
➤ Progressive muscle relaxation
➤ Massage
➤ Aromatherapy
➤ Yoga, Tai Chi, and Qi Gong

Coping Activities Schedule

Schedule at least one individual and one family activity per day. *Put this schedule in a place in your home where you will see it often,* such as on your refrigerator.

	MON	TUES	WED	THURS	FRI	SAT	SUN
0600 hrs							
0700 hrs							
0800 hrs							
0900 hrs							
1000 hrs							
1100 hrs							
1200 hrs							
1300 hrs							
1400 hrs							
1500 hrs							
1600 hrs							
1700 hrs							
1800 hrs							
1900 hrs							
2000 hrs							
2100 hrs							
2200 hrs							
Night ⇩							

Family Handout Step 3.2

In an Emergency! Reactive Coping Activities

Reactive coping tools are skills and behaviors that we do in response to a problem. Like firefighters responding to a fire in progress, reactive strategies are focused on reducing or removing a problem that is already there. If you are stressed and feel overwhelmed, but you use meditation to help calm yourself down, you are using a reactive coping tool.

There are several reactive coping tools that can help reduce stress and promote or restore the ability to think during stressful times. Some examples include:

- Laughing and crying are natural ways to relieve stress and release tension. They are both part of the emotional healing process. Tell a joke, laugh at a comedy, or cry during sad movies. All of these can be an excellent way to help release stress. Even though we often think that we should not cry, or that it is a sign of weakness, the reality is that crying is an important and natural part of the overall grieving process, and it can be part of getting better.
- Listening to positive music
- Practicing deep breathing, meditation, or progressive muscle relaxation
- Taking a relaxing bath or shower
- If you can do so without becoming angry, discussing situations with each other
- Discussing situations with a close friend, clergy member, a counselor, parent, or other relative
- Praying or going to a house of worship
- Writing or journaling
- Relaxing using mindfulness activities or body-centered exercises:
  - Autogenic, self-hypnosis, and meditation (including mindfulness meditation) training to focus your attention on feeling calm and having a clear awareness about your life
  - Guided imagery (visualization): Using your imagination to help you relax and release tension caused by stress
  - Deep breathing exercises
  - Progressive muscle relaxation
  - Massage
  - Aromatherapy
  - Yoga, Tai Chi, and Qi Gong

Family Handout Step 3.3

Reactive Coping Activities—Downshifting

An important reactive coping skill for families to develop is to know when and how to downshift. When your car is facing a challenging hill, it is time to downshift to a lower gear. When downshifting, the car's transmission works more slowly. However, this slower action allows the car to have the power needed to surmount the hill. When problems become challenging, it is easy to become overwhelmed. However, it is very important for family members to identify when problems begin to overwhelm them. When you recognize that problems are building, it is time to downshift. Downshifting involves five steps:

Step 1: Recognize that problems are becoming overwhelming. Recognize that it is time to give yourself and each other a break.

Step 2: Let others know you need to downshift.

Step 3: Slow down and breathe. Just like downshifting a car to a lower gear allows the car to have the power to surmount a hill, slowing down and breathing will help us have the strength and wherewithal to cope.

Step 4: Decide which reactive coping tool to use.

Step 5: Focus on one task at a time.

Family Handout Step 3.4

Practicing Reactive Coping Skills

The goal of this exercise is to help your family recognize future times when problems are building and help you plan ahead to cope with the situation.

Which reactive coping strategies can you use when needed?

_____

_____

_____

_____

_____

How will you know when you need to step back from a situation and downshift?

_____

_____

_____

_____

_____

Can you give me an example of a time when you may need to downshift, and how you would go through the steps?

_____

_____

_____

_____

_____

Family Handout Step 3.5

Negative Coping

We all find ways of coping with stress. Some coping methods are helpful, whereas others are harmful and can make the problems much worse. Negative coping makes families vulnerable to more problems.

Here are examples of negative coping responses:

- Driving too fast in your car
- Becoming aggressive or violent (hitting someone, throwing, or kicking something)
- Eating too much or too little, or drinking a lot of caffeinated beverages
- Smoking or chewing tobacco
- Drinking alcohol or taking recreational drugs
- Ruminating about problems
- Criticizing yourself (negative self-talk)
- Yelling at your spouse or partner, children, co-workers, or friends
- Avoiding social contact
- Dropping out of recreational activities
- Working long hours to avoid thoughts or people
- Playing video games for hours to avoid thoughts or people

Family Handout Step 3.6

Positive or Negative Coping?

Which type of coping do you think your family is primarily using? How is it positive or negative?

_____

_____

_____

_____

_____

What do you see as being the positive or negative impact of using these coping skills?

_____

_____

_____

_____

_____

What are some positive coping activities you can replace the negative ones with?

_____

_____

_____

_____

_____

When will you be willing to schedule those positive activities into your life from now on?

Weekdays:

Times:

Step 4: Empower

Focusing on Strengths

Family Handout Step 4.1

Identifying Feelings

1. How good or bad are you feeling on a scale from one to ten?

2. What feeling word best describes how you are feeling now?

Feeling Words

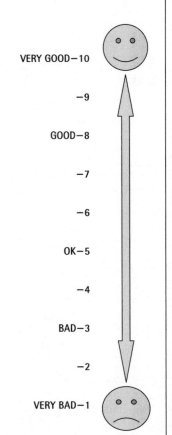

Joyful

Happy   VERY GOOD—10

Proud   —9

Content

Optimistic   GOOD—8

Trusting   —7

Numb

Stressed   —6

Nervous or Anxious   OK—5

Irritated

Fearful   —4

Disappointed   BAD—3

Remorseful (Sorry)

Angry   —2

Overwhelmed   VERY BAD—1

Disgusted

Family Handout Step 4.2

Sharing Emotions

Emotions serve important functions. These functions include:

- When people share emotions with others, doing so makes emotions less intense.
- Sharing emotions helps connect people with others, and so can help people feel less isolated from others.
- Avoiding talking about emotions and problems usually just makes the problems worse.
- Sharing emotions is associated with better physical and emotional health.

Here are some guidelines for listening to others when they are expressing how they feel:

1. First, take time to provide the person with your full attention.
2. When your family member shares, just listen. Focus on what the other person is communicating. Do not interrupt or think about what you want to say next.
3. Let the person know that you support them and are there for them by nodding or encouraging them to share more.
4. Last, ask the person if there is anything you can do to help.

Family Handout Step 4.3

Deepening Communication

In this exercise, we get to a deeper level of communication and trust among family members. To help clarify your feelings, you can write about them here.

Please share and describe your experience. What emotions are you feeling and why?

_____

_____

_____

_____

_____

Please write about your experience with sharing your emotions with your family members. What is it like for you?

_____

_____

_____

_____

_____

What can your family members do to support you when you feel upset?

_____

_____

_____

_____

_____

Step 5: Improve

Changing Negative Thoughts

Family Handout Step 5.1

Exploring Intimate Needs and Feelings

It is very important for partners to understand how they feel about each other on an intimate level. Please answer these questions openly and honestly.

THOUGHTS AND FEELINGS ABOUT INTIMACY:

When my partner and I are intimate, I feel . . .

_____

_____

_____

After we have sex, I feel . . .

_____

_____

_____

As far as our love life, lately I have been wondering . . .

_____

_____

_____

When it comes to sex these days, I would describe myself as . . .

_____

_____

_____

I would describe my partner as . . .

_____

_____

_____

When it comes to our sex life and level of intimacy in our relationship, I am concerned that . . .

_____

_____

_____

Sometimes I think . . .

_____

_____

_____

Family Handout Step 5.2

Defining Intimacy in the Relationship

It is important for spouses or partners to become very clear about how each of them defines intimacy in their relationship. It also helps partners to clarify expectations they have for one another specific to intimacy and sexuality. Please answer each of the following questions openly and honestly.

DEFINING INTIMACY:

To me, intimacy means . . .

_____

_____

_____

As far as our relationship, my idea of what sex should be like is . . .

_____

_____

_____

My expectations for myself in our relationship are . . .

_____

_____

_____

My expectations for my partner in our relationship are . . .

_____

_____

_____

In my ideal fantasy, I would be . . .

_____

_____

_____

In my ideal fantasy, my partner would be . . .

_____

_____

_____

Family Handout Step 5.3

Breaking It Down

This exercise is a very important one because it will bring out your family's underlying fears and perceptions about intimacy. Please complete the following statements openly and honestly.

I realize my biggest fear(s) is/are . . .

_____

_____

_____

_____

_____

_____

In our relationship, on a deep level, I feel . . .

_____

_____

_____

_____

_____

_____

The experience with my partner where I felt closest to him/her and good about myself was (describe it) . . . I felt this way because . . .

_____

_____

_____

_____

_____

The experience with my partner where I felt furthest from him/her and bad about myself was (describe it). . . . I felt this way because . . .

_____

_____

_____

_____

_____

_____

Family Handout Step 5.4

Challenging and Correcting

In this exercise, your family will identify, challenge, and modify negative thoughts, feelings, and beliefs.

What are your negative thoughts, feelings, and beliefs? Please list them here.

_____

_____

_____

_____

_____

_____

After thinking about and considering the "evidence" you have for your belief(s), how valid do you feel your beliefs are now?

_____

_____

_____

_____

_____

_____

Step 6: Process
Taking a Deeper Look

Family Handout Step 6.1

Changing Beliefs About Sharing Emotions

This exercise will help shed more light on how you feel about sharing painful thoughts and emotions with each other as a family.

Please write your responses out to these questions:

When you were young, was there someone you talked to when you felt sad or scared?
If no, what did you do instead when you felt that way? If yes, who was that? What was it like to share with them?

_____

_____

_____

_____

_____

_____

Imagine that you talked to your partner about something that made you feel sad or scared. What would that be like for you?

_____

_____

_____

_____

_____

If you told your partner about a secret you had never shared with anyone, how would you like your partner to respond and show that they are listening to you?

_____

_____

_____

_____

_____

_____

Family Handout Step 6.2

Honoring the Loss

This exercise entails questions to help family members make sense of and pay honor to their losses. Use the worksheet to write out about your loss; take time to really consider each question and spend some time on your answers.

What is it or who was it that you lost?

_____

_____

What was important to you about that person, thing, or event?

_____

_____

_____

When did the loss occur?

_____

_____

_____

How did the loss occur? Describe what took place.

_____

_____

_____

_____

_____

_____

_____

What were your thoughts when the loss occurred?

_____

_____

_____

_____

What are your thoughts now about the loss?

_____

_____

_____

_____

How exactly did having the person, place, or thing in your life change your life?

_____

_____

_____

_____

_____

What can you do to honor the person, thing, or event? (Following are some examples of ways you can honor a loss).

_____

_____

_____

_____

_____

Suggestions for Paying Honor

1. Write a letter to the person or the thing that you lost, whether you know that person or not. If you prefer, you can write a letter to that person's spouse, parent, or child. If your loss was an event, write to somebody about the loss. Light a candle and read the letter out loud.

2. If you were close to the person you lost, create a picture book or scrapbook of that person.

3. Create a ritual that honors your loss; a ritual might entail celebrating the birthday of a person you lost or the anniversary date of an event, or attending a faith-based organization as a tribute to your loss.

4. You may go to a place that means something to the person or signifies something about the thing that you lost (e.g., if you used to love walking in the mountains before you lost your legs, go back to the mountains and spend a day there in honor of your legs. If your buddy used to love the rodeo, attend a rodeo to honor her memory.).

5. Attend a memorial that represents the person, thing, or event.

6. Find an activity to volunteer your time to honor the person, thing, or event. Volunteer or donate money to an organization. Tutor or coach others: coach a children's sports league, tutor an adult who cannot read, or become a Big Brother/Big Sister.

7. Become involved in your community. Join a faith-based organization. Join a community sports league.

8. Help your neighborhood or an organization perform a community service, such as a neighborhood cleanup.

Family Handout Step 6.3

What Is Grief?

Grief is a normal and natural response to loss. Although it can be painful, grieving is an adaptation process that helps you cope with and better understand the world. Many people think grieving is what people go through when a loved one dies. However, grieving can help people cope with many types of losses. Many service members have lost members of their unit over the course of deployment, others have been physically injured themselves, and still others have witnessed the loss of others. Some service members may have experienced the loss of innocence, from witnessing a complete breakdown of moral order—of what they may have believed was right.

There is no right way or wrong way to grieve. In general, a person who has experienced a loss will have distressing thoughts about their loss that they cannot control. Sometimes, feelings of guilt can be associated with the loss. People who are grieving often struggle with trying to make sense of the loss. Some people have trouble feeling anything at all. Others go out of their way to avoid thinking about their loss.

Grief is a normal and natural response to loss, one that allows us to heal from loss. However, grief is a very misunderstood process. Because responding to losses is usually uncomfortable, service members sometimes avoid dealing with grief. Others around you may do the same. For example, friends or family members may make statements such as, "You have to get on with your life" sometimes because the reality is difficult for them as well. Others may believe that it is not appropriate to show emotions related to loss. Or, that recovery should be complete within a prescribed amount of time. These are all misconceptions that can make it more difficult for people to grieve. Although there is no empirically proven treatment for grief, there are recommendations from experts in the field about how to heal from loss.

Here are some suggestions for the grieving process:

Remember. Identify your loss and the details of painful experiences.

Experience your feelings. Most experts agree that experiencing and accepting feelings will allow you to honor the people or things that were lost.

Tell others you trust what happened. Talk to your buddies, your spouse, and other caring family members about what happened; write down your experiences. Chaplains and mental health providers are also available to hear about what happened. If someone is uncomfortable with your emotion or your need to talk about the loss, politely let him or her know that talking out your loss is part of your healing process.

Stay connected. Don't isolate yourself. Surround yourself with your family and military/civilian community.

Honor the loss. People often find healing through conducting an activity that honors the person(s) or thing(s) that was lost. For example, it is healing to respect the fallen through memorial services and other rituals. When a loss is more personal, you may want to write a letter about the loss, attend a faith-based service in honor of the loss, or conduct your own ritual to honor the loss.

Family Handout Step 6.4

Meaning Making

This exercise focuses on helping you honor the person, thing, or event that you lost through meaningful rituals or activities. In this exercise, you will identify an activity or ritual that you can do with the support of your spouse or other family members.

In what way can you honor what or whom you have lost? What ritual(s) can you do with the support of your family? This ritual or activity will symbolize how much the person, thing, or event meant to you. Please write your ideas out here and be specific.

_____
_____
_____
_____
_____
_____
_____
_____
_____
_____
_____
_____

How can this ritual/activity help you make meaning out of what happened?
Please share your thoughts now.

_____
_____
_____
_____
_____
_____
_____
_____
_____
_____
_____
_____
_____

Family Handout Step 6.5

Unconditional Support and Acceptance

In this exercise, your family members will make vows to be there for each other no matter what and "learn how to give out love, and to let it come in." Here are some examples of brief statements you can start with:

- I will love you forever.
- I promise to be there for you no matter what.
- I love you and am proud to be your (husband/wife/father/mother/daughter/son, etc.).
- You are a beautiful person, and I feel very lucky to be your (husband/wife).
- You are an amazing person, and I fully commit myself to you.

Now please write out your statement or vows to your family member(s), promising your unconditional love and commitment to them.

_____

_____

_____

_____

_____

_____

_____

_____

_____

_____

_____

_____

_____

_____

Step 7: Challenge
Setting Higher Life Goals

Family Handout Step 7.1

Assessing Needs and Clarifying Values

In this exercise, your family will talk with one another and discover each other's unfulfilled needs and values. Please openly and honestly answer these questions.

Please write about one of the most important, peak experiences you have had in your personal or professional life. This experience would have made you feel on top of the world, enthusiastic, driven, and fulfilled at a deep level inside. It is one of the most important experiences in your life. Please write about it in detail, sharing everything you remember about it.

_____

_____

_____

_____

_____

_____

_____

_____

_____

_____

_____

_____

_____

Don't be humble: What would you say you value the most about yourself? What are some other things you value about yourself?

_____

_____

_____

_____

_____

_____

_____

_____

_____

_____

_____

What do you see as being your most important strengths? And how do you think these strengths relate to your peak experience(s)?

_____

_____

_____

_____

_____

_____

_____

_____

_____

_____

_____

How do you feel your relationship has helped or hurt your abilities to have more peak experiences like the one you shared in this exercise?

_____

_____

_____

_____

_____

_____

_____

_____

_____

_____

_____

_____

_____

Family Handout Step 7.2

Aligning Visions

In this exercise, we take things to the next level. This exercise can help your family to explore each other's deepest, most personal wishes, visions, and dreams. Please answer the following questions openly and honestly.

If I were a genie and could grant you three wishes in life, what would they be for you? For your family?

_____

_____

_____

_____

_____

_____

_____

_____

_____

_____

_____

_____

_____

How does your reality measure up to what your deepest wishes are for yourself? For your family?

_____

_____

_____

_____

_____

_____

How can you use your strengths and values to fulfill these wishes and make them a reality?

_____

_____

_____

_____

_____

_____

How can your family align these visions and make them happen for you?

_____

_____

_____

_____

_____

_____

Family Handout Step 7.3

Enhancing the Vision

In this exercise, you will further enhance and clarify your vision for your life.

Recall your peak experience. Sit with the experience in your mind for the next couple of minutes. Don't answer these questions aloud. Just remember the details and allow yourself to connect with the passion and purpose you felt at that time. Reconnect with what you were seeing, hearing, smelling, tasting, and touching. Who was with you at the time? What were you doing?

As the family member who is taking notes, please answer these questions as your loved one responds in session.

What is the most significant thing you are experiencing in your peak experience right now? Tell me in detail. (Their family member is taking notes, as verbatim as possible).

_____

_____

_____

_____

_____

_____

What is it you feel the most connected with? How does it make you feel right now?

_____

_____

_____

_____

_____

_____

Describe yourself while you are in your peak experience.

_____

_____

_____

_____

_____

_____

What do you realize are your strengths in this experience?

_____

_____

_____

_____

_____

_____

Describe the passion you are feeling right now in your experience.

_____

_____

_____

_____

_____

_____

What else do you notice about yourself in your experience, that maybe you didn't realize before?

_____

_____

_____

_____

_____

In your peak experience, how did you accomplish all of this? What did it take for you to do it?

_____

_____

_____

_____

_____

Family Handout Step 7.4

Setting Goals for Positive Life Change

In this exercise, your family will take the inner knowledge and passion (based on your peak experience) you learned from doing the last exercise, and you will devise a clear, specific plan to make it happen. Please answer these questions openly and honestly.

What are your most important goals for your life that will help you realize your vision?

_____

_____

_____

_____

_____

_____

_____

_____

_____

_____

What do you see as being all of your options to make your vision a reality?

_____

_____

_____

_____

_____

_____

_____

_____

_____

What are all of the possible obstacles that could get in the way?

_____

_____

_____

_____

_____

_____

_____

_____

_____

_____

How will you do it? What are the steps you need to take now?

_____

_____

_____

_____

_____

_____

_____

_____

_____

Step 8: Grow
Fostering Lifelong Resilience

Family Handout Step 8.1

Our Core Values

Our values are the qualities in life that are most important to us. Even though we all have values that guide the way we live our lives, we rarely take a moment to think about what our values are. However, the closer we follow our values in our day-to-day lives, the more meaningful our lives can be.

Instructions: In the following exercise, rate how often each value in the following list is important to you on a scale from one to four. Circle the number that represents how important the value is for you individually, then place a checkmark over the number that represents how important you think the value is to your family as a whole. Make sure your answer is true for you, and not just what you think most people would expect you to say.

Being honest

Not Important	Sometimes Important	Usually Important	Always Important
1	2	3	4

Being at peace

Not Important	Sometimes Important	Usually Important	Always Important
1	2	3	4

Being ethical and honest

Not Important	Sometimes Important	Usually Important	Always Important
1	2	3	4

Freedom of speech

Not Important	Sometimes Important	Usually Important	Always Important
1	2	3	4

Honoring my country

Not Important	Sometimes Important	Usually Important	Always Important
1	2	3	4

Respecting elders

Not Important	Sometimes Important	Usually Important	Always Important
1	2	3	4

Being a loyal friend

Not Important	Sometimes Important	Usually Important	Always Important
1	2	3	4

Being disciplined

Not Important	Sometimes Important	Usually Important	Always Important
1	2	3	4

Being a positive role model

Not Important	Sometimes Important	Usually Important	Always Important
1	2	3	4

Being a good parent, spouse, son or daughter

Not Important	Sometimes Important	Usually Important	Always Important
1	2	3	4

Having close and loving relationships

Not Important	Sometimes Important	Usually Important	Always Important
1	2	3	4

Honoring God/higher power

Not Important	Sometimes Important	Usually Important	Always Important
1	2	3	4

Being spiritual

Not Important	Sometimes Important	Usually Important	Always Important
1	2	3	4

Being honest

Not Important	Sometimes Important	Usually Important	Always Important
1	2	3	4

Being the best

Not Important	Sometimes Important	Usually Important	Always Important
1	2	3	4

Gaining financial success

Not Important	Sometimes Important	Usually Important	Always Important
1	2	3	4

Being successful

Not Important	Sometimes Important	Usually Important	Always Important
1	2	3	4

Being powerful

Not Important	Sometimes Important	Usually Important	Always Important
1	2	3	4

Being independent

Not Important	Sometimes Important	Usually Important	Always Important
1	2	3	4

Being creative

Not Important	Sometimes Important	Usually Important	Always Important
1	2	3	4

Being physically attractive

Not Important	Sometimes Important	Usually Important	Always Important
1	2	3	4

Living a healthy lifestyle

Not Important	Sometimes Important	Usually Important	Always Important
1	2	3	4

Commitment to a social cause(s)

Not Important	Sometimes Important	Usually Important	Always Important
1	2	3	4

Being responsible for one's duties

Not Important	Sometimes Important	Usually Important	Always Important
1	2	3	4

Being valued by the community

Not Important	Sometimes Important	Usually Important	Always Important
1	2	3	4

Being a model citizen

Not Important	Sometimes Important	Usually Important	Always Important
1	2	3	4

Working hard

Not Important	Sometimes Important	Usually Important	Always Important
1	2	3	4

Gaining education

Not Important	Sometimes Important	Usually Important	Always Important
1	2	3	4

Having intellectual pursuits

Not Important	Sometimes Important	Usually Important	Always Important
1	2	3	4

Being tolerant of differences in others

Not Important	Sometimes Important	Usually Important	Always Important
1	2	3	4

Having fun

Not Important	Sometimes Important	Usually Important	Always Important
1	2	3	4

Learning

Not Important	Sometimes Important	Usually Important	Always Important
1	2	3	4

Being fair

Not Important	Sometimes Important	Usually Important	Always Important
1	2	3	4

Respecting the environment

Not Important	Sometimes Important	Usually Important	Always Important
1	2	3	4

Having compassion for all living things

Not Important	Sometimes Important	Usually Important	Always Important
1	2	3	4

Seeking justice and equality for all

Not Important	Sometimes Important	Usually Important	Always Important
1	2	3	4

Having a sense of humor

Not Important	Sometimes Important	Usually Important	Always Important
1	2	3	4

Helping those who are less fortunate

Not Important	Sometimes Important	Usually Important	Always Important
1	2	3	4

Being adventurous

Not Important	Sometimes Important	Usually Important	Always Important
1	2	3	4

Being famous

Not Important	Sometimes Important	Usually Important	Always Important
1	2	3	4

Being popular

Not Important	Sometimes Important	Usually Important	Always Important
1	2	3	4

Being brave

Not Important	Sometimes Important	Usually Important	Always Important
1	2	3	4

Being happy

Not Important	Sometimes Important	Usually Important	Always Important
1	2	3	4

Other: _____

Not Important	Sometimes Important	Usually Important	Always Important
1	2	3	4

What are some of my core values?

1. _____
2. _____
3. _____
4. _____
5. _____

What are my family's core values?

1. _____
2. _____
3. _____
4. _____
5. _____

Family Handout Step 8.2

Communicating Gratitude

PART 1

Resilient families recognize the positive side of situations and people in their lives. Research shows that listing things we are grateful for on a daily basis helps improve our health and well-being. Once a day, use this format to list things you are grateful for:

Three Things I am Most Grateful About My Day are . . .

(1)_____

(2)_____

(3)_____

Three Things I am Most Grateful About My Life are . . .

(1)_____

(2)_____

(3)_____

Three Things I am Most Grateful About My Family are . . .

(1)_____

(2)_____

(3)_____

PART 2

Sharing with each other things you are grateful for about family members will help increase your family's resilience. Too often, we only focus on the negatives about each other. We know that complaining to others only about the bad things they do makes them do more bad things! Research shows that the opposite is also true. The more you tell someone positive things they are doing, the more they will do positive things! Please complete these statements about your family members.

I am Most Grateful For You, _____, Because . . .

_____

_____

_____

I Admire That You . . .

_____

_____

_____

I am Thankful for Your . . .

_____

_____

_____

Family Handout Step 8.3

A Resilient Future

This exercise entails questions to help family members solidify their new resilience for the future. Please answer these questions openly and honestly.

What are the most important ways your family has grown through therapy?

_____

_____

_____

What do you see as your newfound strengths?

_____

_____

_____

Name three high-risk situations that have caused you and/or your family problems in the past:

1. _____

_____

_____

2. _____

_____

_____

3. _____

_____

_____

What new behaviors or skills will you and/or your family use to manage these challenging situations in the future?

1. _____

_____

_____

_____

2. _____

_____

_____

_____

3. _____
_____
_____
_____

What is the most important thing that has changed about how you behave?

_____
_____
_____
_____
_____
_____

How do you see yourselves as being more resilient as a result of going through this process?

_____
_____
_____
_____
_____
_____

Clinicians' Resource Guide

Clinicians' Resource Guide

The Center for Deployment Psychology (CDP) trains military and civilian clinicians to provide deployment-related behavioral health services to military personnel. They host trainings and conferences in various communities across the United States. Additionally, they provide a variety of online resources that can aid civilian therapists to better understand and effectively communicate with service members and their families.

http://deploymentpsych.org/

We recommend that clinicians who are not familiar with military culture and organization take the CDP's interactive online course located at:

http://deploymentpsych.org/training/training-catalog/military-cultural-competence

The National Center for Post-Traumatic Stress Disorder (NCPTSD) website is a comprehensive source for information related to trauma and deployment-related stress developed by leaders in the field of PTSD. The website contains online interactive trainings, hundreds of fact sheets, downloadable articles, videos, and a searchable database of journal articles for clinicians. Another helpful tool is the Iraqi War Clinician's Guide, developed collaboratively by top clinicians and researchers in the Department of Defense and the National Center for PTSD. It is an excellent resource for clinicians who are addressing various issues posed by returnees. In addition to material for clinicians and researchers, a great deal of information is available for military populations and family members.

www.ncptsd.va.org

Additionally, clinicians who are not familiar with military culture and organization will benefit from the National Center for PTSD online course on military culture located at:

http://www.ptsd.va.gov/professional/ptsd101/course-modules/military_culture.asp

MilitaryHOMEFRONT is the Department of Defense website for official Military Community and Family Policy program information. The website policy information and guidance for troops, their families, and service providers. The site links users to program staff who are able to provide the documents and information related to housing, children, and a wide range of other services. Their casualty assistance program provides many services, including transportation assistance; help applying for and receiving benefits and entitlements; help obtaining copies of records, reports, and investigations; legal assistance; mortuary and funeral honors assistance; and relocation assistance.

http://www.militaryhomefront.dod.mil/

Courage to Care was developed by leading military health experts from Uniformed Services University of the Health Sciences. Courage to Care consists of electronic fact sheets on health topics relevant to military life. Fact sheets target military and civilian professionals serving the military community, as well as information for service members and families.

http://www.usuhs.mil/psy/courage.html

Navy and Marine Corps Public Health Center is the Navy and Marine Corps center for public health services. The site, discussed further in the "Resources for Service Members and Families" section, includes the Sesame Street video "Talk, Listen, and Connect," which was created to help injured returnees and their spouses to prepare for reunions with their children.

http://www.nmcphc.med.navy.mil/

National Center for Telehealth & Technology (T2) is a Department of Defense Agency developing web, mobile, and virtual reality tools targeting PTSD, mTBI, and suicide prevention in the military community. There are several websites connected with T2, as well as mobile applications that can help service members, returnees, and veterans.

www.T2health.org To find out about T2's latest PTSD, TBI, and suicide prevention efforts.

www.AfterDeployment.org A one-stop website that can help service members and returnees deal with the stresses of military life and service.

www.SuicideOutreach.org Fast, free, anonymous help and information for service members who are in crisis.

T2 mobile apps currently available for iPhone and Android platforms:

Breathe2Relax
PTSD Coach
T2 MoodTracker
Tactical Breathing Trainer
mTBI Pocket Guide

Defense and Veterans Brain Injury Center is an organization whose mission is to serve active duty military, their beneficiaries, and veterans with traumatic brain injuries (TBIs) through state-of-the-art clinical care, innovative clinical research initiatives, and educational programs.

http://www.dvbic.org

WebMD is recommended for both clinicians and clients. On this site, veterans and family members can find stress management techniques and hundreds of additional resources.

www.webmd.com/

Service Members and Military Families Resource Guide

Service Members and Military Families Resource Guide

Military Programs and Services

Programs provided for service members and their families vary by location. Service members and spouses can access their installation's support services for information about where to find mental health services. Larger installations will have a Military Treatment Facility on-site that may provide treatment for PTSD. Many of these centers provide individual, group, marriage, and family counseling. These might include:

➤ Air Force Life Skills Clinics
➤ Army Community Centers
➤ Marine Corps Community Services
➤ U.S. Coast Guard Work-Life Center

Family programs may be available to support families in military and civilian settings. Such centers also can provide information and updates on available benefits, entitlements, and services (e.g., medical care).

These might include:

➤ Airman and Family Readiness Programs
➤ Army Family Advocacy Programs
➤ Army National Guard
➤ State Family Program Office
➤ Fleet and Family Support Center
➤ Marine & Family Services Counseling Services

Military ONESOURCE is an organization that provides services, including brief counseling to active-duty military personnel, reservists, and the National Guard members (1-800-342-9647; www.militaryonesource.com).

MilitaryHOMEFRONT is the Department of Defense website for official Military Community and Family Policy Program information. The website provides policy information and guidance for troops, their families, and service providers. The site links users to program staff who are able to provide the documents and information related to housing, children, and a wide range of other services. Their casualty assistance program provides many services, including transportation assistance; help applying for and receiving benefits and entitlements; help obtaining copies of records, reports, and investigations; legal assistance; mortuary and funeral honors assistance; and relocation assistance.

http://www.militaryhomefront.dod.mil/

The National Center for Post-Traumatic Stress Disorder (NCPTSD) website is a comprehensive source for information related to trauma and deployment-related stress developed by leaders in the field of PTSD. The website contains online interactive trainings, hundreds of fact sheets, and videos for veterans, service members, and their families. Their "Returning from the Warzone: A Guide for Families" interactive audio presentation provides guidance concerning common family issues, and when and how to get help for problems.

www.ncptsd.va.org

Navy and Marine Corps Public Health Center is the Navy and Marine Corps center that provides leadership and expertise to promote health and mission readiness. Their "Healthy Living" link provides information on early intervention and prevention of chronic problems, such as smoking, anger management, stress, and post-deployment health.

http://www.nmcphc.med.navy.mil/

Within the "Healthy Living" link, their operational stress control link provides a variety of trainings, posters, videos, and information on resilience. We recommend the Sesame Street video "Talk, Listen, and Connect," which helps injured returnees and their spouses to prepare for reunions with their children.

http://www.nmcphc.med.navy.mil/healthy_living/psychological_health/stress_management/operandcombatstress.aspx

National Center for Telehealth & Technology (T2) is a Department of Defense Agency developing web, mobile, and virtual reality tools targeting PTSD, mTBI, and suicide prevention in the military community. There are several websites connected with T2, as well as mobile applications that can help service members, returnees, and veterans.

www.T2health.org To find out about T2's latest PTSD, TBI, and suicide prevention efforts.

www.AfterDeployment.org A one-stop website that can help service members and returnees deal with the stresses of military life and service.

www.SuicideOutreach.org Fast, free, anonymous help and information for service members who are in crisis.

T2 mobile apps currently available for iPhone and Android platforms:

Breathe2Relax

PTSD Coach

T2 MoodTracker

Tactical Breathing Trainer

mTBI Pocket Guide

Defense and Veterans Brain Injury Center is an organization whose mission is to serve active duty military, their beneficiaries, and veterans with traumatic brain injuries (TBIs) through state-of-the-art clinical care, innovative clinical research initiatives, and educational programs.

http://www.dvbic.org

Comprehensive Soldier Fitness (CSF) is a program the United States Army launched in 2009 to help soldiers cope with financial, marital, and other personal problems related to serial deployments and spending significant periods of time away from their families. The Comprehensive Soldier Fitness website provides information about the Army's assessment and development program that is designed to build the resilience and enhance the performance of soldiers, family members, and civilians.

http://csf.army.mil/

Battlemind.org helps recent returning veterans to develop a realistic preview, in the form of a briefing, of the stresses and strains of deployment on soldiers. It was developed by leading military professionals at Walter Reed Army Institute of Research. Training briefs are available for service members, leaders, national guard members/reservists, and families.

http://www.battlemind.org/

The Department of Veterans Affairs Programs and Services

The *Department of Veterans Health Affairs* has developed several comprehensive web pages to help veterans and their loved ones become familiar with VA services, as well as other community resources. Under the mental health umbrella, a variety of subheadings are offered on topics such as suicide, PTSD, and substance abuse. The link for substance abuse, for example, provides an overview of issues relevant to substance abuse as well as tabbed sections on "VA Programs and Services," and "Articles and Fact Sheets." Additionally, the "Other Resources" subtab on that site contains contact information for Alanon and NarAnon, links to fact sheets from the National Institute on Drug Abuse and the National Institute on Alcohol Abuse and Alcoholism, and more. A link for "Returning Veterans" provides an overview of issues as well and tabbed sections on "VA Programs and Services," "Articles and Fact Sheets," and "Other Resources."

The overall site is located at:

http://www.mentalhealth.va.gov/VAMentalHealthGroup.asp

Within the www.mentalhealth.va.gov website is a 20-page "Guide to VA Mental Health Services for Veterans and Families" at:

http://www.mentalhealth.va.gov/docs/Guide_to_VA_Mental_Health_Srvcs_FINAL12-20-10.pdf

My HealtheVet is a free, online personal health record for veterans enrolled in the VA. If veterans choose to enroll in the program, they have access to their confidential health records and opportunities to monitor their well-being.

http://www.myhealth.va.gov/

The *VA Caregivers* webpage informs users about services that the VA provides to support caregivers, ranging from help for injured veterans in the home to listening support for caregivers. The site also includes links to sections for self-care, a support line number, tips to avoid burnout, caregiver checklists, and connections to their local VA Caregiver Support Coordinator.

http://www.caregiver.va.gov/index.asp

VA Medical Centers

The VA Medical Centers and Vet Centers provide veterans with health services that health insurance will not cover and that cost little or nothing, according to a veteran's ability to pay. A variety of mental health services are available. For example, VA Medical Centers' specialized PTSD clinics and programs provide eligible veterans with educational information, diagnostic assessment, and treatment for PTSD and other mental health and medical disorders. To find a VA Medical Center near you, call 1-800-905-4675 or look on the web at http://www1.va.gov/directory/guide/home.asp?isFlash=1.

Vet Centers

Community-based Vet Centers provide benefits information, evaluations, and counseling for any veteran who served in a war zone or in a military conflict (such as in Panama, Grenada, or Somalia) or who were sexually harassed or sexually assaulted while on active duty. There are no co-payments or charges of any kind for Vet Center confidential services. To find a Vet Center near you, call 1-800-905-4675 or look on the web at http://www1.va.gov/directory/guide/home.asp?isFlash=1.

Tragedy Assistance Program for Survivors (TAPS)

The Tragedy Assistance Program for Survivors (TAPS) is a nonprofit Veterans Service Organization that provides a wide range of free services to all those affected by the death of a loved one in the armed forces. To find a TAPS program, call 1-800-959-TAPS (1-800-959-8277) or look on the web at www.TAPS.org.

Office of Veterans Services

The Office of Veterans Services acts as a liaison between the Department of Veterans Affairs and individual veterans and between the governor and veterans' organizations. The Office assists veterans in obtaining state and federal entitlements, supplies the latest information on veterans' issues, and provides advice and support to veterans who are making the transition back into civilian life. To find an office near you, please visit http://www.va.gov/statedva.htm.

VA Benefits

The Office of Veterans Benefits Administration provides information about service-connected compensation and other types of benefits available to veterans. To find out more about VA health benefits, call 1-877-222-VETS. The website provides information about a VA Medical Center in your area at: http://www.va.gov/rcs/.

References

Alexander, M. P. (1995). Mild traumatic brain injury: Pathophysiology, natural history, and clinical management. *Neurology, 45,* 1253–1260.

Auerbach, J. (2001). *Personal and executive coaching: The complete guide for mental health professionals.* Pismo Beach, CA: Executive College Press.

Beck, A. T., & Emery, G. (1985). *Anxiety disorders and phobias: A cognitive perspective.* New York, NY: Basic Books/HarperCollins.

Beck, A. T., Rush, A. J., Shaw, B. F., & Emery, G. (1979). *Cognitive theory of depression.* New York, NY: Guilford Press.

Becker, J. V., Skinner, L. J., Abel, G. G., & Treacy, E. C. (1982). The incidence and types of sexual dysfunctions in rape and incest victims. *Journal of Sex and Marital Therapy, 8,* 65–74.

Benge, J. F., Pastorek, N .J., & Thornton, G. M. (2009). Postconcussive symptoms in OEF-OIF veterans: Factor structure and impact of posttraumatic stress. *Rehabilitation Psychology, 54*(3), 270–278.

Bowman, E.K. & Walker, G.A. (2010). Predictors of men's healthcare utilization. *Psychology of Men and Masculinity, 11,* 113–122.

Brewin, C. R., Andrews, B., & Valentine, J. D. (2000). Meta-analysis of risk factors for posttraumatic stress disorder in trauma-exposed adults. *Journal of Consulting and Clinical Psychology, 68*(5), 748–766.

Buehlman, K. T., Gottman, J. M., & Katz, L. F. (1992). How a couple views their past predicts their future: Predicting divorce from an oral history interview. *Journal of Family Psychology, 5,* 295–318.

Campbell, T. A., Nelson, L. A., Lumpkin, R., Yoash-Gantz, R. E., Pickett, T. C., & McCormick, C. L. (2009). Neuropsychological measures of processing speed and executive functioning in combat veterans with PTSD, TBI, and comorbid TBI/PTSD. *Psychiatric Annals, 39*(8), 796–803.

Clark, M. E., Bair, M. J., Buckenmaier, C. C. III, Gironda, R. J., & Walker, R. L. (2007). Pain and OIF/OEF combat injuries: Implications for research and practice. *Journal of Rehabilitation Research and Development, 44,* 179–194.

Clark, M. E., Scholten, J. D., Walker, R .L., & Gironda, R. J. (2009). Assessment and treatment of pain associated with combat-related polytrauma. *Pain Medicine, 10*(3), 456–469.

Clark, M. E., Walker, R. L., Gironda, R. J., & Scholten, J. D. (2009). Comparison of pain and emotional symptoms in soldiers with polytrauma: Unique aspects of blast exposure. *Pain Medicine, 10,* 447–455.

Cooper, D. B., Mercado-Couch, J. M., Critchfield, E., Kennedy, J., Vanderploeg, R. D., DeVillibis, C., & Gaylord, K. M. (2010). Factors influencing cognitive functioning following mild traumatic brain injury in OIF/OEF burn patients. *NeuroRehabilitation, 26,* 233–238.

Cordova, M. J., Ruzek, J. I., Benoit, M., & Brunet, A. (2003). Promotion of emotional disclosure following illness and injury: A brief intervention for medical patients and their families. *Cognitive and Behavioral Practice, 10*(4), 358–371. doi:10.1016/S1077-7229(03)80053-6

Cozza, S. J. (2005). Combat exposure and PTSD. *PTSD Research Quarterly, 16*(1), 1–7.

Defense Veterans Brain Injury Center. (2006a). Defense and Veterans Brain Injury Center Working Group on the Acute Management of Mild Traumatic Brain Injury in Military Operational Settings: Clinical Practice Guidelines and Recommendations. [Online]. Retrieved from: http://www.pdhealth.mil/downloads/clinical practice guideline recommendations.pdf

Defense Veterans Brain Injury Center. (2006b). Provider TBI Facts. [Online]. Retrieved from http://www.dvbic.org

DePalma, R. G., Burris, D. G., Champion, H. R., & Hodgson, M. J. (2005). Blast injuries. *The New England Journal of Medicine, 352*(13), 1335–1342.

Department of Defense (DoD). (2011, March). U.S. Department of Defense Annual Report on Sexual Assault. [Online]. Retrieved from http://www.defense.gov/releases/release.aspx?releaseid=14340

Department of Defense (DoD). (2011). *2010 WGRA.* Washington, DC: DMDC. [Online]. Retrieved from http://www.sapr.mil/index.php/research

Department of Defense (DoD). (2010, April). Month of the military child. [Online]. Retrieved from http://www.defense.gov/home/features/2010/0410_military child/

Department of Health and Human Services (HHS), Centers for Disease Control (CDC). (2009a). *Understanding Sexual Violence Fact Sheet, 2009* [Online]. Retrieved from http://www.cdc.gov/violenceprevention/pdf/SV_factsheet-a.pdf

Department of Health and Human Services (HHS), Centers for Disease Control (CDC). (2009b). *Sexual violence: Consequences* [Online]. Retrieved from www.cdc.gov/ViolencePrevention/sexualviolence/consequences.html

Department of Veterans Affairs. (2009). *Veterans Health Administration Directive 2009-2028: Polytrauma: Traumatic brain injury (TBI) system of care.* Washington, DC: Author.

Emmons, R. A., & Crumpler, C. A. (2000). Gratitude as a human strength: Appraising the evidence. *Journal of Social and Clinical Psychology, 19,* 56–69.

Emmons, R. A., & McCullough, M. E. (2003). Counting blessings versus burdens: An experimental investigation of gratitude and subjective well-being in daily life. *Journal of Personality and Social Psychology, 84*(2), 377–389.

Feder, A., Southwick, S. M., Goetz, R. R., Wang, Y., Alonso, A., Smith, B. W., . . . Vythilingam, M. (2008). Posttraumatic growth in former Vietnam prisoners of war. *Psychiatry: Interpersonal & Biological Processes, 71,* 359–370.

Feldman-Summers, S., Gordon, P. E., & Meagher, J. (1979). The impact of rape on sexual satisfaction. *Journal of Abnormal Psychology, 88*, 101–105.

Foa, E. B., & Kozak, M. J. (1986). Emotional processing of fear: Exposure to corrective information. [DOI:10.1037/0033-2909.99.1.20]. *Psychological Bulletin, 99*(1), 20–35.

Foa, E. B., & Rothbaum, B. (1998). *Treating the trauma of rape: Cognitive-behavioral therapy for PTSD.* New York, NY: Guilford Press.

Frankl, V. (1946). *Man's search for meaning.* Boston, MA: Beacon Press.

Galovski, T., & Lyons, J. A. (2004). Psychological sequelae of combat violence: A review of the impact of PTSD on the veteran's family and possible interventions. *Aggression and Violent Behavior, 9*, 477–501.

Gawande, A. (2004). Casualties of war: Military care for the wounded from Iraq and Afghanistan. *New England Journal of Medicine, 351*, 2471–2475.

Glaze, M. (2010). Team building is more than a strategy. [Online]. Retrieved June 23, 2011 from http://www.powerbasketball.com/100302.html

Goff, B. S., Crow, J. R., Reisbig, A. M., & Hamilton, S. (2007). The impact of individual trauma symptoms of deployed soldiers on relationship satisfaction. *Journal of Family Psychology, 21*(3), 344–353.

Goldberg, M.C. (1998). *The art of the question: A guide to short-term question-centered therapy.* New York, NY: Wiley.

Gottman, J. M., Gottman, J. S., & Atkins, C. L. (2011). The comprehensive soldier fitness program. *American Psychologist, 66*(1), 52–57.

Gottman, J. M., & Levenson, R. W. (1992). Marital processes predictive of later dissolution: Behavior, physiology, and health. *Journal of Personality and Social Psychology, 63*, 221–233.

Green, B. L., Grace, M. C., Lindy, J. D., Gleser, G. C., & Leonard, A. (1990). Risk factors for PTSD and other diagnoses in a general sample of Vietnam veterans. *The American Journal of Psychiatry, 147*(6), 729–733.

Haley, J. (2007). *Directive family therapy.* Binghamton, NY: Hawthorn Press.

Hayward, P. (2008). Traumatic brain injury: The signature of modern conflicts. *Lancet Neurology, 7*, 200–201.

Heltemes, K. J., Dougherty, A. L., MacGregor, A. J., & Galarneau, M. R. (2011). Inpatient hospitalizations of U.S. military personnel medically evacuated from Iraq and Afghanistan with combat-related traumatic brain injury. *Military Medicine, 176*(2), 132–135.

Hoge, C. W., Castro, C. A., Messer, S. C., McGurk, D., Cotting, D. I, & Koffman, R. L. (2004). Combat duty in Iraq and Afghanistan, mental health problems, and barriers to care. *New England Journal of Medicine, 351*, 13–22.

Howard, M. D. (2007). Escaping the pain: Examining the use of sexually compulsive behavior to avoid the traumatic memories of combat. *Sexual Addiction & Compulsivity, 14*, 77–94.

Keane, T. M., Scott, W. O., Chavoya, G. A., Lamparski, D. M., & Fairbank, J. A. (1985). Social support in Vietnam veterans with posttraumatic stress disorder: A comparative analysis. *Journal of Consulting and Clinical Psychology, 53*(1), 95–102.

Kennedy, J. E., Leal, F. O., Lewis, J. D., Cullen, M. A., & Amador, R. R. (2010). Posttraumatic stress symptoms in OIF/OEF service members with blast-related and non-blast-related mild TBI. *NeuroRehabilitation, 26*, 223–231.

Kimerling, R., Street, A., Pavao, J., Smith, M. W., Cronkite, R. C., Holmes, T. H., & Frayne, S. M. (2010). Military-related sexual trauma among Veterans Health Administration patients returning from Afghanistan and Iraq. *American Journal of Public Health, 100*(8), 1409–1412.

King, D. W., Taft, C., King, L. A., Hammond, C., & Stone, E. R. (2006). Directionality of the association between social support and posttraumatic stress disorder: A longitudinal investigation. *Journal of Applied Social Psychology, 36*(12), 2980–2992.

Laffaye, C., Cavella, S., Drescher, K., & Rosen, C. (2008). Relationships among PTSD symptoms, social support, and support source in veterans with chronic PTSD. *Journal of Traumatic Stress, 21*(4), 394–401.

Leider, R. J. (2010). *The power of purpose: Creating meaning in your life and work* (2nd ed.). San Francisco, CA: Berrett-Koehler.

Lepore, S. J., Silver, R. C., Wortman, C. B., & Wayment, H. A. (1996). Social constraints, intrusive thoughts, and depressive symptoms among bereaved mothers. *Journal of Personality and Social Psychology, 70*(2), 271–282.

Levenson, R. W., Carstensen, L. L., & Gottman, J. M. (1994). The influence of age and gender on affect, physiology, and their interrelations: A study of long-term marriages. *Journal of Personality and Social Psychology, 67*, 56–68.

Lew, H. L., Otis, J. D., Tun, C., Kerns, R. D., Clark, M. E., & Cifu, D. X. (2009). Prevalence of chronic pain, posttraumatic stress disorder and postconcussive symptoms in OEF/OIF veterans: The polytrauma clinical triad. *Journal of Rehabilitation Research and Development, 46*(6), 697–702.

Lewinsohn, P. M., Muñoz, R., Youngren, M. A., & Zeiss, A. (1986). *Control your depression.* Englewood Cliffs, NJ: Prentice Hall.

Lichtenthal, W. G., Cruess, D. G., & Prigerson, H. G. (2004). A case for establishing complicated grief as a distinct mental disorder in the *DSM-V. Clinical Psychology Review, 24*, 637–662.

Litz, B. T., Orsillo, S. M., Friedman, M., Ehlich, P., & Batres, A. (1997). Post-traumatic stress disorder associated with peacekeeping duty in Somalia for U.S. military personnel. *American Journal of Psychiatry, 154*, 178–184.

Lorber, W., & Garcia, H. S. (2010). Not supposed to feel this: Traditional masculinity in psychotherapy with male veterans returning from Afghanistan and Iraq. *Psychotherapy Theory, Research, Practice, and Training, 47*, 296–305.

Mansfield, A. J., Kaufman, J. S., Marshall, S. W., Gaynes, B. N., Morrissey, J. P., & Engel, C. C. (2010). Deployment and the use of mental health services among U.S. Army wives. *New England Journal of Medicine, 362*(2), 101–109.

Masi, R. (2010). The coming Afghanistan surge—and the severely wounded. [Online]. Retrieved January 19, 2010 from *The Providence Journal and GlobalSecurity.org.*

Maslow, A. (1970). *Motivation and personality.* New York, NY: Harper-Row.

McCall-Hosenfeld, J. S., Liebschutz, J. M., Spiro, A. V., & Seaver, M. R. (2009). Sexual assault in the military and its impact on sexual satisfaction in women veterans: A proposed model. *Journal of Women's Health, 18*(6), 901–909.

McCubbin, H. I., McCubbin, M. A., Patterson, J. M., Cauble, A. E. Wilson, L. R., & Warwick, W. (1983). *Journal of Marriage and the Family, 45*, 359-370.

Military culture: A primer. (2011). [Online]. Retrieved on June 22, 2011 from: http://militarywives-matter.org/militaryculture.html

Monson, C. M., Schnurr, P. P., Resick, P. A., Friedman, M. J., Young-Xu, Y., & Stevens, S. P. (2006). Cognitive processing therapy for veterans with military-related posttraumatic stress disorder. *Journal of Consulting and Clinical Psychology, 74*(5), 898–907.

Moore, D. F., & Jaffee, M. S. (2010). Military traumatic brain injury and blast. *NeuroRehabilitation, 26*, 179–181.

Morrow, C. E., Bryan, C. J., & Isler, W. C. (2011). Concussive and psychological symptom predictors of aeromedical evaluation following possible brain injury among deployed military personnel. *Psychological Services, 1*, 1541–1559.

Norris, J., & Feldman-Summers, S. (1981). Factors related to the psychological impact of rape on the victim. *Journal of Abnormal Psychology, 90*, 562–567.

Okie, S. (2005). Traumatic brain injury in the war zone. *New England Journal of Medicine, 352*, 2043–2047.

Orlando, J. A., & Koss, M. P. (1983). The effects of sexual victimization on sexual satisfaction: A study of the negative-association hypothesis. *Journal of Abnormal Psychology, 92*, 104–106.

Pennebaker, J. W. (1989). Confession, inhibition, and disease. In M. Zanna (Ed.), *Advances in experimental social psychology, Vol. 22* (pp. 211–244). San Diego, CA: Academic Press.

Pennebaker, J. W. (1993). Putting stress into words: Health, linguistic, and therapeutic implications. *Behaviour Research and Therapy, 31*(6), 539–548.

Pennebaker, J. W., & Beall, S. K. (1986). Confronting a traumatic event: Toward an understanding of inhibition and disease. *Journal of Abnormal Psychology, 95*(3), 274–281.

Pietrzak, R. H., Johnson, D. C., Goldstein, M. B., Malley, J. C., & Southwick, S. M. (2009). Perceived stigma and barriers to care to mental health service utilization among OEF/OIF veterans. *Psychiatric Services, 60*, 1118–1122.

Prigerson, H., Shear., M., Jacobs, S., Reynolds, C. F. III, Maciejewski, P., Davidson J., & Zisook, S. (1999). Consensus criteria for traumatic grief: A preliminary empirical test. *British Journal of Psychiatry, 174*, 67–73.

Prigerson, H. G., Shear, M. K., Frank, E., Beery, L. C., Silberman, R., Prigerson, J., & Reynolds, C. F. III. (1997). Traumatic grief: A case for loss-induced trauma. *American Journal of Psychiatry, 154*(7), 1003–1009.

Prigerson, H. G., Maciejewski, P. K., Reynolds, C. F. III., Bierhals, A. J., Newsom, J. T., & Fasiczka, A. (1995). Inventory of complicated grief: A scale to measure maladaptive symptoms of loss. *Psychiatry Research 59*(1–2), 65–79.

Reivich, K. J., Seligman, M. E. P., & McBride, S. (2011). Master resilience training in the U.S. Army. *American Psychologist, 66*, 25–34.

Renshaw, K. D., Rodrigues, C. S., & Jones, D. H. Psychological symptoms and marital satisfaction in spouses of Operation Iraqi Freedom veterans: Relationships with spouses' perceptions of veterans' experiences and symptoms. *Journal of Family Psychology, 22(4)*, 586–594.

Resick, P. A., & Schnicke, M. K. (1993). *Cognitive processing therapy for rape victims: A treatment manual*. Newbury Park, CA: Sage.

Rimé, B. (2007). Interpersonal emotion regulation. In J. J. Gross (Ed.), *Handbook of emotion regulation* (pp. 466–485). New York, NY: Guilford Press.

Ruzek, J. (1993). Professionals coping with vicarious trauma. *National Center for PTSD Clinical Newsletter*, Spring 1993.

Sayer, N. A., Friedemann-Sanchez, G., Spoont, M., Murdoch, M., Parker, L. E., Chiros, C., & Rosenheck, R. (2009). A qualitative study of determinants of PTSD treatment initiation in veterans. *Psychiatry, 72,* 238–255.

Shipard, J. C., & Beck, J. G. (2005). The role of thought suppression in posttraumatic stress disorder. *Behavior Therapy, 26,* 277–287.

Simmons, R., Maconochie, N., & Doyle, P. (2004). Self-reported ill health in male UK Gulf War veterans: A retrospective cohort study. *BMC Public Health, 4,* 1–20.

Solomon, Z., Waysman, M. A., Nerial, Y., Ohry, A., Schwarzwald, J., & Wiener, M. (1999). Positive and negative changes in the lives of Israeli former prisoners of war. *Journal of Social and Clinical Psychology, 18,* 419–435.

Southwick, S. M., Vythilingam, M., & Charney, D. S. (2005). The psychobiology of depression and resilience to stress: Implications for prevention and treatment. *Annual Review of Clinical Psychology, 1,* 255–291.

Stecker, T., Fortney, J. C., Hamilton, F., & Ajzen, A. (2007). An assessment of beliefs about mental health care among veterans who served in Iraq. *Psychiatric Services, 58,* 1358–1361.

Stinnett, N. (1979). In search of strong families. In N. Stinnett, B. Chesser, & J. De Frain (Eds.), *Building family strengths: Blueprints for action* (pp. 23–30). Lincoln: University of Nebraska Press.

Stroebe, M. S., Hansson, R. O., & Stoebe, W., & Shut, H. (2001). *Handbook of bereavement research: Consequences, coping and care*. Washington, DC: American Psychological Association.

Summerall, E. L., & McAllister, T. W. (2010). Comorbid posttraumatic stress disorder and traumatic brain injury in the military population. *Psychiatric Annals, 40,* 563–580.

Terrio, H., Brenner, L. A., Ivins, B. J., Cho, J. M., Helmick, K., Schwab, K., . . . Warden, D. (2009). Traumatic brain injury screening: Preliminary findings in a U.S. Army Brigade combat team. *Journal of Head Trauma Rehabilitation, 24,* 14–23.

Thames, B. J. (2008). Building family strengths: Values. [Online]. Retrieved on June 23, 2011 from http://www.education.com/reference/article/Ref_Building_Values/

The Wizard of Oz. (1939). Warner Bros Productions.

Tracy, B. (2010). *Goals! How to get everything you want: Faster than you ever thought possible* (2nd ed.). San Francisco, CA: Berrett-Koehler.

Trivette, C., Dunst, C., Deal, A., & Hamer, W. (1990). Assessing family strengths and family functioning style. *Topics in Early Childhood Education, 10(1),* 16–35.

Tugade, M. M., & Fredrickson, B. L. (2004). Resilient individuals use positive emotions to bounce back from negative emotional experiences. *Journal of Personality and Social Psychology, 86,* 320–333.

Ullman, S. E. (2003). Social reactions to child sexual abuse disclosures: A critical review. *Journal of Child Sexual Abuse, 12*(1), 89–121.

Ullman, S. E., & Filipas, H. H. (2001). Predictors of PTSD symptom severity and social reactions in sexual assault victims. *Journal of Traumatic Stress, 14*(2), 369–389.

Uomoto, J. M., & Williams, R. M. (2009). Post-acute polytrauma rehabilitation and integrated care of returning veterans: Toward a holistic approach. *Rehabilitation Psychology, 54*(3), 259–269.

Wade, A. L., Dye, J. L., Mohrle, C. R., & Galarneau, M. R. (2007). Head, face, and neck injuries during Operation Iraqi Freedom II: Results from the US Navy-Marine Corps Combat Trauma Registry. *Journal of Trauma, 63*, 836–840.

Walker, R. L., Clark, M. E., & Sanders, S. H. (2010). The "Postdeployment Multi-Symptom Disorder": An emerging syndrome in need of a new treatment paradigm. *Psychological Services, 7*(3), 136–147.

Walsh, F. (2006). *Strengthening family resilience.* New York, NY: Guilford Press.

Whealin, J. M., DeCarvalho, L. T, & Vega, E. M. (2008a). *Clinician's guide to treating stress after war: Education and coping interventions for veterans.* Hoboken, NJ: Wiley.

Whealin, J. M., DeCarvalho, L. T., & Vega, E. M. (2008b). *Strategies for managing stress after war: Veteran's workbook and guide to wellness.* Hoboken, NJ: Wiley.

Whealin, J. M., Stotzer, R., Vogt, D., Pietrzak, R. H., Nelson, D., Bozik, S., & Southwick, S. (2011). *Service utilization and barriers to care for veterans in rural and urban setting.* Honolulu, HI: VA Pacific Islands Health Care System National Center for PTSD Report.

Winfrey, Oprah. (2011, May 23). *Finding your life's calling: The final episode.* Chicago, IL: Harpo Productions.

Wolin, S. J., & Bennett, L. A. (1984). Family rituals. *Family Process, 23*, 401–420.

Wood, A. M., Froh, J. J., & Geraghty, A. W. A. (2010). Gratitude and well-being: A review and theoretical integration. *Clinical Psychology Review, 30*, 890–905.

Zouris, J. M., Walker, G. J., Dye, J., & Galarneau, M. (2006). Wounding patterns for U.S. marines and sailors during Operation Iraqi Freedom, major combat phase. *Military Medicine, 171*, 246–252.

About the Authors

Lorie T. DeCarvalho, PhD, is a licensed clinical psychologist and board-certified expert in traumatic stress, and she is also a pain management specialist, and peak performance coach. Dr. DeCarvalho is the founder and medical director of Behavioral Health Services for Adventist Health, Central California Network, as well as founder and CEO of Center for Integrative Psychology & Wellness, Inc., a health care corporation that provides clinical care, consultation, education, and training for individuals and organizations at the national and international levels, including universities, doctoral-training programs, the U.S. Department of Defense, the Department of Veterans Affairs, and county governments to improve services for active-duty service members, veterans, and military families. She is an associate clinical professor of psychiatry at Loma Linda University Medical Center. Prior to this, she served as an education specialist at the National Center for PTSD. Dr. DeCarvalho is the co-author of *The Clinician's Guide to Treating Stress After War: Education and Coping Interventions for Veterans,* and *Strategies for Managing Stress After War: Veteran's Workbook and Guide to Wellness,* both published by Wiley, as well as numerous other professional, educational, general interest, and self-help publications. Dr. DeCarvalho can be contacted at: drdecarvalho@centerpsychwellness.com.

Julia M. Whealin, PhD, is a licensed clinical psychologist and Senior Education Specialist at the National Center for PTSD, Pacific Islands Division. Dr. Whealin serves as an adjunct associate professor at the University of Hawaii, John A. Burns School of Medicine. She has overseen several nationally funded research projects that examine the needs and preferences of veterans and their family members. Dr. Whealin serves as a consultant to the U.S. Department of Defense, Department of Veterans Affairs, and other federal and local state organizations. Dr. Whealin is the co-author of *The Clinician's*

Guide to Treating Stress After War: Education and Coping Interventions for Veterans, and *Strategies for Managing Stress After War: Veteran's Workbook and Guide to Wellness,* both published by Wiley. She has published widely on a host of military-related mental health issues, including combat stress, family issues, resilience/prevention, and access to care for underserved populations.

Index